Revitalizing
the Older Suburb

Revitalizing
the Older Suburb

David Listokin
W. Patrick Beaton

with
William R. Dolphin
Sandra M. Holler
Carol Baker

CENTER
FOR URBAN
POLICY RESEARCH

Published in the United States of America
by the Center for Urban Policy Research
Building 4051 - Kilmer Campus
New Brunswick, New Jersey 08903

Library of Congress Cataloging in Publication Data

Listokin, David.
  Revitalizing the older suburb

  Bibliography: p. 227
  1. Local finance--United States. 2. Urban renewal--United States. 3.
Suburbs--United States. 4. Municipal services--United States--Finance.
I. Beaton, W. Patrick. II. Rutgers University. Center for Urban Policy
Research. III. Title
HJ9145.L57 1983   352.073   83-7376
ISBN 0-88285-094-6

Contents

List of Exhibits

CHAPTER 4. STRENGTHENING THE RETAIL SECTOR OF THE OLDER SUBURBS

CHAPTER 5. THE ARTS AS A DOWNTOWN REVITALIZATION MECHANISM

CHAPTER 6. RETHINKING MUNICIPAL EXPENDITURES AND SERVICE STRATEGIES

Foreword

The older suburb is the forgotten frontier of America. It is coupled with its near relative, the free-standing smaller city, as elements of our society that have largely been overlooked by academics and planners as well. On the one hand, the trauma of the central city has dominated the scene. On the other, there is the issue of coping with the growth problems of the outer suburbs and exurbs. Lost in the middle are the older suburbs.

And yet the older suburb can and should be viewed as the new frontier of our society. It provides a potential safety valve for the new minority outmigration from core areas. The older suburb still maintains a competitive infrastructure, not uncommonly has housing available at prices to which moderate-incomed people can aspire, and thus can be a crucial stepping stone toward full middle-class status for those who cannot afford the full costs of fashionable suburbia.

But this role is threatened as the capacity of such municipalities to deliver the support structures and stability of services for which they are sought, begins to be threatened. The problems of optimizing municipal operations and budget stringencies are linked. The smaller community has not fallen heir to the levels of transfer payments from states and federal governments that dominate the ledgers of larger cities. Thus their operations are much more a function of self-raised revenues. The harsh realities of limited tax bases, and dependency on local real estate taxes, impose a harsh calculus.

There is little growth and indeed frequently the real decline of older economic functions. These dynamics threaten the income base of the community. This is particularly the case in terms of the historic market functions of major retailing. Though perhaps not incorporating significant department stores -- the older suburb in the past typically had a strong quanta of specialty stores. In the face of the suburban shopping center, in all but rare cases, these crucial elements have disappeared and with them not only their accompanying tax base, but also much of the identity of the community.

Within the communities' delivery systems, they partake of the problems of age, of infrastructure that has all of the geriatric problems requiring large levels of maintenance and expensive operations. And this too is further complicated by the encrustation of costs as a function of seniority which dominates their staffing. With little in the way of growth and thus limited new hires, there is a tendency to have a proliferation of staff at senior salary levels. The very scale

xiii

of the personnel base may reflect older glories rather than present limitations.

The relatively quiet desperation of the fiscal imbalance in the older suburb is not the stuff of newspaper headlines or television shows -- it is nonetheless of vital importance. And yet within the trauma both of fisc and economic function, there are the beginnings of revitalization. The reality of intolerable tax rates, self-destructive as the ratable base declines in their face, is beginning to develop a new generation of inputs. Older suburbs are undergoing a painful reexamination of municipal costs and benefits, a new willingness to face the necessity of reshaping their expenditures to meet a limited purse. This is not enough; it must be coupled with efforts at securing new forms of function, new capacities for pulling power with which to ultimately secure a renewed place in the market. While the staple retailing of yesterday may well have moved to the highway, this is far from the growth sector of distribution. Instead, there is the rise of shopping as a "fun" exercise. The very splintering of the monolith of the baby boom generation, of the classic expenditure patterns of child-dominated households, has created a boom in one-of-a-kind type retailing. Those communities in the forefront of revitalization are seeking out unique market segments. The older suburb at its best, is establishing a new identity to consumers -- one which has a penetration capacity -- and a scale sufficient to support its future. Within this context, the rise of the performing arts within the city can play a very important role. The challenge of losing the old is not a tragedy unless it is met with passive acceptance; the response must be to seek out new forms and new functions. Self-evaluation can be a sparkplug for opportunity. And bringing this to fruition indeed is the challenge of the future.

In the study at hand, the authors bring together not only the literature of the field, but also provide an intensive case analysis of the present realities and the beginnings of positive response. The work is at one and the same time dedicated to helping the city fathers of a specific municipality, Englewood, New Jersey, yet also securing a broader oversight for deeply-troubled communities facing comparable issues. The authors have incorporated detailed methodologies which are both practical and applicable to other municipalities. The focus is first on securing a baseline: Where does our community stand within the context of other comparables? Secondly, to analyze the results of this investigation; and third, to look at some of the meliorative measures which can be implemented.

It is our hope that this work will be of utility to planners, municipal officials and concerned citizenry in the field as well. The issues are substantial, the potential of appropriate responses must match the significance of the arena. The authors have made a very important step in this direction.

GEORGE STERNLIEB

Acknowledgments

The preparation of this study would have been impossible without the assistance and cooperation of many individuals. Dr. George Sternlieb, director of the Center for Urban Policy Research, must be singled out for his patience and guidance. Mr. Kennedy Shaw, Englewood's City Manager at the inception of the research, served an invaluable role in shaping the analysis and establishing contacts with municipal officials and local business and civic leaders. Mr. William Sommers, Englewood's current City Manager, Mr. Robert Benecke, Englewood's Finance Director, and Mr. Joseph Murphy, Englewood's Planner, also served key advisory roles.

Staff members of the Center for Urban Policy Research assembled background data and wrote draft sections of the report. We thank Lizabeth Allewelt, Lynn Kramer, Karen Kaduscwicz, and Rocco Pizzollo.

A key role was played by the study's Advisory Board. In alphabetical order, the Board's members included: Edward Baczewski, Robert Benecke, William Brown, Norman Davis, Betty Frank, Frank W. Haines, Stan Jeter, Aaron Knight, Joseph Murphy, Phillip E. Leahy, Kennedy Shaw, and Barry Skokowski.

The authors also wish to extend their gratitude for the financial support offered by Bergen County and the City of Englewood.

Mrs. Joan Frantz, Mrs. Lydia Lombardi and Mrs. Arlene Pashman, the mainstays of the Center for Urban Policy Research's typing staff, all performed valuable duties in preparing the manuscript. Mrs. Mary Picarella assisted its editing and final publication. Ms. Jean Acker also warrants thanks for her publication efforts.

The authors assume reponsibility for any errors or misinterpretations that remain.

David Listokin
W. Patrick Beaton

Study Background
Methodology, and Organization

Introduction
Suburbanization and Its Study

America has been "suburbanizing" -- leaving the central city of metropolitan areas to outside central city locations -- for almost 150 years. First there was a trickle of the affluent who did not need to commute to the city for employment or else could do so at their own leisure and schedule.[1] Thus the mid-to-late 19th century saw the establishment of such premier enclaves as Llwellyn Park, Tuxedo Park, Shaker Heights, and Lake Forest.[2] Shortly thereafter at around the turn of the 20th century, transportation improvements in the form of horse-drawn trolleys, electrified street cars, and steam railroads, opened suburbia for middle-income families.[3] These second-generation suburbs such as the north shore of Long Island and Chicago, the Oranges of New Jersey, Brookline and Newton outside of Boston, and the lower San Francisco peninsula, typically were located right off the expanding trolley car and train lines.

The movement outward from the central city is reflected in the following changing decennial census counts. By 1910, almost one-quarter of the metropolitan population lived outside of cities (see Exhibit I-1). This share increased slightly over the next three decades as growing availability and use of the automobile made it easier than ever to live in suburbia. By 1930, almost one-third of metropolitan residents lived outside central cities. In the post-World War II era, a return to readily accessible and affordable automobiles, the building of interstate highways, and pent-up demand for housing, fueled a suburban explosion that has slowed but not abated until today. By 1960, the metropolitan population was split between central and outside central city residents; by 1970, suburbanites became the majority; and by 1980 they constituted an overwhelming 60 percent share (see Exhibit I-1).

How have social scientists responded to this monumental population shift? For many years the suburbs did not figure prominently in their research agenda.[4] Suburbia was treated more as a state of mind or a social phenomenon than a place that many people lived or worked. Perhaps because of this perspective, there isn't an official census definition[5] of a suburb -- how can one give physical strictures to an ephemeral social state? Unofficial definitions, such as "territory within the standard metropolitan statistical area other than central cities,"[6] are wanting in their amorphousness.

1

EXHIBIT I-1

Percentage Distribution of U.S. Population,
By Metropolitan and Central City Status: 1910 to 1980

	1910	1920	1930	1940	1950	1960	1970	1980
Metropolitan Population@	28.3	34.0	44.6	47.8	56.1	62.9	68.6	72.8
Inside central cities	21.7	25.3	30.8	32.5	32.8	32.3	31.4	29.4
Outside central cities	6.6	8.7	13.8	15.3	23.3	30.6	37.2	43.4
Nonmetropolitan Population	71.7	66.0	55.4	52.2	43.9	37.1	31.4	27.2
Percent of Metropolitan Population								
Inside central cities	76.7	75.4	70.1	68.0	58.5	51.4	45.8	40.4
Outside central cities	23.3	25.6	30.9	32.0	41.5	48.6	54.2	59.6

@ Data for 1910 through 1940 are for metropolitan districts as officially defined at each date. Data for 1950 through 1980 are for standard metropolitan statistical areas as defined at each date.

Source: John Long, Population Deconcentration in the United States (Washington, D.C., Government Printing Office, 1981), p. 65.

The sociological emphasis of the suburban literature is illustrated in the following Cooks tour of some of the more important studies[7] (see bibliography in this study for a comprehensive listing). In 1953, William H. Whyte described suburban society as a filiarchy -- a society "ruled" by child rearing.[8] In 1957, Max Lerner bemoaned the anti-individual characteristics of suburban living.[9] In 1959, Ktsanes and Reissman described suburbia as a "new home for old values held by a resettled middle class."[10] In the 1960's, Herbert Gans[11] and Bennett Berger[12] sought to debunk the "myth" of suburbia as a uniform and complacent and indeed separate society, a theme dwelled on by Scott Donaldson in The Suburban Myth.[13] Researchers also sought to identify varying suburban community patterns and roles. Thus, Dobriner[14] considered division by socioeconomic status, Logan factored age,[15] Schnore employment,[16] and others such as Farley[17] and Duncan[18] "ecological niche" or "ecological complex." Thus, for most of the post-World War II period, suburbia was studied mostly as a social phenomena and little else.

As with any such sweeping generalization, there were some exceptions to the rule. For instance, in 1968, then President Johnson called the Task Force on Suburban Problems into existence.[19] It is interesting to note, however, that this group was formed after sister national study groups considering urban disorders and decline were created such as the Kaiser and Douglas Commissions. Moreover, while the latter focused on the distress of urban areas caused by their decline, the problems identified by the Suburban Task Force -- environmental degradation, exclusionary zoning, and inadequate highways -- were consequences of the rapid out-of-city growth and business expansion.

It was not until the early 1970's that decline-associated problems of suburbia were first pointed to in the literature. This effort was spearheaded by Louis Masotti.[20] In the Urbanization of the Suburbs, he spoke of the outward spread of many of the functions and distresses of central cities:[21]

> ...Contemporary suburbia...is becoming increasingly less suburban and more urban. More and more of what have historically been central city functions are now being shared by suburbia. The net effect is to urbanize suburbia....[The] process...has resulted in "an outer city" that is rapidly becoming more like the inner city in social structure, economy, problems, and life style.

Writing in 1973, Masotti urged that suburbs begged for serious scholarly attention.[22] Ten years later we can say that much work has been done. Sociological studies have continued, often conducted with increasingly sophisticated factor analysis and other statistical tools.[23] Changing demographics have also been examined,[24] most notably the increasing size of the suburban population, as well as its aging,[25] and more pronounced minority share.[26] Employment analyses have been made showing that suburbs are rapidly becoming the workplace rather than the bedroom of contemporary America.[27] Other areas of suburban research range from the political to the religious[28] (see bibliography in this study).

The topic of suburban fiscal stress manifested by rising governmental expenditures and tax rates, has also begun to be explored. One of the first efforts in this regard was a 1969 essay by Dick Netzer tracing a four-step evolutionary cycle of suburban communities and associated financial problems.[29] The first stage was a rural to suburb transformation forcing the provision for the first time of such services as municipal sewerage and refuse disposal. In the second stage, suburbs grew quickly, thereby necessitating a commensurate acceleration of service provision. In the third and final stages, suburban growth slowed but local resident "appetite" for second-generation services such as recreation grew with attendant cost increases. A not infrequent imbalance between service expenditures and local financial resources added to fiscal stress.

Netzer pointed to the full life-cycle[30] of suburban fiscal problems; however, with few exceptions,[31] the trickle of research on this topic over the 1960's and 1970's focused on birth and growing pains rather than the financial headaches of aging. This emphasis is evident in such titles as "Growing Suburbs and Town Finance,"[32] "The Impact of New Industry on Revenues and Expenditures of Suburban Communities,"[33] and "City and Suburb: The Economics of Metropolitan Growth.[34] Such an expansive orientation was not surprising given the fact that these analyses were conducted in the very years when American suburbs were experiencing vigorous increases in population and business activity.

Starting in the mid-to-late 1970's, researchers of the suburban fiscal condition became more sensitive to financial distress associated with community aging and maturity. Culver spoke of older "suburban distress";[35] RAND of "troubled suburbs."[36] There was growing realization that increasing numbers of suburbs were becoming "urbanized" to use Masotti's term or "mature" or "long-settled" to use Netzer's, in the sense that they too were experiencing population/economic stagnation and attendant fiscal problems. As with their urban brethren, "urbanized" or "mature" suburbs were displaying such financial hardship symptoms as rising per capita expenditures, rising tax rates, shortfalls in collecting taxes, growing debt, and so on.

STUDY FOCUS: FISCAL PROBLEMS AND
RESPONSES OF MATURE SUBURBS

This study continues the research theme of suburban financial stress associated with community maturity as opposed to growth. It examines the municipal fiscal problems and responses of "older hub suburbs," focusing on a case study community: Englewood, New Jersey. The research agenda and terminology are described below.

The study analyzes municipal as opposed to school outlays and revenues. It examines the municipal fisc in a particular class of suburbs, "hub communities" -- localities serving as central activity nodes (e.g. transportation, economic, cultural, etc.) for surrounding suburbs. As other communities, hubs often go through a cycle of first growth when they gain population, jobs, retail sales and so on, followed in time by stabilization and then decline. As our interest is in the fiscal issues of community maturity rather than expansion, we focus on older as opposed to newer, emerging hubs. The former are a compelling group to study because they were the center of many aspects of suburban society for most of this century. To illustrate as well as to gain insight into the financial problems of mature hubs, we refer to one such case study suburb, Englewood, New Jersey. As we shall see shortly, Englewood personifies many hub traits. Englewood's expenditures are reviewed, its revenue sources and emphases are described, and a detailed agenda is presented to improve its financial posture.

Before proceeding, it is important to clarify our terminology and research intent. To avoid jargon, "older hub suburbs" are referred to in an abbreviated fashion simply as "mature" or "older" suburbs, both terms used synonymously. The reader must realize, however, that not all older suburbs are hubs nor are all hubs older suburbs. For instance, an older, predominantly residential community would not be a hub -- a multifunctional center for its neighbors -- while a relatively young suburb containing a recently built regional shopping center or office complex would be a hub but not a mature one. Our analysis thus focuses on the specialized case of the hub suburb in its later years as it experiences and attempts to deal with financial stress.

With this clarification behind us, we can now turn to describing the traditional and changing role of the mature suburb, the linkage of these functional shifts to fiscal stress, and the introduction of the case study community, Englewood.

THE HUB/MATURE/OLDER SUBURB DESCRIBED

Mature or older suburbs historically served as central activity nodes (e.g. transportation, economic, social and cultural) for surrounding suburbs. Hubs were the suburb's "cities." In years past, in the pre-interstate era when bus, trolley, and train were paramount, the hub suburb often served as a transportation terminous. Its downtown was the region's shopping promenade. When one did not need or want to go to the central city to shop, the mature suburb's central business district was a satisfactory alternative. Cheek by jowl to the main shopping street, commonly named according to its function (e.g. "main," "grand," "central," "broadway," etc.), was often found another regional attraction -- the first-run movie house-cum-vaudeville theatre with its neighboring restaurants, arcades, and other amusements. For the more serious minded, the older suburb housed numerous social and educational institutions such as churches, civic clubs, vocational schools, etc. Not infrequently, hospital and other medical facilities were found. Government offices also often sought mature suburban locations as did professional firms and other employers.

Our description of hub communities in terms of activities past was deliberate. It reflects the fact that many of the older suburbs' economic, social, and cultural functions are no longer concentrated in individual communities but instead are dispersed across the suburban

landscape. For instance, with the coming of the interstate, suburban
transportation has decentralized to individual automobile trips; yesteryear's train, trolley, and bus terminals housed in the older suburb
have either closed or have become shells of their former selves. In
other instances, activities clustered in mature suburbs are now concentrated elsewhere. The older suburb's shopping prominence has been
lost to newer, free-standing shopping centers located off the interchanges of interstate and other major highways. The large downtown
movie house has fared even worse. Changes in America's leisure-time
pursuits, and the advent of cinemas at malls, have forced many a downtown theatre to close or else limp along with pornographic or other
peripheral showings. Other hub functions -- medical, educational, government, and professional -- are still to be found and in some cases
are thriving, yet even here their vibrancy and surely their regional
dominance of the past are often lost.

Our description of mature suburbs surely masks variations in individual community histories. Some hubs have fared very poorly to the
point that they are more impacted from an economic, social, and physical perspective than central cities.[37] Others, in contrast, are
thriving and have become the preferred location for professional
space, expensive residential infilling, etc. While surely one cannot
generalize concerning the fate of all mature suburbs, as a group these
communities are being challenged in their historical role as the suburb's center of activity.

Examples of Mature Suburbs

The hub's traditional functions and the challenge to these activities are illustrated by the following historical overview of an important Long Island suburb, Hempstead.[38] For over two centuries, this
community served as an important transportation, cultural, and retail
center:[39]

> Through the 1700's Hempstead served as the principal junction for
> Long Island produce destined for markets....One of the earliest
> terminals of the Long Island Rail Road opened...in 1839....By the
> turn of the century Hempstead sat astride Long Island's transpor-
> tation arteries and was acknowledged to be a leading population
> and commercial center.

The first 50 years of the twentieth century were good ones for Hempstead. During World War I, it lay astride a major embarcation center,
Camp Mills, and an important airport, Mitchell Field. To better accommodate the more than 300,000 soldiers and aviators passing through
these facilities, the Army upgraded Hempstead's sewage facilities and
train service -- improvements which helped spur development in the
post-war era. Hempstead became the region's central hub. Retail sales
exceeded $20 million by the late 1920's; a branch of New York Univer-
sity (Nassau College-Hofstra) was opened; New York Telephone built its
Long Island headquarters there, and so on.[40] Prosperity continued in

the 1940's and early 1950's. Abraham and Strauss opened Long Island's then target department store in the downtown, and the community served as a regional center for automobile sales and service stations.

Prosperity soon ended as Hempstead lost many of its hub functions in the late 1950's and throughout the 1960's.[41] Important nearby military posts such as Mitchell and Roosevelt Fields were closed. Adding insult to injury, many of these surplus facilities (e.g. Roosevelt Field) were soon converted to regional shopping, office and other centers located outside Hempstead's borders and devastating the community's traditional retail and related economic activity. Retail sales, for instance, fell from a 12 percent share of total Nassau County sales in 1950, to 6 percent in 1970.[42] With its tax base eroded, property taxes increased. The middle-class soon fled, leaving a more impoverished and welfare-dependent population. Housing was abandoned, and the CBD became a shabby shell of its former self. Hempstead was suffering the full spectrum of urban woes.

Hempstead's fortunes were dramatic in their turnabout. They are not unique. Plainfield, New Jersey, was once an important hub suburb. By the 1970's, however, it lost many of its regional functions:[43]

> Plainfield was once the dominant retail locus within its region. Increasingly, however, this function has been usurped by the highway-oriented facilities outside the city's boundaries. Plainfield was, classically, a commuter town dating back to the development of the Jersey Central Railroad. The city acquired a major Mack Truck assembly plant located on the railroad line and drew workers from outlying areas. The assembly plant, however, moved out more than six years ago. While Plainfield sits proximate to the great band of industrial development between New York and Philadelphia, the new highway network has provided a host of alternate locations for new job growth. The former Mack Truck works is reoccupied, but by low-paying operations in search of cheap labor and cheap sites. The potential for increased economic development within the municipality is not encouraging.

The shifts buffeting Hempstead and Plainfield are borne by other mature suburbs across the country. Examples include: Newton, Massachusetts; Evanston, Illinois; Highland Park, Michigan; East Cleveland, Ohio; University City, Missouri; and Pasadena, California.[44]

FISCAL STRESS OF MATURE SUBURBS

The older suburb's traditional role as the suburb's "city" and the loss of this role contribute to the fiscal stress many such communities are experiencing.

Historical hub functions as transportation, retail, and entertainment centers demanded a wide range of typically costly municipal services. Roads had to be built and maintained to service the multitude entering and leaving the hub. Shoppers, employees, and visitors needed the protection of a full-scale police force. Physically large residential and nonresidential structures such as theatres, hospitals, and government-buildings, prompted the establishment of a full-fledged paid fire department as opposed to volunteers. Movie theatres, restaurants, arcades, and similar businesses demanded municipal food, safety and other inspectors. The diversity of local properties -- residential, commercial, and industrial -- necessitated the hiring of sophisticated, full-time assessors and other tax officials. As a suburban center, hubs often assumed regional cultural, recreational, and welfare functions in the form of building major library facilities, operating swimming pools, and leading the way in clinic, child care and similar services. Creation of this far-flung municipal service corporation, in turn, demanded that a commensurately large, sophisticated, and ultimately expensive administrative apparatus be formed.

The costs of the mature suburb's comprehensive service structure were bearable as long as these communities reaped the financial gain from serving as the region's central node. This fiscal windfall was not to last, however. Loss of retail, industrial, and other business sector vitality denuded the older suburb's property tax base and induced the more affluent to leave. Decline not only depleted the local ability to pay for services, it fostered heightened municipal spending pressure in the form of added patrols to police the declining downtown, increased fire calls to abandoned properties, and the care and feeding of an increasingly dependent population.

Our description thus far of mature suburbs -- their historical function, role today, and fiscal stress -- is based on the admittedly sparse literature[45] on this subject. The objective of the study is to expand our knowledge, especially of the fiscal dynamic. Are mature suburbs as a class characterized by high municipal outlays? If so, why does this occur? Does their range of local activities from residential to industrial play a role? Are a large bureaucracy and high civil service salaries -- legacies of their past role and affluence -- factors in explaining their spending profile today? Does their increasing "urbanization" contribute to expenditure pressures? What is their revenue posture, and how does income compare to outlays? What does this spending versus revenue comparison augur for future fiscal stress? What should be done to ameliorate such strain?

Insight into these financial dynamics is provided by the case study community, Englewood. To understand this locality's fiscal profile today we must first turn back the historical clock to the community's roots, two centuries ago.

ENGLEWOOD, NEW JERSEY: THE DEVELOPMENT OF A HUB SUBURB

Englewood is a physically compact locality (5 square miles), located in Bergen County, New Jersey. It lies just north of the great New Jersey meadowlands, three miles from the George Washington Bridge, and ten miles from midtown Manhattan[46] (see Exhibit I-2).

This portion of New Jersey was first settled in the late 1600's, first by the Dutch and then the English. The latter soon prevailed and the area from Ridgefield north to Closter (see Exhibit I-2) became known as "English Neighborhood."[47]

EXHIBIT I-2

Englewood, New Jersey and Adjacent Area

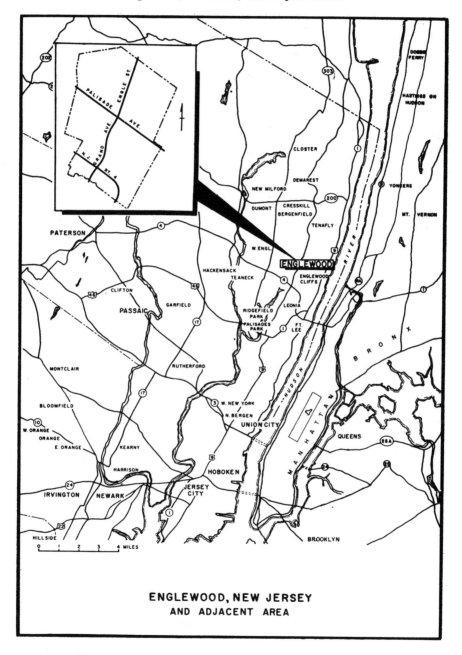

ENGLEWOOD, NEW JERSEY
AND ADJACENT AREA

Source: The League of Women Voters of the Englewood Area, New Jersey, <u>Englewood: A Community Handbook</u> (Englewood: League, 1977), p. 2.

The site of modern-day Englewood was first settled in the early 1700's as a six-farm land grant to Gerrit Lydecker.[48] The area was soon known as "Liberty Pole" after such a monument was erected in 1766 to commemorate the repeal of the Stamp Act. "Liberty Pole" soon assumed an important role as a result of its location near a critical road intersection:[49]

> Liberty Pole was at a major intersection of the Colonial Road system where English Neighborhood Road (the major route from the south) turned west and intersected both northbound, Tenafly Road and several routes westbound across solid land to the Hackensack River at New Bridge. This was the furthest point where the marshes...could be transversed and New Bridge was the furthest point south where the limited technology of the day would allow construction of a bridge over the Hackensack....

"Liberty Pole's" strategic location near the English Neighborhood Road intersection prompted early hub roles as a meeting place and transportation center:[50]

> At this strategic intersection stood a tavern which...came to be known as Liberty Pole Tavern....[It] played an important role in the early history of the area since it served as a meeting place for the entire county and a point from which information about the growing revolution was brought by travelers and disseminated to the entire community.

> The...Tavern was torn down in 1813....Another...was constructed ....It became a tavern and a hotel. It served not only as a resting place for travelers, but also as a local political and social meeting place....

> Sometime before 1850, the Liberty Pole Tavern became the starting point of a stage line between Liberty Pole and the ferry at Hoboken.

While this stage was an improvement over the ad-hoc arrangements of the day (e.g. walking to Hackensack and taking the stage there), it did not open the area to rapid settlement because the stage-ferry combination took three hours (each way) to reach Manhattan. The advent of the railroad and other transportation improvements changed all this. In the mid-nineteenth century, a railroad was built from Jersey City to English neighborhood (see Exhibit I-2).[51] It was only a matter of time before a trunk (ultimately to be known as the Northern Railroad) would be extended to "Liberty Pole," already established as a transit center. In anticipation of the opportunities for growth the Northern Railroad would bring, in the late 1850's, J. Wyman Jones, a friend of the Northern's chief engineer, purchased roughly 600 acres of farmland from the Lydecker family. Jones incorporated his purchase as a village called Englewood, supposedly a contraction of "English

Neighborhood."[52] Politically, Englewood would remain a village within Hackensack until the 1870's, an independent village until the
1890's, and incorporated as a city at the turn of the century.

This period, spanning the late 19th to early 20th century, was a
prosperous one for both the Northern Railroad and Englewood. In 1859,
one train daily stopped in Englewood, shortly afterwards, three, and
by 1915, 42. Convenient train service to Jersey City and from there by
ferry to Chambers Street in lower Manhattan took a total of only 45
minutes each way -- the same as today. Englewood's accessibility to
Wall Street, the elevation and physical beauty of its East Hill (an
ideal setting for the romantic suburb of the late 19th century), and
the affluent circle of friends of Jones and other early Englewood pro-
moters (e.g. I. Sheppard Homans, publisher of Banker's Magazine),[53]
soon brought to the community a "who's-who" of the American financial
world such as the presidents of both the New York and the American
Stock Exchanges. They built East Hill mansions, many of which still
stand today.

Englewood's role as a hub was accentuated by the prestige and affluence of its founding fathers and early citizens. The Englewood hospital was founded in this period. Regional cultural facilities were
built such as the opera house and Athenaeum (a grand four-story building containing a post office, stores, and 800 seat theatre). A bus-
tling commercial district developed adjacent to the Palisade Avenue
Railroad station. This too served the surrounding area, not only
Englewood:[54]

> As the post-Civil War decades passed, Englewood quickly grew into
> the regional shopping center of the Northern Valley. The activi-
> ties present were not only more numerous, but also of a higher
> order than those of the communities around it, with the exception
> of Hackensack, the county seat.

Transportation improvements strenghtened Englewood's position as a
regional center. In the late 1860's, its main commercial street, Palisade Avenue (see Exhibit I-2), was widened to 70 feet. Intersecting
English Neighborhood Road, the northern valley's main north-south
route was also widened, renamed (to Grand Avenue), and aligned with an
important Englewood thoroughfare, Engle Street (see Exhibit I-2).
These improvements enhanced Englewood's accessibility and role as a
regional thoroughfare:[55]

> New roads approached Englewood from the South and aided in the
> development of the downtown area by increasing accessibility from
> that more densely populated direction....Englewood, thus found
> itself not only astride the foot of the Northern Valley, but also
> containing two major traffic routes, one at each end of the town.
> The first was the Grand Avenue-Engle Street route which skirted
> the meadows from Hudson County and ran up the length of the
> Northern Valley. The other had as its focal point the intersec-
> tion at Liberty Pole which tied the West Bank communities of the
> Overpeck (and the Hackensack) to the Northern Valley.

Englewood benefited from other transportation advances. A trolley
line to Hackensack to the west and the Leonia-Fort Lee-Edgewater ferry
to the east (see Exhibit I-2) was opened in the late 1890's. Horse-
drawn and then steam bus service was inaugurated shortly afterwards.
Improved accessibility spurred Englewood's growth. At the turn of the
century, it contained roughly 6,500 residents; by 1910, about 10,000;
1920, 12,000; and 1930 almost 18,000. The train, trolley, and bus network enhanced Englewood's role as a hub:[56]

> Englewood's commercial expansion continued with this increased
> accessibility for residents of other communities who could now
> travel there via the greatly expanded public transportation
> system. Two theatres were constructed, 18 automobile dealers
> appeared, banks, and a variety of specialty stores could be
> found.... According to older residents, Englewood had become
> known as "the shopping hub of the Northern Valley." It was an era
> of great prosperity for Englewood merchants. According to Joseph
> Carney, former City Clerk, "the twenties were great."

Englewood's growth slowed during the Depression; its 1940 census
count of 19,000 was only marginally higher than that a decade earlier.
In the early post-World War II era, the community grew to 23,000 in
1950 and peaked at 26,000 in 1960. Since then, the number of residents
has declined to 25,000 in 1970 and 24,000 ten years later. Other social shifts occurred. For example, the community's traditionally high
minority share, a legacy of the many domestics working on East Hill,
accelerated from one-third of the total population in 1970 to one-half
in 1980.

Much of the post-World War II era was one of decline for Englewood
as a regional hub. The following transportation changes were both
symptom and cause of this diminution. Railroad service limped along
until the 1960's when only two trains daily stopped at Englewood --
down from over 40 two decades earlier. Railroad service ceased alto-
gether in 1966. Englewood still retained its important Grand-Engle-
Palisade thoroughfares (see Exhibit I-2), but these were no longer the
region's through routes. They were replaced by limited access roads
such as Routes 1, 4, and 9, and the New Jersey Turnpike (see Exhibit
I-2).

Englewood lost other hub functions. Industrial and related firms
left the city. Its last movie theatre closed in the early 1970's. Its
commercial district was an earlier victim. In the 1950's, a succession
of shopping centers was built in nearby Paramus at the intersection of
Routes 4 and 17 (see Exhibit I-2). They took their economic toll on
Englewood's CBD:[57]

> In the 1948 to 1954 period, the city, once known as the shopping
> hub of Bergen, was not holding its own with the rest of Bergen
> County. Its sales, 8 percent of the county total in 1948, had
> slipped to 6.2 percent in 1954, and by 1958, the number of firms
> would decline to 327 and its sales to 5.4 percent of the total.

Englewood's retail duress would continue. By 1977, it captured only 4 percent of Bergen's sales. From 1958 to 1977, one-fifth of its retail establishments closed. Sales of shoppers goods (excluding automotive transactions such as car and gasoline purchases) declined in real (inflation-adjusted dollars) over this period. A succession of downtown revitalization plans was commissioned; few were effected and what little was done was ineffectual in stemming the increasing encroachment of nearby shopping centers. Thus on many fronts, Englewood was in its maturity as a hub suburb.

STUDY METHODOLOGY

Examination of Englewood's fiscal profile can provide insight to the financial problems facing mature suburbs. Similarly, investigation of strategies to ameliorate Englewood's fiscal stress can prove instructive to comparable communities elsewhere.

Our methodology is thus the case study -- "a comprehensive description and explanation of the many components of a given situation."[58] This method's intensity of investigation offers the promise, if not always the realization, of insight into complex social interactions. It is particularly appropriate in "relatively unformulated areas where there is little experience to serve as a guide (and where) intensive study (can be) a particularly fruitful method for stimulating insight and suggesting hypotheses."[59] The authors feel that the fiscal dynamic of older suburban hubs is such an "unformulated area" where much can be gained from a case study analysis such as that of Englewood. Furthermore, examining mature suburb responses to fiscal stress, encompassing actions ranging from CBD revitalization to cutbacks in service standards, is most meaningful when conducted on a concrete basis under real world constraints. Our analysis of Englewood thus considers such real world issues as what is the fiscal impact of new development in mature hubs; what are the lingering attractions of the older suburb CBD and how can these be strengthened; and how might local public service standards be adjusted to reflect growing financial austerity? These are not questions to be considered in the abstract.

The source of the case study's strength -- intensive investigation of one or the few -- is also its weakness. If the subject of analysis is idiosyncratic, the research findings cannot be generalized. This is a major potential flaw. As expressed by one text on social science methods: "Ultimately the researcher executing a case study typically seeks insight that will have a more generalized applicability beyond the single case under study, but the case study itself cannot assure this."[60]

This methodological danger prompts the following modification. While we shall continue to focus on Englewood as a case study subject, other New Jersey communities (a total of 50 including Englewood) are added for perspective. (See Appendix A to the Introduction for discussion of how the 50 communities were chosen.) This 50-member sample

comprises roughly one-tenth the total municipalities in New Jersey and
contains about 30 percent of the state's population. With this addition, we can reap the advantage of examining a larger group rather
than a single community while at the same time enjoying the insight of
the detailed Englewood case study.

The 50 localities span a range of community types (see Exhibit I-3
for a roster of individual members). If we list Englewood separately,
they comprise the following four groups.

1. Urban centers – New Jersey cities. A total of 5 were selected.

2. Englewood – the case study community.

3. Mature suburbs – Englewood's sister older New Jersey hubs. A total of 25 including Englewood were chosen.

4. Growing suburbs – newer and emerging hub communities. A total
   of 20 were selected.

This four-community typology was formed to: 1. better examine variations in municipal expenditures/fiscal stress by different classes of
localities; and 2. explore municipal outlays/stress by community evolutionary cycle.

Researchers of municipal expenditure determinants[61] have linked
heightened municipal outlays and attendant financial strain to growing
density or "urban" characteristics (see detailed discussion in chapter
two). Analysts of suburban public spending[62] have pointed to similar
density and urbanism influences. As is evident from Exhibit I-4, our
four community typology -- urban, Englewood, mature, and growing suburbs -- span a density and urban continuum. The urban group has an
average density of 21,000 population per square mile. Densities then
fall to 5,000 for Englewood, 2,800 for mature suburbs, and 2,200 for
growing suburbs. "Urbanism" also varies by community category, albeit
this trait is difficult to define formally. By popularly accepted urban attributes (e.g. crime rate, employment gains/loss, percentage
minority population, etc.), our city group is "most urban" followed
successively by Englewood, mature suburbs, and then growing suburbs
(see Exhibit I-4). By selecting and categorizing our study communities
by a density-urbanism scale, we can test the veracity of the linkage
of these characteristics to municipal outlays and fiscal stress.

A less technical consideration also compels the multi-community
grouping. By focusing on Englewood, even when sister mature suburbs
are included, we are examining municipal characteristics frozen at a
moment of time. Lost is the dynamic cycle of community evolution and
concomitant financial attributes. Adding the growing suburban hub and
urban cohorts gives us a cyclical perspective; it allows examination
of the fiscal profile of the community stage whence the older suburb
evolved -- the newer/growing hub suburb -- as well as the community
type -- urban -- which the mature suburbs may ultimately resemble, at
least on selected attributes. Our point is not to argue for a direct

EXHIBIT I-3

New Jersey Urban, Mature, and Growing Suburbs: Community List

I. *URBAN*	*II.* *MATURE SUBURBS*	*III.* *GROWING SUBURBS*
Elizabeth	Bergenfield	Bernards
Jersey City	Clifton	Cherry Hill
Newark	Cranford	East Brunswick
Paterson	Dover	East Hanover
Trenton	Englewood	East Windsor
	Flemington	Florham Park
	Fort Lee	Holmdel
	Hackensack	Lawrence
	Hillside	Montvale
	Lodi	Moorestown
	Long Branch	Morris Township
	Lyndhurst	New Providence
	Maplewood	Parsippany-Troy
	Millburn	Pennsauken
	Montclair	Piscataway
	Morristown	Rockaway
	New Brunswick	Roseland
	Plainfield	South Brunswick
	Red Bank	Voorhees
	Ridgewood	Warren
	Roselle	
	Scotch Plains	
	Summit	
	Teaneck	
	Wayne	

EXHIBIT I-4

New Jersey Urban and Suburban Communities: Selected Social and Economic Characteristics, 1970–1980

YEAR/AREA	Total Population (in 000s)	Density (a)	% Minority Population (b)	Per Capita Real Income (c)	Crime Rate Per 1,000 Population	Police Per 1,000 Population	Employment (Jobs (d)/ratio of jobs to local population (e))					
							Manufacturing	Wholesale	Retail	Financial	Service	Total (f)
1970												
Urban	201.2	20,763	31.1	$5,400	49	3.4	24,881/.13	5,931/.03	8,876/.05	6,711/.03	12,319/.07	73,397/.38
Englewood	25.0	5,102	32.8	8,700	45	4.0	3,150/.13	2,096/.08	1,554/.06	980/.39	2,278/.09	11,359/.45
Mature Suburbs	29.8	2,838	11.3	7,600	26	2.0	3,482/.13	698/.03	2,150/.09	539/.20	1,458/.05	8,858/.33
Growing Suburbs	20.6	2,168	2.2	7,600	20	1.8	2,234/.14	306/.13	1,098/.05	201/.11	1,290/.09	6,105/.31
1980												
Urban	178.0	18,369	60.8	4,800	106	4.0	20,114/.11	4,216/.03	7,233/.04	5,311/.02	13,135/.07	50,893/.34
Englewood	23.7	4,836	49.4	8,400	97	3.0	2,938/.12	1,497/.06	1,488/.06	652/.28	4,870/.21	12,406/.52
Mature Suburbs	28.0	2,667	22.5	9,900	58	2.0	2,978/.10	811/.03	2,189/.09	964/.39	3,523/.14	11,787/.45
Growing Suburbs	22.0	2,315	4.6	10,800	41	2.0	3,223/.19	918/.05	2,286/.10	1,191/.71	2,963/.16	10,581/.63
1980 As Share of 1970 Value												
Urban	.88	.88	1.95 (f)	.89	2.16	1.18	.81	.71	.81	.79	1.07	.83
Englewood	.95	.95	1.51	.97	2.16	.75	.93	.71	.96	.67	2.14	1.09
Mature Suburbs	.94	.94	1.99	1.30	2.23	1.00	.86	1.16	1.02	1.79	2.42	1.33
Growing Suburbs	1.07	1.07	2.09	1.54	2.05	1.11	1.44	3.00	2.08	5.93	2.30	1.73

Notes: (a) Population per square mile.
(b) Includes Blacks and Spanish-speaking in 1980 and Blacks only in 1970.
(c) In constant (inflation-adjusted) dollars; 1978 used as a base case. *NOTE:* 1980 income data are projected from 1970–1975 trends.
(d) Indicates covered employment by economic sector.
(e) Indicates ratio of local employment to local population; these figures were obtained for each community within the four groups and then averaged. It therefore differs slightly from the ratio which would be yielded by dividing the average population and employment counts shown in the exhibit.
(f) Total is greater than sum of categories shown because not all employment groups are indicated.

NOTE: Where 1980 data were unavailable, 1978 information was utilized and/or projections to 1980 were made from the most current data.

Source: U.S. Census, New Jersey Department of Labor and Industry.

newer hub-older hub-urban evolutionary cycle which may not exist, nor to speak of a linear community change which surely oversimplifies reality, but, rather to sensitize us to the changing nature of community identity and related fiscal attributes.

How well have we chosen our four community typologies? Appendix A describes the selection process in detail. It is instructive here to briefly consider how these different groupings conform to expected patterns as far as local employment is concerned. Cities have traditionally been the nation's job centers. This factor is reflected in the high total employment counts of our urban set relative to the suburban cohorts (see Exhibit I-4). Urban centers have been buffeted by recent employment losses, especially in manufacturing and related industrial areas. Our New Jersey urban group lost 20 percent of its total employment between 1970 and 1980; certain nonresidential sectors of these communities were harder hit, such as wholesale experiencing a 30 percent job drop. In contrast to urban job diminution, suburbs have fared better -- on average our New Jersey suburban groups enjoyed roughly a 50 percent job gain between 1970 and 1980.

This half-again suburban employment increase is an average. It is instructive to compare the variations in job vigor of the mature versus newer New Jersey suburban hubs. If we selected our groups properly, the former should experience slow to middling employment growth, the latter strong expansion. This is the pattern shown. Between 1970 and 1980, employment in the mature New Jersey suburbs grew by relatively small amounts (10 percent for Englewood, 30 percent in sister older hubs) compared to the vigorous expansion (75 percent) displayed by the growing suburbs (see Exhibit I-4).

Exhibit I-5 gives a visual presentation of the growing suburbs' "pulling away" from their older counterparts in an important hub activity, retail trade (as measured by retail employment). This graph has two axes: the horizontal shows different time periods between 1970 and 1980 (e.g. 1970, 1974, 1976, etc.); the vertical indicates employment-to-residence ratios (e.g. a community with 5,000 jobs and 10,000 population would have a .5 ratio; see Appendix A). The 20 individual growing suburbs are each displayed by the letter "G"; the 25 individual declining or mature suburbs by the letter "D" (Englewood is shown by an "E"). Exhibit I-5 indicates that in the early 1970's the mature hubs had the more significant retail employment; by the end of the decade the growing suburbs pulled even and then some (see also Exhibit I-4). In summary, the different New Jersey community cohorts "behave" in expected patterns at least as far as job vigor or lack of vigor is concerned.

STUDY OUTLINE

Our analysis consists of two sections comprising a total of six chapters.

The first section presents the problem of financial hardship in older suburbs. Chapter one examines the revenue and expenditure profiles of urban areas, Englewood, other mature suburbs, and growing

EXHIBIT 1-5

Plot of Retail Employment to Population Ratio by Year:
Growing Suburbs ("G"), Declining/Mature Suburbs ("D"), and Englewood ("E")

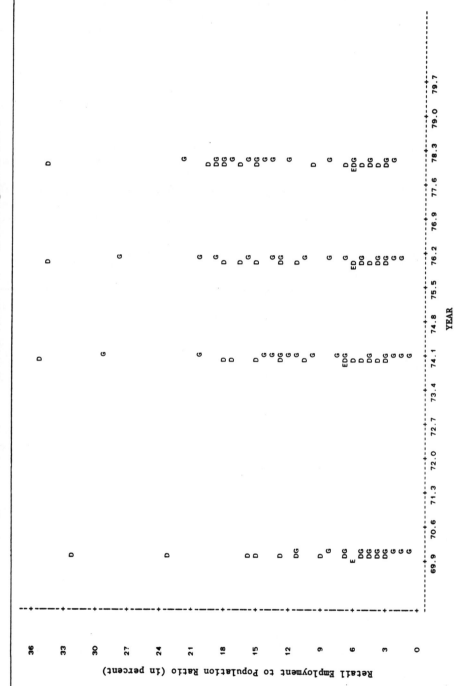

suburbs. It concludes that relative to newer suburban communities and sometimes even urban centers, mature suburbs and most particularly Englewood, have high municipal outlays. This spending relationship is paralleled in the tax burden profile. While mature suburbs typically do not shoulder the tax obligation of urban communities, the former, especially Englewood, impose far higher taxes than their newer suburban counterparts. By these expenditure and tax load criteria, residents in older suburbs in general and Englewood in particular are characterized by relative fiscal strain.

Chapter two explores why these fiscal patterns occur, focusing on the influences on municipal expenditures. While surely fiscal stress encompasses both expenditure and revenue considerations, we focus on the former for the following reasons. By any measure of community wealth (e.g. per capita income or property value), mature suburbs are usually quite affluent. Their financial stress is a function of extremely high municipal spending. Englewood, for example, is quite well-to-do as far as resident income or property value is concerned, yet experiences fiscal strain because of its very high municipal outlays (e.g. on a per capita basis, two-thirds higher than sister mature suburbs and twice that of growing suburbs). Another reason prompting focus on expenditures is that the municipal reaction to the fiscal crunch of the past few years has typically emphasized reducing public outlays rather than raising often already high taxes; improving our understanding of the factors prompting municipal spending can thus assist such expenditure cutback management.

Section two of the study turns from exploring the presence, nature, and underlying causes of mature suburb fiscal stress to examining how such strain can be ameliorated. Selected strategies for older suburbs in general and Englewood in particular are explored in chapters three through six. Chapter three examines the fiscal impact of new residential and nonresidential development. Chapter four explores the dynamics of retail activity in the older suburb and considers how this important business sector can be invigorated. Chapter five examines new uses for the older suburb downtown, specifically development of cultural facilities. Chapter six considers various municipal service cutback strategies ranging from lowering service quality sights to rethinking traditional service delivery by public departments.

It is hoped that this study will assist older hubs to adjust to the changing condition of the suburban landscape.

Appendix A
Technical Appendix
Englewood and New Jersey
Study Communities

This appendix is divided into two sections. The first considers how the New Jersey urban and suburban localities were selected for analysis. The second highlights social, economic, and racial variations <u>within</u> Englewood.

SELECTION OF THE NEW JERSEY STUDY COMMUNITIES

The 50-community New Jersey sample referred to in this monograph was chosen as follows:

1. Urban - New Jersey's 5 largest cities were selected (see Exhibit I-3).

2. Englewood - This community was chosen for detailed case study analysis. Englewood has many accentuated mature suburb traits. The latter have traditionally been central activity nodes for surrounding communities. Englewood has served in this capacity and then some (see discussion in text). Mature suburbs often exhibit more pronounced "urban social traits" relative to their newer or growing counterparts -- a profile strongly evident in Englewood (see Exhibit I-4). Mature suburbs typically provide extensive municipal services. Few communities offer a more luxurious service slate than Englewood (see chapter two). Older suburbs often have high municipal expenditures. Englewood personifies this trait; its per capita municipal outlays are twice those of newer suburban hubs (see chapter two). Mature suburbs pay a price for their expenditure and service profile in the form of relatively high taxes and growing fiscal stress. These burdens are accentuated in Englewood (see chapter one).

3. Older hub suburbs - Twenty-five mature New Jersey suburban hubs were selected (see Exhibit I-3). They were chosen on the basis of their economic activity (present and past), population size, and other considerations.

A. Economic Activity. One indicator of a hub community is a relatively high proportion of local jobs to local population. This relationship can be expressed as a ratio (e.g. .5 in a community with

5,000 jobs and 10,000 residents). We therefore established a criteria that to be included within our older suburban group, communities had to have a rather high 1980 jobs-to-population ratio (roughly .5).

We wished to identify older hubs. A good indication of such a role is that of being an early, say pre-1950, retail center. We therefore established a criteria that not only did communities to be included within the older suburban cohort have to be in the 1948 Census of Retail Trade (only a third of New Jersey's 567 minor civil divisions were considered important enough retail areas to be listed), but in addition their 1948 retail sales had to exceed the median for the state.

B. Population. Municipal expenditures have a "U"-shaped relationship with community size. They are relatively high in both very small and very large localities. To avoid examining expenditures in such "extreme" population cases, we limited our examination to communities with at least 10,000 residents and no greater than about 50,000.

C. Other. From the full group of mature suburb candidates, 25 finalists were chosen based on numerous considerations such as: similarity to Englewood so that the case study locality could be analyzed against "comparables"; geographical diversity -- avoiding concentrations in one or two counties; and recommendations by knowledgeable New Jersey planners, geographers, and economists, as to which of the state's localities were "truly" older hubs. Upon the latter's recommendation, we included communities nominally "violating" some of the economic activity and/or population criteria discussed above (e.g. Clifton was chosen despite a 70,000 population).

4. Growing Hub Suburbs - Twenty newer, or growing suburban hubs were selected (see Exhibit I-3). They were also chosen on the basis of population, economic activity, and other considerations.

The same community population standard (roughly over 10,000, less than 50,000) was adhered to. Economic activity was also examined. As we wished to identify newer as opposed to older suburban centers, we established a criteria that localities to be included in the growing hub cohort could not be listed in the 1948 Census of Retail Trade. They did, however, have to show recent economic vigor and concentration as indicated by such indicators as high employment-to-population ratios (roughly .5), recent (1970-1980) rapid increases in employment, and/or the presence of a regional shopping center or other major employment complex (e.g. Fortune 500 corporate headquarters). For example, of the communities chosen, Florham Park had an employment-to-residence ratio of 1.2; Bernard's employment climbed from 1,000 to 5,000 over the 1970's; Lawrence contains the super regional Quaker Bridge Mall (1.1 million ft.), while Prudential Casualty Insurance is headquartered in Holmdel.

From the full group of growing suburban hub candidates, 20 finalists were chosen based on the same "other" considerations described
for mature suburbs such as geographical diversity and recommendations
by knowledgeable observers that certain communities were "truly" the
emerging suburban centers of New Jersey.

The reader should realize that there is some overlap between the
different community groups. For instance, Elizabeth, included in the
urban category, might have been slotted in the older suburb cohort.
The converse is true with respect to New Brunswick. Similarly, Wayne,
identified as an older suburb, might have been categorized in the
emerging hub category because this locality contains the Willowbrook
Mall. In such grey areas, a judgement call was made as to the most
appropriate community group.

INTRA-ENGLEWOOD SOCIAL AND ECONOMIC VARIATIONS

The introduction to this study noted overall Englewood community
traits such as its affluence, racial composition, etc. It is important to recognize that significant distinctions exist within Englewood
itself. Intra-community contrasts are illustrated by reference to
racial incidence and income. While Englewood's population as a whole
is about half non-white (1980), there are very clear spatial concentrations of its white and non-white households. Exhibit I-6 indicates
that non-whites predominate in the northwestern portion of the city,
comprising over 75 percent of the residents there. In contrast, there
are relatively few minority families in the northeastern quadrant.
Remaining areas are characterized by greater racial mixing.

There are also spatial cleavages regarding affluence. Exhibit I-7
displays the median property value per block as of the 1980 census.
The community's most expensive homes are in the northeastern and portions of the southwestern quadrant. Less expensive dwellings are found
elsewhere. A similar pattern is evident when the prices of recent home
sales (1979 and 1980) are plotted (see Exhibit I-8). Household income
displays a comparable distribution. According to the 1970 census, Englewood as a whole is quite well-to-do; almost one-fifth of its residents earned over $25,000. (1970 data are used because 1980 income
information by census tract are unavailable as of the time of this
writing.) There are clear areal distinctions, however. In the northeast portion of the community, over one-half the households earned
over $25,000 in 1970; in the northwest sector only 10 percent earned
this amount. A greater diversity of incomes was found in the other
portions of the community.

In sum, the overall Englewood community profile masks considerable
intra-local distinctions. While it is an oversimplification, the
northeast sector of the community is almost entirely white and very
affluent; the northwest is largely minority and far less wealthy, and
the other areas are far more mixed from a socioeconomic perspective.
Similar cleavages are apparent when other variables are examined. A
1975 study of Englewood's ecology and social patterns, for example,
concluded that the community displayed distinct areal variations:[63]

EXHIBIT I-6

Englewood, New Jersey: Percent Population Black by Area (1980 Census)

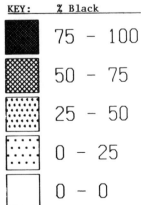

KEY: % Black

75 - 100

50 - 75

25 - 50

0 - 25

0 - 0

EXHIBIT I-7

Englewood, New Jersey: Median Block Property Value

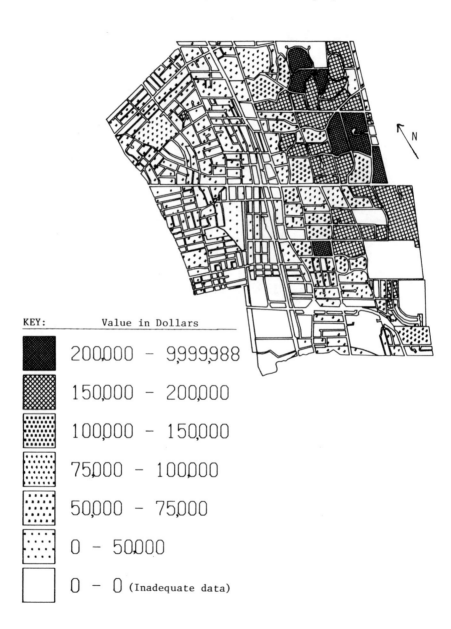

KEY: Value in Dollars

200,000 - 9,999,988

150,000 - 200,000

100,000 - 150,000

75,000 - 100,000

50,000 - 75,000

0 - 50,000

0 - 0 (Inadequate data)

EXHIBIT I-8

Englewood, New Jersey: Home Sales Prices 1979 and 1980

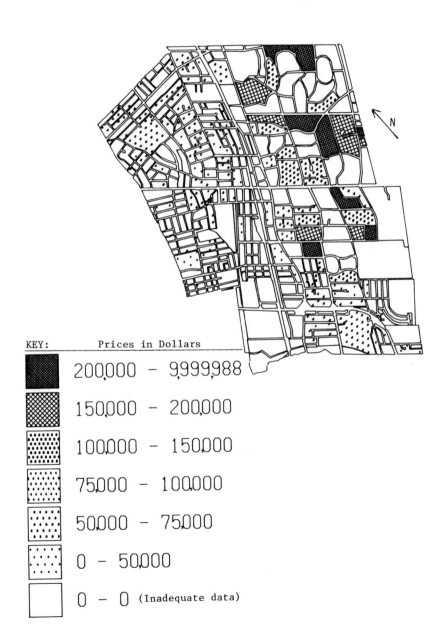

KEY: Prices in Dollars

200,000 — 9,999,988

150,000 — 200,000

100,000 — 150,000

75,000 — 100,000

50,000 — 75,000

0 — 50,000

0 — 0 (Inadequate data)

Housing quality patterns, therefore, coincide with previously mentioned racial and income distribution patterns, activity patterns, and perceived neighborhood environments, thus reinforcing the impression that Englewood is divided into several separate environments.

NOTES

1. John Long, Population Deconcentration in the United States (Washington, D.C.: Government Printing Office, 1981), p. 63.

2. Scott Donaldson, The Suburban Myth (New York City: Columbia University Press, 1969), p. 64.

3. Amos Hawley, Urban Society (New York: Ronald Press, 1971).

4. Louis Masotti and Jeffrey K. Hadden, The Urbanization of the Suburbs (Beverly Hills: Sage Publications, 1973), p. 21.

5. Andrew Isserman and Marilyn Brown, Measuring Suburban Need and Distress. (Washington, D.C.: Government Printing Office, 1981), p. 2.

6. Ibid. See also Norvald Green, "Suburbanization in the United States Since World War II" in Masotti, The Urbanization of the Suburbs, pp. 52-53; Robert Lineberry, "Suburbia and the Metropolitan Turf," Annals of the American Academy of Political and Social Science, Vol. 442, (November 1975), p. 2.

7. This section is derived in part from Masotti, "Prologue: Suburbia Reconsidered -- Myth and Counter Myth" in Masotti, The Urbanization of the Suburbs, pp. 20-22. See also bibliography to this study.

8. William H. Whyte, Jr. "How the Suburbia Socializes," Fortune (August, 1953); See also Seth Richlin, "The Aging of the Suburbs," Fortune (December 15, 1980), p. 67.

9. Max Lerner, "The Suburban Revolution," America as a Civilization (New York: Simon and Schuster, 1957).

10. T. Ktsanes and L. Reissman, "Suburbia -- New Homes for Old Values," Social Problems, Vol. 7, (Winter 1959-60), pp. 187-195.

11. Herbert Gans, The Levittowners (New York City: Panthean Books, 1959).

12. Bennett Berger, "The Myth of Suburbia," Journal of Social Issues, Vol. 17, (November 1961), pp. 38-49.

13. Donaldson, The Suburban Myth.

14. William Dobriner (editor), Class in Suburbia (Englewood Cliffs: Prentice-Hall, 1963).

15. John Logan, "Industrialization and the Stratification of Cities in Suburban Regions," American Journal of Sociology, Vol. 84, (1976), pp. 404-416.

16. Leo Schnore, The Urban Scene (New York: Free Press, 1965).

17. Renolds Farley, "Suburban Persistence," American Sociological Review, Vol. 29, (February 1964), pp. 38-47.

18. Otis Duncan and Leo Schnore, "Cultural Behavior: An Ecological Perspective in the Study of Social Organizations," American Journal of Sociology, Vol. 65, (September 1959), p. 132.

19. Charles Haar (editor), United States President's Task Force on Suburban Problems. Final Report (Cambridge, MA: Ballinger, 1974); Charles Haar, The End of Innocence: A Suburban Reader (Chicago, IL: Scott-Foresman, 1972).

20. Masotti, The Urbanization of the Suburbs.

21. Ibid., pp. 17, 533.

22. Ibid., p. 21.

23. See for example John Stahura, "The Evolution of Suburban Functional Roles," Pacific Sociological Review, Vol. 21, No. 4, (October 1970), pp. 423-439; John Stahura, "A Factorial Ecology of Suburban America: 1960-1970," Sociological Focus, Vol. 12, No. 1, (January 1979), pp. 8-19; Eugene Perle, "Perspectives of the Changing Ecological Structure of Suburbia," Urban Geography, Vol. 2, No. 3 (1981, pp. 237-254).

24. Barry Schwartz, (editor), The Changing Face of the Suburbs (Chicago, University of Chicago Press, 1976); Peter O. Muller, Contemporary Suburban America (Englewood Cliffs, NJ: Prentice-Hall, 1981); Peter O. Muller, The Outer City: Geographical Consequences of the Suburbs (Washington, D.C.: Association of American Geographers, 1976).

25. Michael Gutowski and Tracey Field, The Graying of Suburbia (Washington, D.C.: Urban Institute, 1979).

26. Robert Lake, Race and Housing in the Suburbs (New Brunswick, NJ: Center for Urban Policy Research, Rutgers University, 1980); Robert Lake, "Racial Transition and Black Homeownership in American Suburbs," Annals of the American Academy of Political and Social Sciences, Vol. 441, (January 1979), pp. 423-440; Avery Guest, "The Changing Racial Composition of Suburbs 1950-1970," Urban Affairs Quarterly, Vol. 14, No. 2, (December 1978), pp. 195-206; George Grier, "Black Suburbanization: Desegregation or Resegregation?" Urban Concerns, (May/June 1979), pp. 42-44.

27. Muller, Contemporary Suburban America; George Sternlieb and James Hughes (editors), Post-Industrial America: Metropolitan Decline and Inter-Regional Job Shifts (New Brunswick, NJ: Center for Urban Policy Research, Rutgers University, 1975); Arthur Solomon, The Prospective City: Economic, Population, Energy, and Environmental Developments Shaping Our Cities and Suburbs (Cambridge, MA: The MIT Press, 1980).

28. J. Stahura, et al. "Crime in the Suburbs: A Structural Model," Urban Affairs Quarterly, Vol. 15, No. 13, (March 1980), pp. 291-316; Edward Loucks, "The New Federalism and the Suburbs," Growth and Change, Vol. 9, (October 1978), pp. 2-7.

29. Dick Netzer, "Financing Suburban Development," in Dieter Zschock (editor), Economic Aspects of Suburban Growth: Studies of the Nassau-Suffolk Planning Region (Stony Brook, NY: State University of New York at Stony Brook, Economic Research Bureau, 1969).

30. See Edgar Hoover, "Introduction -- Suburban Growth and Regional Analysis," in Zschock, Economic Aspects of Suburban Growth, p. 9.

31. See George Sternlieb and W. Patrick Beaton, The Zone of Emergence (New Brunswick, NJ: Transaction Books, 1972).

32. Beldon Schaffer, <u>Growing Suburbs and Town Finance</u> (Storrs, CT: University of Connecticut Press, 1964).

33. L.K. Lowenstein, "Impact of New Industry on the Fiscal Revenues and Expenditures of Suburban Communities: Case Study of Three Phila- delphia Townships: Lower Merion, Upper Merion, and Radner," <u>National Tax Journal</u> (June 1972).

34. Benjamin Chinitz, <u>City and Suburb: The Economics of Metropoli- tan Growth</u> (Englewood Cliffs: Prentice Hall, 1964).

35. Lowell Culver, "The Politics of Suburban Distress," <u>Journal of Urban Affairs</u>, Vol. 4, No. 1 (Winter 1982), p. 1.

36. Judith Fernandez, et al. <u>Troubled Suburbs: An Exploratory Study</u> (Santa Monica: RAND, 1982).

37. Isserman and Brown, <u>Measuring Suburban Need and Distress</u>.

38. Susan Tenenbaum, "Hempstead: Can the "Hub" be Recapped?" <u>New York Affairs</u>, Vol. 2, No. 2, (1982), pp. 81-88.

39. Ibid. p. 82.

40. Ibid. p. 82.

41. Ibid. pp. 82-83.

42. Ibid. p. 84.

43. Sternlieb and Beaton, <u>The Zone of Emergence</u>, pp. 3-4.

44. See Fernandez et al., <u>Troubled Suburbs: An Exploratory Study</u>.

45. See bibliography to this study.

46. League of Women Voters of the Englewood Area, New Jersey, <u>Engle- wood: A Community Handbook</u> (League: 1977), p. 2.

47. Ibid. p. 4.

48. Ibid.

49. D. Bennett Mazur, <u>People, Politics, and Planning: The Compara- tive History of Three Suburban Communities</u>. Ph.D. Dissertation, Rutgers University, May 1981, pp. 96-97.

50. Ibid. p. 97-100.

51. League of Women Voters, <u>Englewood</u>, p. 4.

52. Ibid. p. 5.

53. Mazur, <u>People, Politics and Planning</u>, p. 119.

54. Ibid. p. 120.

55. Ibid. p. 129.

56. Ibid. p. 150.

57. Ibid. P. 512.

58. Earl R. Babbie. <u>Survey Research Methods</u> (Belmont, CA: Wadsworth Publishing, 1973), p. 37. See also Claire Sellitz, et al., <u>Research Methods in Social Relations</u> (New York: Holt, Rinehart and Winston), p. 59.

59. Sellitz, <u>Research Methods in Social Relations</u>, p. 59.

60. Babbie, <u>Survey Research Methods</u>, p. 37.

61. See chapter two in this study and Thomas Muller, "Fiscal Prob- lems of Smaller and Declining Cities," in Herrington Bryce, <u>Small Cities in Transition</u> (Cambridge: Ballinger, 1977), p. 167.

62. Masotti, <u>The Urbanization of the Suburbs</u>; Fernandez, et al. <u>Troubled Suburbs</u>.

63. See Charles Bradley Jr. and Jay Sanders, <u>Englewood: A Quality of Life Study</u>, Masters Thesis, University of Pennsylvania, Department of Landscape Architecture and Regional Planning, December 1975.

SECTION ONE

The Fiscal Problems of Older Suburbs

Chapter One
Fiscal Stress
In Older Suburbs

INTRODUCTION

The introduction to this study theorized that mature suburbs would be more prone to heightened municipal spending, tax rates, and other symptoms of fiscal stress. This chapter empirically examines whether this is indeed the case. It analyzes the fiscal condition of the case study community, Englewood, as well as other New Jersey mature suburbs, growing suburbs, and urban centers.

The chapter proceeds as follows. Techniques for measuring community distress in general, and local fiscal condition in particular, are examined first. This evaluation suggests a list of financial distress indicators, encompassing both municipal expenditure and revenue characteristics. These financial factors are then used as a basis for examining the level of fiscal strain in Englewood as well as the other New Jersey communities. A factor-by-factor analysis indicates that while urban areas are the most distressed from a financial perspective, mature suburbs in general, and Englewood in particular, are symptomatic.

MEASURING DISTRESS: HISTORICAL BACKGROUND

There has been interest in identifying and dealing with impacted areas for many decades. At first the perspective of distress was one of a localized physical malady within an overall healthy community.[1] For instance, the Urban Renewal program of the 1950's viewed distress as a neighborhood problem of largely physical guise. Various remedies were prescribed for different levels of neighborhood deterioration. Core slum areas would be revitalized by demolition and new construction; areas of lesser blight -- "grey" neighborhoods -- would receive housing rehabilitation assistance.

The 1960's saw further attention paid to both "grey" as well as "slum" areas.[2] The gestalt of distress was still one of a neighborhood nature, albeit there was greater sensitivity to local social and economic strain and not only physical decay. Model Cities, for example, was designed to tackle the spectrum of inner-city socioeconomic problems such as unemployment, inadequate health care, educational disadvantage and so on.[3]

In time, the perspective of distress widened from neighborhood(s) to regions. Thus in the 1960's and 1970's, the Area Development Administration (ARA) was formed to deal with problems of long-term unemployment and underemployment in rural areas. The Economic Development Administration (EDA), the successor to the ARA, continued assistance to depressed regions.

In going from neighborhood to region, an intermediate level, overall community distress, was passed over. This oversight did not last long; starting in the late 1970's, city distress became a central topic of concern and analysis. A major urban policy review was entitled "Cities and People in Distress."[4] Congress, financial analysts, and academicians studied the common and individual problems faced by New York, St. Louis, Cleveland, Newark, and sister communities.[5] An article disputing the thesis of crisis afflicting America's major cities was met by a vigorous rebuttal from HUD and others.[6] Even the popular press discussed the continued problems of older industrial localities in the Northeast and Midwest in a post-industrial society.[7]

The measurement of urban distress -- the determination of the level of physical, economic, and social hardship encountered by different communities -- is a central interest of the burgeoning literature on city problems. Measurement is a key concern because it draws explicit attention to the components of distress and also serves as an operational device for directing relief to those cities with the greatest hardship. As of 1980, approximately fifteen urban distress measures had been developed.[8] These rankings were followed, in 1981-82, by roughly comparable suburban stress rankings. The following section examines the intent and operation of some of the more important indices, focusing on those measuring municipal financial strain or at least encompassing this dimension in their enumeration of need.

MEASURING DISTRESS: SPECIFIC INDICES

Overall City Measures

The 1976 Brookings Institution's hardship indices[9] (intercity and intrametropolitan) were the first distress measures to be developed and are still cited as leading examples of the state-of-the-art (see Exhibit 1-1). Their goal was to provide a relative ranking of "city hardship" by examining various local population and shelter characteristics, e.g., educational attainment, income, poverty incidence, and age and quality of housing. Ratios were derived for each of these variables. The ratios were city-to-city in the case of the intercity index, city-to-suburb for the intrametropolitan measure. These ratios were then expressed in standard value format and the average value of these standardized scores was used to rank distress.

The Brookings efforts were followed by several later overall city distress measures, most encompassing a broader array of indicators and utilizing more sophisticated statistical approaches. For instance, the Congressional Budget Office (CBO) urban need index incorporated social, economic, and fiscal need.[10] Each of these three dimensions was scrutinized by examining appropriate local variables, e.g., social and economic need by considering changes in income, population characteristics, and employment; fiscal need, by examining the local

EXHIBIT 1-1
Urban and Suburban Municipal Fiscal Indicators

	MUNICIPAL FISCAL INDICATORS							Other	
	Municipal Expenditures				Municipal Revenues/Wealth				
DISTRESS INDICES	Total Expenditures	Expenditure Burden	Expenditure Service Emphasis in	Stress-Indicative Categories	Total Taxes/ Tax Burden	Local Affluence	Intergov. Revenue Share	Fiscal	Social
I. OVERALL URBAN DISTRESS									
Brookings Hardship Index (1976) [a] HUD Need Index (1979) [b] Other [c]									Unemployment, housing deficiency, poverty, crime, population loss
Institute for the Future Evaluation Index (1976) [d]					Total taxes	Total Property Value			Poverty, overcrowded housing, death rate, aged population
Urban Institute Municipal Danger Signals (1976) [e]				PC debt	PC* taxes				Unemployment, private job loss
Congressional Budget Office Urban Need Index (1978) [f]					Taxes**/ income	PC income PC* property value			Unemployment, density, aged housing, Brookings indices
II. URBAN FISCAL DISTRESS									
U.S. Treasury Urban Fiscal Strain Index (1978) [g]				Δ PC debt/ Δ PC income		PC income Δ Total property value	Δ PC own-source revenue/ Δ PC income		Population change, Brookings and other indices
Municipal Finance Officers Financial Difficulty Measures (1978) [h]	Total expenditures		Police Welfare Statutory	Debt	ΔProperty tax rate	PC income PC property value	% Intgov.		
Touche Ross Urban Fiscal Stress Index (1979) [i]	PC operating expenses			PC debt	Taxes/ income PC taxes		% Intgov.	City, local employ., PC interest cost	

EXHIBIT 1-1 (continued)

MUNICIPAL FISCAL INDICATORS

DISTRESS INDICES	Municipal Expenditures				Municipal Revenues/Wealth			Other	
	Total Expenditures	Expenditure Burden	Expenditure Service Emphasis in	Stress-Indicative Categories	Total Taxes/Tax Burden	Local Affluence	Intergov. Revenue Share	Fiscal	Social
Advisory Commission on Intergovernmental Relations City Fiscal Disparity-Distress (1980)	PC expenditures		PC welfare		PC taxes	PC income	PC intergov.		Retail sales
Urban Institute, Municipal Fiscal Indicators (1980)	PC expenditures			Long and short-term debt		PC income	% intergov.		
ICMA Fiscal Trend Monitoring (1981)	PC revenues		Statutory	% Uncollected taxes	% Change property base	PC income	% intergov.	Pension funding	Employment, Retail sales
Clark and Ferguson Fiscal Strain Indices (1981)	ΔExpenditures/Δlocal population	Municipal expenditures/family income; Municipal expenditures/city wealth		PC short and long-term debt				Liquidity, pension funding	
Joint Economic Committee Fiscal Condition Measure (1981)	PC expenditures		Police, fire		PC taxes			Assets/liabilities; Surplus public employees	
III. OVERALL SUBURBAN DISTRESS									
U.S. Census Suburban Classification Project (1977)	PC expenditure		Police		PC property tax				
Isserman and Brown Suburban Need/Distress Measures (1981)									Poverty, housing quality, crime, employment
RAND Troubled Suburbs (1982)	PC expenditure; ΔExpenditure/ΔPopulation			PC debt			% intergov.		Population, crime, poverty

EXHIBIT 1-1 (continued)

	MUNICIPAL FISCAL INDICATORS								
	Municipal Expenditures				Municipal Revenues/Wealth			Other	
DISTRESS INDICES	Total Expenditures	Expenditure Burden	Expenditure Service Emphasis in	Stress-Indicative Categories	Total Taxes/ Tax Burden	Local Affluence	Intergov. Revenue Share	Fiscal	Social

Notes:

*Per Capita

**Indicates division, e.g., taxes divided by income.

① Richard B. Nathan and Charles Adams, Jr., "Understanding Central City Hardship," Political Science Quarterly, Vol. 91, No. 1 (Spring 1976).

② Harold L. Bunce and Robert L. Goldberg, City Need and Community Development Funding (Washington, D.C. Government Printing Office, January 1979), U.S. Department of Housing and Urban Development.

③ See Robert W. Burchell et al., "Measuring Urban Distress: A Summary," in Burchell and Listokin (editors), Cities Under Stress (New Brunswick: Rutgers University Center for Urban Policy Research, 1981), p. 159.

④ Gregory Schmid, Hubert Lupinski and Michael Palmer, An Alternative Approach to General Revenue Sharing: A Needs Based Formula (Menlo Park, CA: Institute for the Future, 1975).

⑤ Thomas Muller, "Statement on the Fiscal Outlook for State and Local Governments." Presented to the Subcommittee for Urban Affairs of the Joint Economic Committee, U.S. Congress, Washington, D.C., January 22, 1976.

⑥ Subcommittee on the City of the Committee on Banking, Finance and Urban Affairs, House of Representatives, City Need and the Responsiveness of Federal Programs. (Written by Peggy L. Cuciti of the Congressional Budget Office.)

⑦ U.S. Department of the Treasury, Office of State and Local Finance, Report on the Fiscal Impact of the Economic Stimulus Package on 48 Large Urban Governments (Washington, D.C.: Treasury, January 1978).

⑧ Municipal Finance Officers Association, "Measuring Governmental Financial Condition," in MFOA, Elements of Financial Management, No. 5 (Washington, D.C.: MFOA, 1980).

⑨ Touche Ross & Co. and the National Bank of Boston, Urban Fiscal Stress: A Comparative Analysis of 66 U.S. Cities (New York: Touche Ross, 1979).

⑩ U.S. Advisory Commission on Intergovernmental Relations, Central City-Suburban Fiscal Disparity and City Distress (Washington, D.C.: Government Printing Office, 1980).

⑪ Peterson, et al., Monitoring Urban Fiscal Conditions (Washington, D.C.: Urban Institute, 1981).

⑫ Sanford, Groves, et al., "Financial Indicators for Local Government," Public Budgeting and Finance (Summer 1981), p. 5.

⑬ Terry Clark and Lorna Ferguson, "Fiscal Strain: Indicators and Sources." Political Processes and Urban Fiscal Strain (forthcoming).

⑭ Joint Economic Committee, Congress of the United States, Trends in the Fiscal Condition of Cities, 1979-1981 (Washington, D.C.: Government Printing Office, 1981).

⑮ U.S. Bureau of the Census, Suburban Classification Project (Washington, D.C.: Government Printing Office, 1977).

⑯ Andrew Isserman and Marilyn Brown, Measuring Suburban Need and Distress (Washington, D.C.: Government Printing Office, 1981). Study conducted for the U.S. Department of Housing and Urban Development.

⑰ Judith Fernandez et al., Troubled Suburbs: An Exploratory Study (Santa Monica: RAND, 1982). Study conducted for the U.S. Department of Housing and Urban Development.

property-tax base and tax effort (see Exhibit 1-1). A composite score
for each of the three need dimensions was derived by converting all of
the local indicator variables into standard scores and an overall
average measure secured. The community need index developed by HUD[11]
gathered over 20 local variables, incorporating elements of demog-
raphy, poverty, economic activity, and social trauma. Factor analysis
was then applied to reduce this broad data set into a smaller group of
need dimensions and the factors were then combined into a composite
distress score.

For the most part, these overall city measures were aggregative indices of a community's social and economic profile (see Exhibit 1-1).
Not touched upon, or else handled in passing fashion, was community
fiscal condition, defined by the International City Management Association (ICMA) as the "local ability to maintain existing service
levels, fund normal demands for additional services, withstand local/
regional economic trauma, and meet demands of natural growth and
change."[12] For instance, neither the Brookings nor the HUD need indices contained any municipal expenditure or revenue traits. Others,
such as the CBO need index, included some fiscal variables; however,
these indicators were largely secondary to the primary socioeconomic
characteristics emphasized by the overall city distress measures (see
Exhibit 1-1).

Urban Fiscal Stress Measures

Brookings and sister rankings satisfied a demand by Congress, academicians, and others for an objective, generalized account of city
hardship. These indices were not, nor were they designed to be, fiscal
measures. The near or actual financial bankruptcy of New York City,
Yonkers, Cleveland, and other communities in the late 1970's pointed
to the urgency for a specialized fiscal index.

State-of-the-art municipal financial ratings prevalent at that time,
for the most part developed by bond underwriters or analysts, were too
technical or were inadequate in other ways. One "extreme" measure was
default -- an inability to meet payrolls, current bills, and/or debt
service.[13] Default was a very poor indicator, for a municipality
could financially be very distressed yet technically not be in default. Other measures conveyed a better sense of municipal financial
strain yet were still deficient. To illustrate, bond ratings by
Moody's and Standard and Poor's were found wanting, as they failed to
predict the financial trauma to engulf many of the nation's cities in
the late 1970's:[14]

> Bond ratings have sometimes been considered to reflect fiscal
> strain of city governments. But the specific procedures used ....
> are admittedly "judgmental" and may include population change and
> economic base measures, political processes, as well as more spe-
> cific fiscal measures of the city government. The lack of clear
> criteria and heavy workload on small staffs makes the rating
> agencies' results too unsystematic for careful analysis. The

limitations of defaults and bond ratings as indicators of fiscal strain necessitate a different type of measure, conceptually prior to default and available for all cities. Such strain measures should capture the propensity for fiscal difficulties, even if actual default is never realized.

Starting in the late 1970's, numerous measures were developed to capture the "propensity for fiscal difficulty." One of the first was the strain index of the U.S. Treasury.[15] It encompassed the local revenue sources to be tapped (e.g. total property value and per capita resident income) and conversely the degree of non-local municipal income such as state and federal aid. Significant intergovernmental assistance signaled fiscal danger, both because of its vulnerability to cutbacks, as well as the fact that such aid was usually targeted to local fiscal stress and other need. Hence, communities receiving the most generous allotments of state-federal stipends were considered by the respective funding agencies to be the most distressed and therefore the most appropriate candidates for assistance.

The Treasury's fiscal strain index emphasized the municipal revenue profile. Later fiscal indicators included as well municipal expenditure indicators. For instance, the fiscal stress index, developed by Touche Ross and the First National Bank of Boston,[16] included numerous expenditure characteristics such as per capita operating expenses, and various revenue profiles spanning the tax burden (ratio of local taxes to local income) to the share of revenue coming from state and federal sources. Similarly, the Municipal Finance Officers' (MFO) financial difficulty measure[17] itemized revenue factors ranging from the property tax to the percentage share of intergovernmental assistance (see Exhibit 1-1). It also encompassed numerous expenditure items such as total municipal outlays and spending in stress-indicative categories such as police, welfare, statutory, and debt. Considerable spending in these areas signals danger because it is symptomatic of community aging and growing resident population demand on and need for certain, and often quite expensive, public services. Thus, community maturity is often accompanied by enhanced pressures on the police and fire departments. As the municipal service sector and public employment expand, overhead expenses in the form of statutory outlays, increase. Debt may also grow to finance a more comprehensive inventory of public capital facilities and also to cover any shortfalls in paying for rising municipal expenses from current revenues.

Many other financial ranking systems such as the Urban Institute's municipal fiscal indicators,[18] Clark and Fergusons' fiscal strain indices,[19] and the ICMA's fiscal trend monitoring factors[20] encompass similar municipal expenditure and revenue factors as those discussed above (see Exhibit 1-1). Prevalent expenditure characteristics are: the level of spending (e.g., total outlays), the relationship of spending to local income (expenditure burden), and the emphasis of spending in stress-indicative areas. Roughly analogous to these expenditure items are such common revenue indicators as: the level of taxation (e.g., per capita taxes), the relationship of taxes to local

income (tax burden), and stress-indicative revenue traits such as the
level of intergovernmental aid (see Exhibit 1-1).

One final observation concerns the manner in which these different
expenditure and revenue variables are expressed and combined in the
community distress measures. While it is difficult to generalize, many
of the characteristics are referred to in a per capita form. This
basis allows ready comparison across municipalities of greatly varying
population. Thus common inclusive traits are per capita expenditures,
per capita property taxes, per capita intergovernmental aid, and so
on. How are these disparate variables combined into an aggregate fiscal stress measure or ranking? In some cases, sophisticated statistical techniques are employed, reminiscent of those utilized in the
overall city distress measures. To illustrate, the Treasury's fiscal
strain index converted individual variables into standard deviation
units (Z scores) which were then weighted and summed. In most instances, however, a much simpler aggregation approach is utilized,
such as ranking the communities under analysis according to their
"performance" on each individual variable and then averaging the rankings for all the inclusive characteristics. As shall be discussed
shortly, the latter technique is utilized in analyzing the fiscal
condition of the New Jersey study communities.

Suburban Fiscal Stress Measures

The analyses cited thus far and summarized in Exhibit 1-1 focus on
the measurement of urban hardship in general and urban fiscal stress
in particular. What about suburban hardship and fiscal strain? A very
limited literature has considered the former: a 1977 census study
classified suburbs by varying socioeconomic characteristics;[21] a
1981 monograph developed specialized suburban need measures, in part
modeled on, in part differing from urban counterparts such as the
Brookings indices;[22] while a 1982 RAND investigation sought to identify troubled suburbs by a range of variables.[23] The more specialized topic of measuring suburban fiscal stress has not, however, been
addressed in the literature outside of passing reference to this subject in the RAND and other work cited above (see Exhibit 1-1).

Since a comprehensive suburban fiscal measure has not yet been developed, we shall construct one of our own. The encompassing variables, summarized in Exhibit 1-2, are derived from the extant work on
urban financial evaluation. Both expenditure and revenue indicators
are therefore included. The expenditure category consists of:

a. the level and direction of spending as reflected by the per cap-
    ita municipal outlay and the percentage change in this sum;

b. the burden of municipal spending as shown by the relationship
    between per capita expenditures and per capita income; and

c. spending emphasis in stress-indicative categories such as public
    safety, overhead (statutory), and debt (as indicated by their
    respective percentage shares of total municipal outlays).

EXHIBIT 1-2

Fiscal Distress Rating By Distress Indicators: New Jersey Urban and Suburban Communities

FISCAL DISTRESS INDICATORS	COMMUNITY GROUPS			
	Urban	Englewood	Mature Suburbs	Growing Suburbs
	Relative Fiscal Distress Ranks: 4=Most Distressed ... 1=Least Distressed			
I. *Municipal Expenditure Indicators*				
Total				
Per capita expenditures	3	4	2	1
% change in per capita expenditures (early 1970s/late 1970s)	2/3	3/1	1/2	4/4
"Burden"				
Per capita expenditure "burden"	4	3	2	1
Service Emphasis in Stress-Indicative Categories				
Public safety as % of operating expenditures (early 1970s/late 1970s)	3/3	4/2	2/4	1/1
Statutory as % of operating expenditures	3	4	2	1
Debt as % of operating expenditures	4	3	1	2
II. *Municipal Revenue Indicators*				
Total				
Per capita property tax levy	2	4	3	1
"Burden"				
Per capita tax "burden" (early 1970s/late 1970s)	4/3	3/4	2/2	1/1
Property tax rate	4	3	2	1
Uncollected taxes as % of total tax levy	4	3	2	1
Local Affluence				
Per capita property value (early 1970s/late 1970s)	4/4	1/2	3/3	2/1
Per capita income (early 1970s/late 1970s)	4/4	1/3	2/2	3/1
Intergovernmental				
Intergovernmental revenue as % of total revenue	4	1	3	2
AVERAGE DISTRESS RANK (EARLY 1970s/LATE 1970s)	3.46/3.46	2.85/2.85	2.08/2.31	1.62/1.38

Notes:
- Most or least distressed relative to the four community groups.
- See Exhibit 1-3.
- See Exhibit 1-5.
- See Exhibit 1-10.
- See Exhibit 1-6.
- See Exhibit 1-7.
- See Exhibits 1-8 and 1-9.
- See Exhibits 1-9 and 1-10.

The municipal revenue group includes many analogous factors:

  a. the level of taxation as reflected by the per capita municipal
     property tax;

  b. the municipal tax burden as shown by: 1) the ratio between per
     capita property taxes and per capita income; 2) the ratio between
     per capita municipal property taxes and per capita property value
     (e.g. the property tax rate); and 3) the percentage share of un-
     collected taxes;

  c. local affluence -- the resources to be drawn upon as indicated
     by both the per capita property value and income; and

  d. the share of intergovernmental revenue -- a factor reflecting
     vulnerability to cutbacks as well as a targeting to the most dis-
     tressed communities.

These dozen or so variables offer an ordered roster for considering
the fiscal stress of the New Jersey study communities. We shall test
the veracity of the hypothesis discussed in the introduction to the
study that mature suburbs are prone to heightened financial strain,
perhaps not to the degree of central cities but more so than growing
hubs. Our testing procedure is as follows. First we examine the performance of the four New Jersey community groups (cities, Englewood,
mature suburbs, and growing suburbs) on each of the fiscal stress
indicator variables. We then derive a composite fiscal stress score
used to rank the overall financial strain of the four community cohorts.

NEW JERSEY STUDY COMMUNITIES: PERFORMANCE
ON THE MUNICIPAL EXPENDITURE INDICATORS

Per Capita Municipal Expenditures

  The level of municipal spending is a measure of local fiscal stress
in that it is a dual indication of the scope of local service operations as well as ultimately the quantity of revenues which must be
raised to meet these obligations. It is found in some form in almost
all the fiscal hardship indices (see Exhibit 1-1).
  Which communities have the highest municipal outlays? Researchers of
both urban and suburban municipal expenditure determinants have linked
generous spending with growing municipal or "urban" characteristics.[24] An "urban"-expenditure linkage is suggested by the New Jersey study localities, for the most urbanized (ranging in descending
order from cities, Englewood, mature suburbs, to growing suburbs; see
introduction) have the steepest municipal outlays. New Jersey cities
spend twice as much for total municipal operating purposes than
growing suburbs and half again more than mature suburbs (see Exhibit

1-3). The latter in turn outspend their sister growing suburbs by roughly a third. The urbanized communities' outlays are especially pronounced in certain municipal functions. Health and welfare and statutory are illustrative. In the former service area, in 1970, the New Jersey cities and mature suburbs outspent growing suburbs by over ten times and two times, respectively; in the latter service category, the spending overage vis a vis growing suburbs was about four times for cities and over two times for mature suburbs. While the spending emphasis of cities and mature suburbs relative to growing suburbs narrowed over the decade (see Exhibit 1-3), perhaps reflecting the latter's growing "urbanization" and consequent municipal service cost spiral, a considerable differential was still to be found.

What about Englewood? Our case study locality was the spending champion of the four New Jersey community groups examined. In 1970, Englewood's per capita municipal operating outlay was about $350 (in 1978 real dollars) -- one-sixth higher than the $300 expenditure in the New Jersey cities, two-thirds greater than the $210 spent by mature suburbs, and over two times the $150 cost of growing suburbs (see Exhibit 1-3). A decade later, the numbers changed slightly but not these overall relationships. Englewood's high spending is found across the spectrum of municipal services. This community expended considerably more for general government, public safety, public works, recreation, statutory obligations, and debt service than either urban locations or sister suburbs, both mature and growing.

Exhibit 1-4 gives a visual presentation of the spending profiles discussed above. This graph has two axes: the horizontal shows different time periods between 1970 and 1980, the vertical indicates per capita municipal outlays for operating functions. Spending for individual cities, mature/declining suburbs, and growing suburbs is indicated by the letters "U," "D," and "G," respectively; Englewood's outlays are indicated by the letter "E." Over the 1970 to 1980 period, the New Jersey cities and Englewood spent the most for municipal services. The "U" and "E" values are therefore dispersed towards the top of the graph. Mature suburbs spend less, and growing suburbs were the least spendthrift. Consequently the "D" values congregate above the "G" values, which cluster towards the bottom of the exhibit.

Percent Increase in Per Capita Municipal Expenditures

This measure indicates the direction and pace of municipal outlays. It is incorporated in the Clark and Ferguson and RAND fiscal strain indices[25] (see Exhibit 1-1).

Municipal spending in all the New Jersey study communities increased fastest in the early 1970's and then stabilized and in some cases declined in real (inflation-adjusted) terms towards the end of the decade. This reversal reflects numerous factors ranging from the imposition of municipal expenditure "caps" to cutbacks in state and federal assistance for municipal services.

Some variations by community category are apparent, however, with respect to the vigor of the spending cutbacks. In general, the more

EXHIBIT 1-3

Real Per Capita Municipal Expenditures [a] of New Jersey
Urban and Suburban Communities, 1970–1980

YEAR/AREA	General Government	Fire	Police	Public Safety	Public Works	Health and Welfare	Recreation	Library	Recreation and Culture	Statutory	Total [e] Operating	Debt [e] Service	Total Municipal [f] Expenditures
1970													
Urban [b]	$28	$40	$68	$108	$53	$37	$9	$8	$17	$38	$303	$53	$356
Englewood [c]	39	47	81	128	86	9	22	18	40	45	354	58	412
Mature Suburbs [c]	32	28	47	75	50	7	12	9	21	22	212	20	232
Growing Suburbs [d]	33	6	36	42	42	3	6	5	11	10	146	12	167
1974													
Urban	56	52	81	133	53	28	8	8	16	34	351	57	408
Englewood	67	56	104	160	107	16	20	20	40	35	439	49	439
Mature Suburbs	38	30	55	85	60	7	13	10	23	20	243	19	262
Growing Suburbs	36	7	49	56	53	4	9	7	16	12	182	19	212
1976													
Urban	48	52	69	121	47	31	9	7	16	38	358	62	420
Englewood	64	55	90	145	101	17	13	18	31	49	436	55	491
Mature Suburbs	35	30	54	84	55	7	3	10	23	24	244	21	265
Growing Suburbs	37	7	51	58	51	4	9	8	17	14	185	20	216
1978													
Urban	59	49	69	118	57	34	8	8	16	48	371	73	444
Englewood	83	53	79	132	90	20	17	16	33	54	438	59	497
Mature Suburbs	38	31	54	85	59	7	13	10	23	31	268	32	300
Growing Suburbs	40	7	50	57	46	4	8	8	16	17	192	24	234
1980													
Urban	50	55	69	124	85	26	7	7	14	47	378	63	441
Englewood	61	48	82	130	102	17	16	16	32	48	412	59	471
Mature Suburbs	40	29	53	82	55	7	11	9	20	27	250	28	278
Growing Suburbs	39	6	51	57	45	6	8	8	16	20	187	28	215

Notes: (a) In constant (inflation-adjusted) dollars; 1978 used as the base (see text).
(b) Average profile of 5 largest New Jersey cities; see Exhibit I-3.
(c) Average profile of 25 New Jersey mature suburbs; see Exhibit I-3.
(d) Average profile of 20 New Jersey growing suburbs; see Exhibit I-3.
(e) Sum is larger than total of itemized categories because it includes miscellaneous expenditures not shown here.
(f) Equals "total operating municipal expenditures" and "debt service."

Source: New Jersey Department of Community Affairs, Division of Local Government Services, *Annual Report of the Division of Local Government Services* for indicated years.

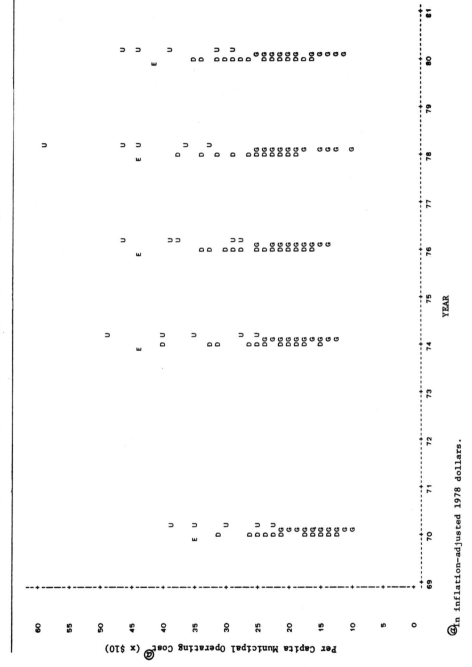

EXHIBIT 1-4

**Real Per Capita Municipal Operating Outlays for Urban ("U"),
Englewood ("E"), Mature/Declining ("D"), and Growing Suburbs ("G")**

urbanized localities experienced the most dramatic turnabout in the
spending direction and pace. Englewood is illustrative. In the first
half of the 1970's, it increased municipal outlays by 6 percent annually on a per capita, real (inflation-adjusted) basis. By the end of
the decade, Englewood curbed spending to the point that its municipal
outlays noticeably declined in real terms (e.g., a 3 percent annual
loss between 1978 and 1980; see Exhibit 1-5). Sister mature suburbs
went from increasing municipal spending by about 4 percent annually in
the early 1970's towards real decreases of that magnitude a few years
later (see Exhibit 1-5). While growing suburbs also witnessed a spending "famine" following the "feast" of the early 1970's, their turnabout was not nearly as dramatic as that of the more urbanized communities, especially Englewood.

Why this differential in spending reversal by community type? One
possible explanation is satiation; once municipal spending reaches the
high plateau achieved by the more urbanized localities, there is perhaps less cause to continue to increase outlays. Growing communities,
not yet at this satiation level, must continue to spend, especially
since they, unlike their sister cities and mature suburbs, are growing
in population and must therefore meet the service demands of new residents. A more detailed analysis of the factors affecting the level and
pace of municipal outlays is presented in chapter two of this study.

Municipal Service Emphasis in Stress-Indicative Categories

Another indicator of fiscal condition is the service expenditure
emphasis within a community. Heightened spending for public safety,
statutory, and debt is a manifestation of community aging, social
change, growing public service sector overhead and other danger signals. The monitoring of spending in stress-indicative areas is incorporated in the MFO, ACIR, ICMA, JEC and other municipal distress measures (see Exhibit 1-1).

What is the expenditure profile of the New Jersey study communities?
Relative to growing suburbs, the most urbanized communities (both
cities and mature suburbs) allocate greater shares of their municipal
spending in stress-suggestive categories. This differential, however,
narrows between 1970 and 1980 so that by the latter period growing
suburbs are symptomatic in this fiscal strain measure.

To illustrate, in 1970, one-third of Englewood's operating outlays
were for public safety purposes, one-eighth for statutory items, and
one-sixth for debt (see Exhibits 1-6 and 1-7). New Jersey cities
displayed an almost identical allocation. There was a lesser emphasis
on public safety, statutory, and debt in the mature suburbs and a further decline in the growing suburbs (see Exhibits 1-6 and 1-7). By
1980, there was rough parity in expenditure emphasis amongst the New
Jersey study communities. All allocated about one-third of their
operating expenses for public safety, about one-eighth for statutory,
and about one-seventh for debt. This equivalence in part reflects the
dynamics of the incipient aging process affecting growing suburbs. As
these communities take on the role of the suburbs' hubs, they too must

EXHIBIT 1-5

Annual Percentage Increases in Real Municipal Operating Expenditures Of New Jersey Urban and Suburban Communities, 1970–1980

YEAR/AREA	General Government	Public Safety	Public Works	Health & Welfare	Recreation & Culture	Statutory	Total Operating
			Annual Percentage Increase in Expenditures				
1970–1974							
Urban	+25.0%	+5.8%	0.0%	-6.1%	-1.5%	-2.6%	+4.0%
Englewood	+17.9	+6.3	+6.1	+19.4	0.0	-5.6	+6.0
Mature Suburbs	+4.7	+3.3	+5.0	0.0	+2.4	-2.3	+3.7
Growing Suburbs	+2.3	+8.3	+6.5	+8.3	+11.4	+5.0	+6.2
1974–1976							
Urban	-7.1	-4.5	-5.7	+5.3	0.0	+5.9	+1.0
Englewood	-2.2	-4.7	-2.8	+3.1	-11.3	+20.0	-0.3
Mature Suburbs	-3.9	-0.6	-4.2	0.0	0.0	+10.0	+0.2
Growing Suburbs	+1.4	+1.8	-1.9	0.0	+3.1	+8.3	+0.8
1976–1978							
Urban	+11.5	-1.3	+10.6	+4.8	0.0	+13.2	+1.8
Englewood	+14.8	-4.5	-5.4	+8.8	+3.2	+5.1	+0.2
Mature Suburbs	+4.3	+0.6	+3.6	0.0	0.0	+14.6	+4.9
Growing Suburbs	+4.1	-0.9	-4.9	0.0	-2.9	+10.7	+1.9
1978–1980							
Urban	-7.6	+2.5	+24.6	-11.8	-6.3	-1.0	+0.9
Englewood	-13.3	-0.8	+6.7	-7.5	-1.5	-5.6	-3.0
Mature Suburbs	+2.6	-1.8	-3.4	0.0	-6.5	-6.5	-3.4
Growing Suburbs	-1.3	0.0	-1.1	+25.0	0.0	+8.8	-1.3
1970–1980							
Urban	+7.9	+1.5	+6.0	-3.0	-1.8	+2.4	+2.5
Englewood	+5.6	+0.2	+1.9	+8.9	-2.0	+0.7	+1.6
Mature Suburbs	+2.5	+0.9	+1.0	0.0	-0.5	+2.3	+1.8
Growing Suburbs	+1.8	+3.6	+0.7	+10.0	+4.5	+10.0	+2.8

The column group header reads: **MUNICIPAL SERVICE CATEGORY**

Notes: (a) In constant inflation-adjusted dollars; 1978 used as the base (see text). (b) Average profile of 5 largest New Jersey cities; see Exhibit I-3. (c) Average profile of 25 New Jersey mature suburbs; see Exhibit I-3. (d) Average profile of 20 New Jersey growing suburbs; see text. (e) Sum is larger than total of itemized categories because it includes miscellaneous expenditures not shown here.

Source: New Jersey Department of Community Affairs, Division of Local Government Services, Annual Report of the Division of Local Government Services, for indicated years.

EXHIBIT 1-6

**Allocation of Municipal Operating Expenditures by Service Category:
New Jersey Urban and Suburban Communities, 1970–1980**

| YEAR/AREA | MUNICIPAL SERVICE CATEGORY | | | | | | |
	General Government	Public Safety	Public Works	Health & Welfare	Recreation & Culture	Statutory	Total Operating[e]
	Percentage of Total Operating Expenses						
1970							
Urban[a]	9.2%	35.3%	17.5%	12.2%	5.6%	12.5%	100.0%
Englewood[b]	11.0	36.2	24.3	2.5	11.3	12.7	100.0
Mature Suburbs[c]	15.0	24.3	23.6	3.3	9.9	10.4	100.0
Growing Suburbs[d]	22.6	28.8	28.8	2.1	7.5	6.8	100.0
1974							
Urban	16.0	37.9	15.1	8.0	4.6	9.7	100.0
Englewood	5.2	36.4	24.4	3.6	9.1	8.0	100.0
Mature Suburbs	15.6	35.0	24.7	2.9	9.5	8.2	100.0
Growing Suburbs	19.7	30.8	29.1	2.2	8.8	6.6	100.0
1976							
Urban	13.4	33.7	13.1	8.7	4.5	10.6	100.0
Englewood	14.7	33.2	23.2	3.9	7.1	11.2	100.0
Mature Suburbs	14.3	34.4	22.5	2.9	9.4	9.8	100.0
Growing Suburbs	20.0	31.3	27.6	2.2	9.2	7.6	100.0
1978							
Urban	15.9	31.8	15.4	9.2	4.3	12.9	100.0
Englewood	18.9	30.2	20.5	4.6	7.5	12.3	100.0
Mature Suburbs	14.2	31.7	22.0	2.6	8.6	11.6	100.0
Growing Suburbs	20.8	29.7	24.0	2.1	8.3	8.9	100.0
1980							
Urban	13.2	32.8	22.5	6.9	3.7	12.4	100.0
Englewood	14.8	31.6	24.8	4.1	7.8	11.7	100.0
Mature Suburbs	16.3	33.6	22.5	2.9	8.2	11.1	100.0
Growing Suburbs	20.9	30.5	24.1	3.2	8.6	10.7	100.0

Notes: [a] Average profile of 5 largest New Jersey cities; see Exhibit I-3.
[b] Average profile of 25 largest mature New Jersey suburbs; see Exhibit I-3.
[c] Average profile of 20 growing New Jersey suburbs; see Exhibit I-3.
[e] Sum of the indicated categories equals less than 100 percent because miscellaneous outlays are now shown.

Source: New Jersey Department of Community Affairs, Division of Local Government Services, Annual Report of the Division of Local Government Services for indicated years.

EXHIBIT 1-7

New Jersey Urban and Suburban Communities: Budgetary Shortfalls

YEAR/AREA	Percentage Property Taxes Collected[d]	Municipal Debt as Percentage of Municipal Operating Cost
1970		
Urban[a]	91.0%	17.5%
Englewood	95.9	16.4
Mature Suburbs[b]	96.5	9.4
Growing Suburbs[c]	95.6	8.2
1974		
Urban	91.0	16.2
Englewood	95.7	11.2
Mature Suburbs	96.0	7.8
Growing Suburbs	96.1	10.4
1976		
Urban	90.1	17.3
Englewood	93.6	12.6
Mature Suburbs	95.6	8.6
Growing Suburbs	95.8	10.8
1978		
Urban	90.3	19.7
Englewood	95.3	13.5
Mature Suburbs	96.5	11.9
Growing Suburbs	97.0	12.5
1980		
Urban	90.0	16.7
Englewood	94.5	14.3
Mature Suburbs	97.0	11.2
Growing Suburbs	97.3	15.0

Notes: [a] Average profile of 5 largest New Jersey cities; see Exhibit I-3.
[b] Average profile of 25 New Jersey mature suburbs; see Exhibit I-3.
[c] Average profile of 20 New Jersey growing suburbs; see Exhibit I-3.
[d] Property taxes collected as share of total tax levy.

Source: New Jersey Department of Community Affairs, Division of Local Government Services, Annual Report of the Division of Local Government Services for indicated years.

increase spending for police and fire purposes, take on new debt, and
bear a growing public sector overhead burden. In this respect, growing
suburbs begin to resemble their more urbanized sister communities.

In sum, the New Jersey study localities display the following characteristics with respect to municipal expenditure distress measures
(see Exhibit 1-2):

1. Per capita expenditures are highest in Englewood followed by urban areas, mature suburbs, and then growing suburbs.

2. The pace of municipal spending changes over the decade. In the
   early 1970's, growing suburbs increased outlays the fastest, fol
   lowed by Englewood, cities, and then mature suburbs. In the latter part of the decade, growing suburbs still kept their expenditure lead, but Englewood reversed to the slowest spender, with
   cities and mature suburbs falling in between.

3. In terms of service emphasis in stress-indicative categories, Englewood and cities are the most distressed, followed by mature
   and then growing suburbs. These differences by community type
   narrowed, however, over the 1970's.

Our analysis now turns to the performance of the New Jersey study
localities on municipal fiscal revenue indicators.

NEW JERSEY STUDY COMMUNITIES: PERFORMANCE
ON THE MUNICIPAL REVENUE INDICATORS

Another category of fiscal distress indicators looks at the revenue
side of the fiscal equation. Increasing property tax levies and rates,
growing dependence on intergovernmental transfers, and stagnant or decreasing local property value and/or resident income signal potential
future economic hardship. These measures are incorporated in almost
all the more prominent indices of fiscal strain (see Exhibit 1-1).
They are examined individually below.

Property Taxes/Intergovernmental Aid

The dollar amount of per capita municipal property taxes is an indication of the level of charge to local residents to support local
services. This variable is incorporated in numerous fiscal distress
measures (see Exhibit 1-1).

It is instructive to examine the relationship of the property tax to
other financial traits. The dollar sum of local property taxes imposed
by a municipality is a function of numerous factors of which two prominent ones are: 1) the level of local spending, and 2) the share of
local spending borne locally. As the more urbanized New Jersey study
communities have the highest municipal outlays, they also tend to have
the highest municipal property tax levies. There are differences, however, between cities and urbanized suburbs. The former receive considerable amounts of intergovernmental aid -- itself a sign of municipal

distress. In 1970, New Jersey cities received one-sixth of their total
municipal revenues from state and federal sources; a decade later intergovernmental aid amounted to over 40 percent (see Exhibit 1-8).
This infusion of outside monies reduced the cities' local share of
paying for municipal services and therefore their local property tax
load per capita. In contrast, while the mature suburbs' allocation of
intergovernmental assistance increased dramatically over the 1970's
(from 5 percent of total municipal revenues in 1970 to about 10 percent in 1980), they still receive modest outside aid relative to the
generous allocation to cities. Consequently, the mature suburbs' net
local contribution, for the most part raised from the property tax, is
high.

To illustrate, in 1980, the New Jersey cities spent an average of
$378 per capita for municipal operating purposes. Since they received
a considerable $154 per person in intergovernmental aid and raised
$100 from local non-property sources, the cities imposed a municipal
property tax levy of only $124 per capita -- a third of total revenues
(see Exhibit 1-8). In contrast, while Englewood spent nearly the same
amount per capita ($412) as cities in 1980, it received considerably
less state and federal aid ($32 per person), so that it was forced to
impose a very large property tax levy of $303 per capita -- three-
quarters of total revenues (see Exhibit 1-8). Englewood's municipal
property tax obligation was by far the highest of the New Jersey study
communities. It was roughly double the sum in both cities ($124) and
mature suburbs ($140).

What about growing suburbs? Compared to cities and even sister mature suburbs, they typically receive the least intergovernmental aid
(see Exhibit 1-8). Nonetheless, their municipal property tax load per
capita is quite low because they spend relatively so little to start
with. To illustrate, in 1980, growing suburbs received $17 per capita
in state and federal assistance, compared to $31, $32, and $154 per
person in mature suburbs, Englewood, and cities respectively. Despite
their modest intergovernmental stipend, the growing suburbs imposed a
very low ($91) property tax sum per capita -- a fraction of the $124
to $303 figures in the other communities -- because their per capita
municipal expenditure outlay ($187) was also a fraction of the spend-
ing (ranging from $250 to $378 per person) in the other localities
(see Exhibits 1-8 and 1-9).

Local Affluence

The property tax amount to be paid or raised is made a more meaningful indicator of fiscal strain by relating these sums to the local
ability to pay. The latter can be measured in many ways. Two prominent
indicators are per capita property value and per capita resident income. About half of the rankings of local fiscal strain incorporate
one or both of these measures (see Exhibit 1-1).

Considerable distinctions are found in the property and income profile of the New Jersey study communities. Suburban localities are far
more affluent than cities. There are differences, however, amongst the

EXHIBIT 1-8

Municipal Revenue Composition of New Jersey Urban and Suburban Communities, 1970–1980

YEAR/AREA	REAL PER CAPITA REVENUES BY SOURCE							PERCENTAGE ALLOCATION OF REVENUES BY SOURCE			
	Intergovernmental				Own Source						
	State	Federal Grant	Federal Revenue Sharing	Total	Property	Other	Total Revenues	Total Intergovernmental	Property	Other	Total
1970											
Urban	$46	$3	$0	$49	$177	$77	$303	16.2%	58.4%	25.4%	100.0%
Englewood	12	0	0	12	278	64	354	3.4	78.5	18.1	100.0
Mature Suburbs	10	1	0	11	142	59	212	5.2	67.0	27.8	100.0
Growing Suburbs	7	b	0	7	69	70	146	4.8	47.2	48.0	100.0
1974											
Urban	70	44	27	141	129	81	351	40.2	36.8	23.0	100.0
Englewood	8	2	20	30	336	73	439	6.8	76.5	16.7	100.0
Mature Suburbs	13	6	15	34	158	51	243	14.0	65.0	21.0	100.0
Growing Suburbs	7	0	11	18	94	70	182	9.9	51.6	38.5	100.0
1976											
Urban	59	60	19	138	165	55	358	38.5	46.1	15.4	100.0
Englewood	11	16	19	46	317	73	436	10.6	72.7	16.7	100.0
Mature Suburbs	7	8	13	28	176	40	244	11.5	72.1	16.4	100.0
Growing Suburbs	2	2	10	14	98	73	185	7.6	53.0	39.4	100.0
1978											
Urban	61	98	21	188	149	34	371	50.7	40.2	9.1	100.0
Englewood	11	41	17	69	300	69	438	15.8	68.5	15.7	100.0
Mature Suburbs	15	18	12	45	165	58	268	16.8	61.6	21.6	100.0
Growing Suburbs	8	4	10	24	96	72	192	12.5	50.0	37.5	100.0
1980											
Urban	73	63	18	154	124	100	378	40.7	32.8	26.5	100.0
Englewood	9	11	12	32	303	77	412	7.8	73.5	18.7	100.0
Mature Suburbs	13	8	10	31	140	79	250	12.4	56.0	31.6	100.0
Growing Suburbs	7	1	9	17	91	79	187	9.9	55.6	34.5	100.0

Notes:
- In constant (inflation-adjusted) dollars; 1978 used as the base (see text).
- Average profile of 5 largest New Jersey cities; see Exhibit 1-3.
- Average profile of 25 New Jersey mature suburbs; see Exhibit 1-3.
- Average profile of 20 New Jersey growing suburbs; see Exhibit 1-3.
- Includes only major intergovernmental categories indicated; does not include CETA.
- See Exhibit 1-7.
- Equals "total revenues" less the sum of intergovernmental and property income. Includes such items as fines, fees, business and personal property, utility franchise, etc.
- For calculation purposes, assumed to equal total operating expenditures.
- Equals indicated revenue sums divided by total revenues.

Source: New Jersey Department of Community Affairs, Division of Local Government Services, Annual Report of the Division of Local Government Services for indicated years.

EXHIBIT 1-9

Real Property Tax Profiles of New Jersey Urban And Suburban Communities, 1970–1980

YEAR/AREA	Real Property Value Per Capita [1]	Equalized Property Tax Rate			Real Property Tax Obligation Per Capita		
		Municipal	School	Total Local	Municipal	School	Total Local
1970							
Urban	$ 6,900	$2.57	$2.19	$4.76	$177	$151	$328
Englewood	20,300	1.37	1.98	3.35	278	402	680
Mature Suburbs	15,800	.90	1.80	2.70	142	284	426
Growing Suburbs	18,700	.37	1.90	2.27	69	355	424
1974							
Urban	5,400	2.39	2.16	4.55	129	117	246
Englewood	20,900	1.61	1.98	3.59	336	414	750
Mature Suburbs	17,500	.90	1.70	2.60	158	298	456
Growing Suburbs	23,600	.40	1.70	2.10	94	401	495
1976							
Urban	6,100	2.71	1.64	4.35	165	100	265
Englewood	20,600	1.54	1.91	3.45	317	393	710
Mature Suburbs	17,600	1.00	1.80	2.80	176	317	493
Growing Suburbs	24,500	.40	1.60	2.00	98	392	490
1978							
Urban	6,600	2.25	1.87	4.12	149	123	272
Englewood	19,600	1.53	1.80	3.33	300	353	653
Mature Suburbs	18,300	.90	1.60	2.50	165	293	458
Growing Suburbs	23,900	.40	1.50	1.90	96	359	455
1980							
Urban	6,100	2.04	1.52	3.56	124	93	217
Englewood	20,600	1.47	1.57	3.04	303	323	626
Mature Suburbs	17,700	.79	1.51	2.30	140	267	407
Growing Suburbs	28,400	.32	1.30	1.62	91	369	460

Notes: [a] In constant (inflation-adjusted) dollars; 1978 used as the base (see text).
[b] Average profile of 5 largest New Jersey cities; see Exhibit I-3.
[c] Average profile of 25 New Jersey mature suburbs; see Exhibit I-3.
[d] Average profile of 20 New Jersey growing suburbs; see Exhibit I-3.
[e] Full value tax rate.
[f] Equals inflation-adjusted property-tax base divided by local population.
[g] Equals sum of municipal and school equalized tax rates.
[h] Equals real property valuation per capita multiplied by the equalized property tax rate.

Source: New Jersey Department of Community Affairs, Division of Local Government Services, <u>Annual Report of the Division of Local Government Services</u> for indicated years.

suburban group. While mature suburbs in general, and Englewood in particular, have historically been quite affluent, both, especially Englewood, have lost ground to growing suburbs. In 1970, the New Jersey
cities had an average per capita property value of $6,900 -- about 40
percent of the respective figures for mature ($15,800) and growing
suburbs ($18,700), and a third that of Englewood ($20,300; see Exhibit
1-9). A decade later, the per capita property base in urban areas
dropped in real terms to $6,100 per person in contrast to the gains
recorded by the suburban localities. The rate of gain was not the
same, however, for all suburbs. Growing suburbs experienced a rapid
increase in their per capita property value (from $18,700 in 1970 to
$28,400 in 1980), mature suburbs had slower growth (from $15,800 in
1970 to $17,700 in 1980), while Englewood's property tax base was
stagnant ($20,300 in 1970, $20,800 in 1980). A similar relationship is
evident with respect to the per person income measure of local affluence (see Exhibit 1-10).

Burden

  Our discussion of local affluence leads directly to consideration of
the local burden. Many measures of municipal fiscal distress encompass
different "load" indicators such as the relationship of local municipal expenditures or property taxes to local resident income and/or the
property tax base (see Exhibit 1-1). The burden of the New Jersey
study communities on these respective indices is discussed below.
  A fundamental sense of burden is the ratio of public outlays to local taxpayer affluence. In general, the more urbanized New Jersey communities spend the most relative to their residents' income. In 1970,
the municipal expenditure-to-income share was 5.6 percent in cities,
4.1 percent in Englewood, 2.8 percent in mature suburbs, and 2.1 percent in growing suburbs (see Exhibit 1-10). A decade later the same
sequence is found except the expenditure-to-income ratios increased
for cities and Englewood (to 7.9 and 4.9 percent respectively) and de-
creased for both mature and growing suburbs (to 2.5 and 1.7 percent
respectively). This occurred because the former's local per capita income either declined or was stagnant while the latter's increased, especially for growing suburbs (see Exhibit 1-10).
  Another burden indicator is the relationship of municipal property
taxes to income. This is more complicated than the expenditure-to-
income ratio because of the intervening factor of intergovernmental
aid. Amongst the New Jersey study communities, cities impose relatively low municipal property taxes because they are the recipients of
considerable state and federal support. Counterbalancing this, is the
cities' very modest average resident income so that their share of
municipal property taxes-to-income is quite high -- about 3 percent in
both 1970 and 1980 (see Exhibit 1-10). A slightly different dynamic is
at work for the New Jersey suburbs. As they receive relatively little
intergovernmental aid, their municipal property tax-to-income burden
is more simply a function of their gross expenditures and local resident affluence. Modest spending in a setting of existing or approach-

EXHIBIT 1-10

Relative Expenditure and Property Tax Burden of New Jersey Urban and Suburban Municipalities, 1970–1980

YEAR/AREA	Real Per Capita Municipal Operating Expenditures[a]	Real Per Capita Property Tax Levy[a]			Real Per Capita Income	Relative Municipal Expenditure "Burden"[f]	Relative Property Tax "Burden"[g]		
		Municipal	School	Total Local			Municipal	School	Total Local
_1970_									
Urban[b]	$303	$177	$151	$328	$5,400	5.6%	3.3%	2.8%	6.1%
Englewood[e]	354	278	402	680	8,700	4.1	3.2	4.6	7.8
Mature Suburbs[c]	212	142	284	426	7,600	2.8	1.9	3.7	5.6
Growing Suburbs[d]	146	69	355	424	7,000	2.1	1.0	5.1	6.1
_1980_									
Urban	$378	$124	$ 93	$217	$4,800	7.9%	2.6%	1.9%	4.5%
Englewood	412	303	323	626	8,400	4.9	3.6	3.8	7.4
Mature Suburbs	250	140	267	407	9,900	2.5	1.4	2.7	4.1
Growing Suburbs	187	91	369	460	10,800	1.7	0.8	3.4	4.2

Notes: [a] In constant (inflation-adjusted) dollars; 1978 used as the base (see text).
[b] Average profile of 5 largest New Jersey cities; see Exhibit I-3.
[c] Average profile of 25 New Jersey mature suburbs; see Exhibit I-3.
[d] Average profile of 20 New Jersey growing suburbs; see Exhibit I-3.
[e] See Exhibit 1-9.
[f] Equals per capita municipal expenditure divided by per capita income.
[g] Equals per capita municipal/school/total property levy divided by per capita income.

Source: New Jersey Department of Community Affairs, Division of Local Government Services, *Annual Report of the Division of Local Government Services* for indicated years.

ing community affluence results in a relatively minor burden. For example, the municipal property tax-to-income ratio for growing suburbs was only 1 percent in 1970 and fell to .8 percent a decade later (see Exhibit 1-10). Conversely, high municipal spending in a setting of community impoverishment or stagnant local affluence forces a high property tax burden. Englewood is illustrative. Its municipal property tax-to-income ratio was 3.2 percent in 1970 -- only a hairbreadth lower than the 3.3 percent in cities (see Exhibit 1-10). Over the decade, Englewood increased its municipal outlays and while it is an affluent community, its local resident income was stagnant in this period. Consequently, by 1980, Englewood's municipal property tax-to-income ratio increased to 3.6 percent -- the most burdensome of New Jersey study communities (see Exhibit 1-10).

A roughly similar dynamic is evident with respect to a third municipal burden measure -- the relationship of municipal property taxes to local tax wealth. This ratio can be expressed as a property tax rate -- the dollar tax obligation per $100 of assessed or true local property value (see Exhibit 1-9). Amongst the New Jersey study communities, the municipal property tax rate is highest in cities. While their municipal property tax sum per capita is relatively low, a consequence of generous intergovernmental aid, their property tax base per person is so inconsequential that a high rate must be imposed. The municipal property tax rate is much lower amongst the New Jersey suburban communities, albeit there are considerable variations. To illustrate, in 1980, the equalized or true municipal property tax levy was $2.04 in the New Jersey cities followed by $1.47 in Englewood, $0.79 in mature suburbs, and $0.32 in growing suburbs (see Exhibit 1-9).

One consequence of a high tax burden is growing property owner reluctance to satisfy their municipal tax obligation. This relationship is shown in Exhibit 1-7. The percentage of property taxes collected is highest in lower tax burden communities and conversely is lowest in high tax burden localities. Thus, from 1970 to 1980, the best record of property taxes realized was achieved by growing suburbs, followed in turn by mature suburbs, Englewood, and then cities. (Other factors besides tax burden will affect the collection ratios such as the diligence of municipal tax collectors, property owner views concerning future neighborhood viability, etc.)

In sum, the New Jersey study communities display the following characteristics with respect to municipal revenue distress measures (see Exhibit 1-2):

1. The per capita municipal property tax sum is highest in Englewood followed by mature suburbs, urban areas, and finally cities.

2. The most generous intergovernmental aid is given to cities with the suburban areas receiving many magnitudes less.

3. Cities are the least affluent. Englewood was historically the most affluent, but over the last decade, it has lost ground to sister suburbs.

4. The public sector burden is most severe in cities and Englewood followed by mature suburbs and then growing suburbs.

NEW JERSEY STUDY COMMUNITIES: OVERALL
MUNICIPAL FISCAL DISTRESS SCORE

Our analysis thus far has focused on individual municipal distress factors. It is instructive to derive a composite score of relative municipal fiscal strain. This can be achieved by translating the "performance" of the four New Jersey study groups (cities, Englewood, mature suburbs, and growing suburbs) on each municipal distress variable into a relative distress score. The group exhibiting the highest distress on each factor is given a value of 4; the least distressed is scored a value of 1. To illustrate, with reference to per capita municipal expenditures, Englewood would be accorded a score of 4, growing suburbs, a 1 (see Exhibit 1-2). Individual scores are then averaged to yield a composite measure of relative fiscal position. The higher the composite value, the greater the degree of relative fiscal strain.

Our final results are as follows: urban areas have an average composite score of 3.5, Englewood, 2.9, other mature suburbs, 2.2, and growing suburbs about 1.5 (see Exhibit 1-2). Slight variations are evident if results are differentiated between the early versus late 1970's (e.g. the mature suburbs' score goes up slightly, that of growing suburbs is reduced). The hypothesis that mature suburbs are prone to municipal fiscal strain, if not to the same degree as cities much more so than growing hubs, is confirmed. For a non-central city locality, the case study community Englewood is characterized by an especially severe level of municipal financial strain.

THE COMPOSITE (MUNICIPAL AND SCHOOL) PERSPECTIVE

The analysis in this chapter has focused on the municipal sector only. What are the results if educational expenditures and revenues are considered as well? In some instances, there are differences. For instance, while growing suburbs spend relatively little for municipal purposes and have a low municipal expenditure and tax burden, they are willing (or able?) to spend generously for school purposes and shoulder a rather high, for them, school burden (see Exhibits 1-9 and 1-10). In other cases, school patterns more closely parallel the municipal profile. Englewood is illustrative. This community has a relatively high school burden in terms of the ratios of school property taxes to local property value or local resident income, albeit its educational overage is less pronounced than with respect to the municipal sector (see Exhibits 1-9 and 1-10). The combination of Englewood's very severe municipal burden with its moderately steep school burden results in a very high composite public sector burden. For instance, while Englewood's total local (municipal and school) property tax rate is lower than in the New Jersey cities, it is almost double that found in growing suburbs and is about one-third greater

than the rate in mature suburbs (see Exhibit 1-9). Englewood's total
local property tax obligation per capita -- about $650 per year over
the 1970's -- is roughly 50 to 100 percent larger than the comparable
figures in the New Jersey cities and either mature or growing suburbs
(see Exhibit 1-10). Finally, the ratio of Englewood's total local
property taxes to resident income, about 7.5 percent over the 1970's,
is also very high -- it is three-quarters greater than the burden in
sister suburbs, both mature and growing, and even considerably exceeds
the tax "bite" of urban centers (see Exhibit 1-10). Thus Englewood's
financial stress is present on both a municipal and composite (municipal and school) perspective.

CONCLUSION

   It is instructive to turn from the quantitative aspects of our analysis of fiscal strain to highlighting some of the major underlying
factors and themes.
   A basic driving force of municipal financial distress is local
municipal spending. All other things being equal, communities which
spend more are more prone to financial hardship. Relative to growing
suburbs which have low municipal outlays, urban centers are big municipal spenders. Cities are not alone in this pattern. They are joined
by the suburbs' traditional centers, the mature hubs. The latter outspend their sister growing suburbs by a third or more. What is true
of mature suburbs in general is emphatically the case of Englewood.
This community outspends all of the New Jersey study groups. On a per
capita basis, its municipal operating costs are one-tenth higher than
in cities, two-thirds greater than mature suburbs, and more than twice
that of growing suburbs.
   Contextual spending factors follow the patterns described above.
Relative to growing suburbs, cities, and mature suburbs in general and
Englewood in particular, shoulder a high expenditure burden and spending emphasis in stress-indicative areas such as public safety, statutory, and debt.
   While spending is the driving force of fiscal strain, there are certain mitigating factors. Two important considerations are: 1) the
share of local spending which must be absorbed or paid for locally;
and 2) local affluence, both income and property, available to shoulder the net local cost. The first factor is influenced by, and is the
converse of, intergovernmental aid. The higher the degree of state and
federal assistance, the lower the net local obligation of municipal
spending. This factoring is dramatically evident in cities which spend
a lot for municipal purposes yet receive considerable intergovernmental aid so that their local obligation for local services is reduced considerably. While suburbs have also been beneficiaries of
growing intergovernmental assistance, mature suburbs more so than
growing, even the former receive only modest stipends so that their
burden of paying for municipal services is resoundingly local.
   A local cost assumption does not have adverse consequences as long
as sufficient local resources are available. Mature suburbs histori-

cally had these resources as they were the traditional commercial and other business sector hubs of the suburban landscape. The whittling of the mature suburbs' regional hegemony, however, has depleted their affluence, so much so that they are beginning to feel the pinch of supporting generous municipal outlays from their own means. For instance, relative to the New Jersey growing suburbs, the mature suburbs experienced relatively slow increases in per capita income and local property value. Englewood fared worse, barely holding its own. This laggard affluence profile results in continued municipal fiscal pressures for mature suburbs in general and Englewood in particular.

In sum, local fiscal strain is a function of local spending within the context of local resources and intergovernmental aid. The next chapter focuses on understanding the primary if not driving element -- municipal expenditures. It explores why municipal outlays are so high in mature suburbs in general and Englewood in particular. This chapter attributed these spending patterns to "community aging" or "urban" traits but this begs the question: What are the specific consequences of "aging" or "urban" which prompt outlays? Which service sector traits most significantly influence the level of local municipal spending? Which general community characteristics play a role? Why does Englewood so outspend its sister mature suburbs?

NOTES

1. President's Conference on Home Building and Home Ownership, Slums, Large-Scale Housing and Decentralization, Vol. III (Washington, D.C.: Government Printing Office, 1932); See discussion in Robert W. Burchell and David Listokin, Cities Under Stress (New Brunswick, NJ: Rutgers University Center for Urban Policy Research, 1981).

2. See U.S. Commission on Urban Problems, Building the American City (Washington, D.C.: Government Printing Office, 1968); U.S. Department of Housing and Urban Development, Housing in the Seventies (Washington, D.C.: Government Printing Office, 1975).

3. Comprehensive City Demonstration Program, Public Law 89-754 Sec. 103(2).

4. United States, The President's Urban and Regional Policy Group, Cities and People in Distress: National Urban Policy Discussion Draft (Washington, D.C., U.S. Department of Housing and Urban Development, 1977).

5. United States Congress, Joint Economic Committee, Subcommittee on Economic Growth and Stabilization, Subcommittee on Fiscal and Intergovernmental Policy, The Current Fiscal Condition of Cities: A Survey of 67 of the 75 Largest Cities: A Study...95th Congress, 1st Session, July 28, 1977 (Washington, D.C.: Government Printing Office, 1977); George E. Peterson, et al., Monitoring Urban and Fiscal Conditions (Washington, D.C.: Urban Institute, 1982); Thomas Muller, Growing and Declining Urban Areas: A Fiscal Comparison (Washington, D.C.: Urban Institute, 1975).

6. See T.D. Allman, "The Urban Crisis Leaves Town," Harper's (December 1978), U.S. Department of Housing and Urban Development, "Whither or Whether Urban Stress" (1978).

7. See Burchell and Listokin, Cities Under Stress.

8. Ibid.

9. Richard B. Nathan and Charles Adams, Jr., "Understanding Central City Hardship," Political Science Quarterly, Vol. 91, No. 1 (Spring 1976).

10. Subcommittee on the City of the Committee on Banking, Finance and Urban Affairs, House of Representatives, City Need and the Responsiveness of Federal Programs. (Written by Peggy L. Cuciti of the Congressional Budget Office.)

11. Harold L. Bruce and Robert L. Goldberg, City Need and Community Development Funding (Washington, D.C. Government Printing Office, January 1979), U.S. Department of Housing and Urban Development.

12. Sanford Groves and Maureen Godsey, Evaluation of Local Government Financial Condition: Financial Trend Monitoring System – A Practitioner's Workbook (Washington, D.C.: International City Management Association, 1980).

13. Municipal Finance Officers Association, "Measuring Governmental Financial Condition," in MFOA, Elements of Financial Management, No. 5. (Washington, D.C.: MFOA, 1980), p. 2.

14. Terry Clark and Lorna Ferguson, "Fiscal Strain: Indicators and Sources." Political Processes and Urban Fiscal Strain (forthcoming).

15. U.S. Department of the Treasury, Office of State and Local Finance, Report on the Fiscal Impact of the Economic Stimulus Package on 48 Large Urban Governments (Washington, D.C.: Treasury, January 1978).

16. Touche Ross & Company and the National Bank of Boston, Urban Fiscal Stress: A Comparative Analysis of 66 U.S. Cities (New York: Touche Ross, 1979).

17. Municipal Finance Officers Association, "Measuring Governmental Financial Conditions."

18. George Peterson, et al., Monitoring Urban Fiscal Conditions (Washington, D.C.: Urban Institute, 1981).

19. Clark and Ferguson, "Fiscal Strain: Indicators and Sources."

20. Sanford, Groves, et al., "Financial Indicators for Local Government," Public Budgeting and Finance (Summer 1981), p. 5.

21. U.S. Bureau of the Census, Suburban Classification Project (Washington, D.C.: Government Printing Office, 1981). Study conducted for the U.S. Department of Housing and Urban Development.

22. Andrew Isserman and Marilyn Brown, Measuring Suburban Need and Distress (Washington, D.C.: Government Printing Office, 1981). Study conducted for the U.S. Department of Housing and Urban Development.

23. Judith Fernandez et al., Troubled Suburbs: An Exploratory Study (Santa Monica: RAND, 1982). Study conducted for the U.S. Department of Housing and Urban Development.

24. See detailed discussion in chapter two of this study.

25. See notes 14 and 23.

Chapter Two
The Dynamics of
Municipal Expenditures

INTRODUCTION

Chapter one presented the fiscal patterns of mature suburbs in general and Englewood in particular. Relative to newer suburban communities and sometimes even urban centers, mature suburbs and most particularly Englewood, have high municipal outlays. This spending relationship is paralleled in the tax burden profile. While mature suburbs typically do not shoulder the tax obligation of urban communities, the former, especially Englewood, impose far higher taxes than their newer suburban counterparts. Thus residents in older suburbs in general and Englewood in particular literally pay a high price for their community's spending patterns.

This chapter turns from describing expenditure profiles, to analyzing why there are variations in suburban municipal outlays. Why are Englewood's expenditures higher than those of nominally comparable mature suburbs? Why do older suburbs as a group outspend their younger sister communities? What are the implications of expenditure influences for Englewood's and the mature suburbs' fiscal future?

This chapter responds to these inquiries by undertaking first a quantitative and then a qualitative analysis of suburban public expenditures. The first attempts to mathematically explain spending patterns via an econometric "older suburb expenditure model." The model shows the statistical relationship between local resident community traits and municipal spending preferences. This analysis is followed by a second line of research which goes "beyond the numbers" and considers such qualitative factors as the linkage of public service range, type, and quality, with the local service price tag.

BACKGROUND TO THE QUANTITATIVE AND
QUALITATIVE ANALYSIS OF MUNICIPAL EXPENDITURES

Selection of dual investigative strategies is prompted by the directions and shortcomings of prior research concerning municipal expenditures. Quantitative research in this area originated with municipal outlay determinant analyses begun in the 1950's, and then refined over the next two decades. In a pioneering 1959 study, Harvey Brazer considered the expenditure patterns of hundreds of cities and

concluded that municipal size, growth rate, and degree of urbanism all
were significantly correlated with variations in local costs.[1] Similar investigations followed. In the 1960's, Hirsch examined the
effects of population size and growth;[2] Baumol considered the
influence of governmental size and complexity;[3] Kee studied the
influence of intrametropolitan and intercity fragmentation;[4] Sacks
analyzed the impact of intergovernmental grants;[5] and Osman considered the effect of categorical grants.[6] Determinants analysis was
pursued vigorously in the 1970's. Weicher,[7] Sunley,[8] Gabler,[9]
Booms,[10] Sternlieb,[11] Ladd,[12] and Beaton[13] considered the influence of such "classical" factors as population size and growth
rate. "New" determinants were also analyzed including the composition
of a community's tax base, and the size-nature of a community's nonresidential work force.

The determinants analysis, largely statistical in both its empirical
method and in its conceptual underpinnings, sought to discover the
best equation that would match a set of municipal, social, economic,
and governmental characteristics with local public expenditure levels.
While this equation was quite successful in explaining in a statistical sense the variation in municipal outlays, it had no direct link to
theory. As a consequence, the coefficients derived from the analysis
could in reality be functions of unspecified exogenous and endogenous
variables and, thus, used for specifying marginal municipal expenditures only with a high degree of risk.

A more recent quantitative branch of municipal cost analysis is
derived from the theories of public goods, public choice, and voter
sovereignty and these concepts have been integrated with econometric
techniques to yield a theoretically based and statistically strong
municipal expenditure "system"[14] (see Appendix A for details). The
quantitative analysis in this chapter, culminating in the expenditure
model, incorporates the advances of the public goods-choice econometric approach.

The qualitative analysis of municipal services is prompted by the
research of Nobel Prize economist, Herbert Simon. In the 1940's, Simon
examined municipal expenditure variations amongst San Francisco Bay
Area communities.[15] This work not only laid the analytical foundation for the statistical determinants research to follow two decades
later, it also emphasized the need for considering the different nu-
ances of municipal service outputs -- what services were being provided (e.g., curb versus rear-yard sanitation pick-up) and by whom
(e.g., municipal department versus private scavenger). Such distinctions point to the fact that "municipal services" is not a uniform
entity and that differences in municipal service costs reflect, in
part, substantive service output distinctions. The qualitative analysis of this chapter incorporates the service output sensitivity demanded by Simon.

QUANTITATIVE ANALYSIS OF MUNICIPAL EXPENDITURES

Development of an econometric approach to municipal exenditures involves a three step process of: (1) model specification; (2) model

calibration ("fitting the data"); and (3) model application.

Model Specification

   Econometricians are concerned with the development of an appropriate
structural model. A structural model is a system of equations which
specifies the relevant cause and effect relationships within the economic system being investigated. In general, an economic system is one
where an actor (city manager, consumer, entrepreneur, etc.) must make
decisions as to which package of goods is most desired for consumption or production given scarce resources (budget constraint).
   Each equation within the structural model, unless it is purely def-
initional, identifies a behavioral relationship in which an economic
characteristic or variable such as the amount of municipal goods consumed (q) in jurisdiction (j) is determined by a set of additional
characteristics such as price (p), and consumer tastes (t) and income
(y). The factor that is being acted upon by the other variables (q) is
termed an endogenous variable; those characteristics causing a change
in the endogenous value (p, t, y, etc.) are termed exogenous variables. The important point is that the causal relationships of the
system be specified to the best of our intuitive or deductive knowledge. We shall see momentarily that the municipal expenditure model is
guided by economists' deductive theories concerning public goods and
services.

Model Calibration-Parameter Estimation

   The next step is to place quantitative data specific to the jurisdiction or site into the variables within the structural model and estimate the parameters of each equation.
   Let us assume that a single equation structural model is judged adequate for explaining municipal expenditures. Using the previously defined terms, the equation may be specified as:

$$q_j = \alpha_0 + \alpha_1 p_j + \alpha_2 t_j + \alpha_3 y_j$$

where α_0 through α_3 are termed the equation parameters. The equation
can be interpreted to mean that a specific quantity of municipal goods
or expenditures will be consumed (q) in jurisdiction j; this value can
be calculated as the sum of a fixed amount of goods (α_0), the product
of the parameters α_1 and p_j (that is the change in municipal goods
consumption per a change in one unit in price [α_1] times the actual or
forecasted price [p_j]) and so on through the remaining exogenous
variables (α_2 multiplied by t_j, α_3 multiplied by y_j). However, in
order to calculate q_j one must first know the values for the parameters. This is known as the estimation problem. In this case, the
solution of the estimation problem involves the location of quantitative terms representing municipal goods, price, taste, etc. Once
these data have been collected and it is judged appropriate for use in
the specific structural model, then multivariate statistical techniques such as regression analysis can be used to estimate the values

of the parameters. We shall see momentarily that the municipal expenditure equation is calibrated on the basis of the municipal spending
profiles exhibited by mature New Jersey suburbs (see chapter one) over
the 1970's.

Model Application

The third step in the forecasting problem is the selection of appropriate forecasts. One possibility is to project the future endogenous
variable, in our case municipal expenditures (q_j), given "guessti-
mated" future exogenous variables (p_j, t_j, and y_j). More technically, for the calculation of q_j, each of the terms in the right
hand side of the equation would have to be expressed in quantitative
terms:

$$q_j = \alpha_0 + \alpha_1 p_j + \alpha_2 t_j + \alpha_3 y_j$$

In the above calculation fixed exogenous values are utilized. It is
also possible to vary the exogenous parameters in order to determine
consequent differences in the endogenous municipal expenditure variable. To illustrate, q_j may increase or decrease if base conditions
concerning municipal good's price (p_j) or consumer tastes (t_j) or
income (y_j) themselves change. Such sensitivity analysis provides
policymakers with important insight concerning the range of future
municipal scenarios. One of the key objectives of this chapter is to
develop such sensitivity for mature suburbs in general and Englewood
in particular.

OLDER SUBURB MUNICIPAL EXPENDITURE MODEL

The older suburb model was derived and applied in the three-step
fashion described above: (a) model specification; (b) model calibration; and (c) model application.

Model Specification

The theoretical approach used for the older suburb model is that
developed by Theodore Bergstrom and Robert Goodman.[16] Application of
their research to municipal expenditure forecasting is summarized below (see Appendix A for detailed discussion).
Bergstrom and Goodman explore the demand for municipal goods and
services and develop a structural model where the endogenous variable
is municipal expenditures. Exogenous factors influencing municipal
outlays encompass characteristics of the municipality's median voter.
In a majoritarian election process, it is hypothesized that over the
long run the median voter's tastes and budget constraint determine the
demand for municipal goods. For the purposes at hand, the median voter
is assumed to possess the jurisdiction's median income level and own
residential property valued at the average for the community. In addition to median voter traits, community characteristics also influence
municipal expenditures (see Appendix A). These community profiles

include total population, nonresidential activity (e.g., level of nonresidential employment) prevailing input or factor costs (e.g., salaries of public employees), and the level of intergovernmental (state and federal) assistance.

These variables affect municipal expenditures in different ways. Median voter traits are crucial. The higher this individual's income, the greater his/her "taste" for municipal services. The median voter's property value is also important. It is firstly indicative of median voter wealth and therefore a demand for services. In addition, it roughly gauges the level of exposure to paying for local public sector activity for public expenditures are typically funded mainly by ad valorem taxation. The higher the median voter's property value, the greater the potential property tax bill to finance public services.

Community traits are also influential. All other things being equal, total municipal expenditures are correlated with the number of residents to be serviced: larger communities spend more, smaller communities spend less. In addition, local nonresidential activity poses special demands for police, fire, and other public services; municipal expenditures will therefore increase as nonresidential uses proliferate. Input or factor costs are a further consideration; public expenditures will be higher in instances of generous public employee salaries/benefits. Intergovernmental assistance is a final community influence, one relating to the burden of payment alluded to previously. As the level of outside (federal and state) funding of services increases, the local financial "pain" of municipal spending lessens, so that there is greater demand, or at least receptivity for, "bargain" public sector involvement.

The municipal expenditure model encompasses these median voter-community traits. It was developed by referring to the basic Bergstrom and Goodman theoretical work and integrating their research with empirical analysis of municipal outlays in the mature New Jersey suburbs identified in chapter one (see Appendix A for detailed discussion).

The reduced form equation of the expenditure model is shown in Exhibit 2-1. Certain features deserve comment. Dollar terms (municipal expenditures, intergovernmental aid, etc.) are expressed in real values -- inflation adjusted 1978 dollars. The 1978 base was chosen for this was the latest year for which complete data to fit the model were available. Another consideration is that factor or input costs are measured by teacher salaries. This was done because there is no source of consistent information for municipal costs in New Jersey municipalities. It is assumed, however, that local teacher salaries reflect the overall community attitude towards public employee compensation; generous teacher salaries will thus often be accompanied by similarly handsome municipal staff remuneration and vice versa. Finally, all the endogenous and exogenous variables are expressed in logarithmic terms. Such an approach was followed under the assumption that municipal expenditures display constant elasticity -- a change in the exogenous variable induces a constant percentage change in the endogenous (municipal expenditure) term.

EXHIBIT 2-1

Components of the Mature Suburb Municipal Expenditure Model

$$ln \; M = ln \; a + ln \; Y + ln \; \tau + ln \; n + ln \; z_i$$

where:

ln is the logarithmic value;

a is a constant;

M represents real municipal operating expenditures;

Y is per capita income;

τ is the median value homeowner's property tax share in relation to the total municipal property tax levy;

n is municipal growing or declining population; and

z_i represents a set of aggregate municipal characteristics. The set of z_i expenditure determinants include the following:

    S employment in the service sector;

    C employment in the commercial trade sector;

    I employment in the industrial sector;

    q municipal factor cost index: average salary of local public employee;

    FA federal grants;

    RS federal revenue sharing; and

    U utility tax receipts.

Source: See text and Appendix A.

More important are the model's substantive assumptions. It encompasses two median voter traits -- income and property. The former is expressed in per capita terms, the latter as a fraction indicating the relationship of: (1) the median value homeowner's property tax share or obligation to (2) the total municipal property tax levy. To illustrate, in a community with a $2.00 equalized (full-value) tax rate, a resident with a $50,000 median property value home would pay $1,000 in property taxes. If the community's total property tax levy were $1,000,000, the $1,000 obligation would constitute a .000001 tax share. The higher the tax share, the greater the financial burden to the median voter and the greater his/her incentive to press for a reduced municipal service profile. The converse is true in situations of a relatively low property tax ratio. The magnitude of the property tax share itself is influenced by such factors as median home value, local tax rate, and the share of total property taxes paid by the local residential as opposed to nonresidential sector.

The municipal expenditure model also includes numerous community traits such as population, nonresidential activity (as measured by nonresidential employment), service factor costs (as measured by public employee salaries) and intergovernmental aid. As we shall see shortly, the model is sensitive to both increases and decreases in population: a growing community will experience added costs; a declining community will also be subject to spending pressures reflecting the social problems of shrinkage. The model also refines the nonresidential activity and intergovernmental aid variables: employment is differentiated by business sector (service, commercial, and industrial); intergovernmental assistance is segregated into the categories of federal grants, federal revenue sharing, and state aid. These population, employment, and intergovernmental distinctions were added because they improved the model's ability to "explain" municipal expenditure variations amongst older New Jersey suburbs.

In summary, the expenditure model suggests that municipal outlays will be higher in instances where the median voter is affluent and has a relatively low property tax share and where the community is growing and/or is losing population, has a significant nonresidential sector, and receives reasonable levels of intergovernmental aid. As we shall see momentarily, these traits characterize older suburbs in general and Englewood in particular relative to growing suburbs and help explain the former communities' considerable municipal expenditures.

Model Calibration-Parameter Estimation

The municipal expenditure equation was calibrated from 1970 to 1978 (1970, 1974, 1976, and 1978) municipal cost profiles exhibited by the 25 mature New Jersey suburbs. The final "fitted" equation is displayed in Exhibit 2-2.

Interpretation of this equation is relatively simple. Each of the parameter estimates associated with an exogenous variable represents the percentage change in municipal expenditures linked to a 1 percent change in the exogenous variable. "Total municipal expenditures" is

EXHIBIT 2-2

Mature Suburb Municipal Expenditure Equation

$$
\left\{ \begin{array}{l} \textit{Total Municipal} \\ \textit{Functions' Operating} \\ \textit{Expenditures in} \\ \textit{1978 Dollars (x1000)} \end{array} \right\} \quad = \quad -5.4461
$$

$$
-.4201 \; x \; \begin{pmatrix} \textit{Median Voter} \\ \textit{Property} \\ \textit{Tax Share} \end{pmatrix} \qquad + .6383 \; x \; \begin{pmatrix} \textit{Population} \\ \textit{x 100} \\ \textit{Growing Cities} \end{pmatrix}
$$

$$
+ .1723 \; x \; \begin{pmatrix} \textit{Population} \\ \textit{x 100} \\ \textit{Declining} \\ \textit{Cities} \end{pmatrix} \qquad + .1337 \; x \; \begin{pmatrix} \textit{Municipal} \\ \textit{Service} \\ \textit{Employment} \end{pmatrix}
$$

$$
+ .0326 \; x \; \begin{pmatrix} \textit{Municipal} \\ \textit{Industrial} \\ \textit{Employment} \end{pmatrix} \qquad - .0473 \; x \; \begin{pmatrix} \textit{Municipal} \\ \textit{Commercial} \\ \textit{Employment} \end{pmatrix}
$$

$$
+ .9493 \; x \; \begin{pmatrix} \textit{Municipal} \\ \textit{Factor of} \\ \textit{Production} \\ \textit{Cost Index} \end{pmatrix} \qquad + .0337 \; x \; \begin{pmatrix} \textit{Federal} \\ \textit{Aid} \\ \textit{Revenues} \end{pmatrix}
$$

$$
+ .0327 \; x \; \begin{pmatrix} \textit{Revenue} \\ \textit{Sharing} \\ \textit{Revenues} \end{pmatrix} \qquad + .5551 \; x \; \begin{pmatrix} \textit{State} \\ \textit{Utility} \\ \textit{Tax} \\ \textit{Receipts} \end{pmatrix}
$$

Source: See text and Appendix A.

merely the sum of each of the product terms to the right of the equals sign. For example, each 1 percent change in the number of service sector employees working within the municipality generates on the average an increase of 0.13 percent in municipal function expenditures; similarly, a 1 percent growth in federal revenue sharing monies brought into the municipal treasury generates on the average a 0.032 percent growth in operating expenditures. One coefficient may appear to be out of place. The coefficient for commercial employment is negative; this does not mean that municipal expenditures decline as commercial employment grows; this seemingly "free lunch" must be put into proper perspective. The negative coefficient has been derived from older suburbs that have lost commercial employment over the past decade. It reflects the overhead costs forced upon local government with the abandonment or reduced utilization of commercial property, and in turn the governmental employment levels and service delivery systems that have evolved to bolster the declining commercial district. Thus, in the calculation of municipal expenditure levels, declining commercial employment translates into higher public costs than if employment remained constant.

Equation coefficients point to the most significant variables influencing municipal expenditures. Strongest, as measured by coefficient size, is factor or input cost (.9493 coefficient). Public expenditures are high when public employees receive generous compensation -- a relationship already assumed (if not statistically proven) by municipal public officials and the public at large. Population change is also influential. Growth (.6383 coefficient) has a strong bearing on inducing added costs. This too has "common-sense" validity. Less obvious, however, is the fact that population decline (.1723 coefficient) offers no relief for it is accompanied by added cost pressures. Some of these costs entail the serving of a more public-dependent population in such areas as welfare, recreation, health, etc., for it is typically the more mobile and affluent families who leave a community, leaving a residue of the less advantaged. Population loss may also be associated with added public safety problems (e.g., vacant buildings are more prone to crime, fire hazards, etc.) which in turn add to police and fire safety expenditures. Decline-induced municipal cost is also evidenced by the negative coefficient (-.0473) shown for commercial employment. An economically stressed downtown poses greater police, fire, public works, and other public service obligations than a thriving business district since in the former case, vacant stores/offices will have to be patrolled, property owners, thinking endgame, will minimize expenditures for capital improvements, and so on.

The net cost of public expenditures -- the burden which must be carried by local taxpayers -- is a further important influence. Median voter property tax share has a reasonably large negative coefficient (.-4201). This is another way of saying that if the tax burden "hits" home, there will be enhanced voter pressure to scale down the public service sector. A similar influence is seen by the effect of intergovernmental aid; as this stipend goes up and therefore net local cost goes down, municipal expenditures will increase. There are several sources of revenue within the intergovernmental category. Federal grants and revenue sharing have relatively small coefficients (.0337 and .0327, respectively), especially in contrast to the rather large coefficient for state utility tax receipts (.5551). It is difficult to explain why the latter is so large. One possibility is that the utility tax receipt is not really an intergovernmental factor. Intergovernmental aid typically consists of the federal/state government according assistance to local governments, typically on the basis of local need or distress. The New Jersey utility tax receipt, in contrast, is not such a state-to-local revenue transfer. Instead, it is a reallocation of revenues which nominally would be available to local governments themselves had they the statutory authority to levy property taxes on utility lines, mains, and other equipment. This revenue "pass-through" as opposed to intergovernmental nature of the utility tax is reflected in its allocation, e.g., not on the basis of local need, as is usually the case with most intergovernmental aid, but rather according to the proportional local value of utility equipment as a share of the total value of utility infrastructure in the state.

If utility tax revenue does not influence municipal expenditures as an intergovernmental aid variable how does it affect local outlays and why is it relatively quite significant as indicated by its rather high equation coefficient (.5551)? One possibility is that, reflecting the basis of its allocation, the utility tax receipt is really an indirect "community density" or "urbanism" factor. As indicated, utility tax revenue is distributed by the state to municipalities on the basis of the proportional value of local utility lines/mains. More intensely settled communities, typically characterized by a more dense and valuable utility infrastructure, therefore receive relatively larger amounts of utility tax revenues. These very same localities may also be characterized by greater "urbanism"-related service demands and consequent higher municipal costs -- an association pointed to by the rather high utility tax receipt coefficient.

It is important to note that there is considerable "noise" in the utility tax-"urbanism" association. Rural communities, for instance, may receive considerable utility revenues if a nuclear facility or other significant utility plant is located within their borders. Newly developing suburbs may also benefit from substantial utility tax largesse if they have experienced shopping center and comparably intensive nonresidential development. In short, there is only a rough association between local utility tax allocation, community "urbanism" profile, and local expenditures.

Nonresidential use is the remaining factor in the expenditure equation. There is a rather weak association between nonresidential uses and municipal costs. Nonresidential coefficients range from .0326 to .1337 depending on the category of nonresidential employment. (These costs will have to be matched against generated nonresidential facility revenues, an exercise undertaken for Englewood in chapter three of this study.) Nonresidential uses also indirectly "induce" added municipal outlays by their effect on the median voter's property tax load because the entry of nonresidential ratables reduces the share of the total property tax levy borne by residential homeowners.

A final comment concerns the effect of median voter income. The public goods-services literature indicates a theoretical linkage between voter income and "taste" and thus, the demand for municipal services. In the regression analysis of the mature New Jersey suburbs' municipal expenditures, voter income was not found to be significant and thus does not appear in the final reduced equation (see Appendix A). It is possible, however, that an income effect is being picked up indirectly by some of the exogenous variables which are included and are correlated with median voter income. For example, there is a close association between community per capita income and community factor costs -- more affluent jurisdictions have the wherewithal, if not always the desire, to offer their public employees higher salaries.

Model Application

Before considering the model's application, it is important to point to its limitations. In general, there is a problem in using any statistical technique to explore complex, multifaceted interactions. There is an added difficulty in considering municipal expenditure determinants, for community decisions regarding public spending are so complicated; they reflect historical influences, a sense of community "identity," future perceptions, and so on. The model presented here is clearly a preliminary attempt suggesting important variables rather than a polished schema fully reflecting the complexity of the municipal fiscal dynamic.

While bearing in mind this caveat, the mathematical model can be applied in three useful ways:

(1) Validity testing -- How well does the model predict known values?

(2) Conceptual analysis -- How well does the model help explain municipal expenditure patterns? For instance, why does Englewood spend more than its sister older suburbs, or why do these suburb as a group exhibit higher municipal outlays than growing suburbs?

(3) Sensitivity analysis -- What are future Englewood municipal expenditure scenarios given changes in this locality's median voter-community profile characteristics?

Validity Testing

Operational validity concerns predictive power. In our case, to what extent does the model yield a municipal expenditure forecast that, when tested against known expenditures, is reasonably free from error? In 1978, Englewood spent $10.383 million for municipal services. How closely can the mathematical model developed for older suburbs predict this figure?

The answer is provided in Exhibit 2-3, which applies the forecast equation summarized in Exhibit 2-2. Column 1 of Exhibit 2-3 lists the

EXHIBIT 2-3

**Calibration/Testing of Mature Suburb Municipal
Expenditure Equation: Englewood, 1978**

Equation Argument or Variable	Equation Constant or Coefficient[a]	Actual or Forecasted Value for Equation Variables[b]	Contribution to Total Municipal Function Expenditures[c]
Intercept	-5.4461		-5.44
Property Tax Share	-.4201	2.5244	-1.06
Population			
Growing	+.6383	0.0000	0.00
Declining	+.1723	5.4680	0.94
Nonresidential Employment			
Service	+.1337	8.4908	1.13
Industrial	+.0326	8.3972	0.30
Commercial	-.0473	7.6686	-0.36
Service Input Cost	+.9493	9.8991	9.39
Intergovernmental Revenue			
Federal Aid	+.0337	6.8855	0.23
Revenue Sharing	+.0327	5.9915	0.19
"Urbanism"			
Utility tax revenue	+.5550	7.09257	3.93
			9.24

*1978 Englewood Municipal
Function Expenditures*

Logarithmic Value: (Computer Estimate): 9.24526[d]
Dollar Value (in $ Millions): $10.355

Notes: [a] Municipal expenditure equation coefficients expressed in logarithmic values (see Exhibit 2-2).
[b] 1978 Englewood values expressed in logarithmic terms.
[c] Equals equation constant multiplied by actual/forecasted value.
[d] Equals sum of all variable contributions.

Source: See text and Appendix A.

median voter-community profile exogenous traits incorporated in the mathematical model. Column 2 displays corresponding coefficients, e.g., .1722 for population (the coefficient for older suburbs like Englewood losing population). Column 3 lists, in logarithmic form, Englewood's values for each of the equation's variables. For instance, as of 1978, Englewood's population was about 23,700, or 2.54680 in logarithmic value. Column 4, the product of columns 2 and 3, represents the total contribution in logarithmic terms of each exogenous variable to total municipal expenditures. Englewood population thus is responsible for 0.94 (.1722 x 5.4680) of municipal costs expressed in logarithmic terms, or \$2.559 million. Adding the contribution from each variable, (e.g., -1.06 for tax share, 0.94 for population, 1.13 for service employment, -0.36 for commercial employment, 9.39 for municipal factor costs, etc.; see Exhibit 2-3), yields a total of 9.24526 in logarithmic terms, or \$10.355 million. This figure is almost identical to Englewood's actual \$10.383 million outlay for 1978. The model thus fares very well from a backcasting perspective.

A similarly strong performance is exhibited when the model is applied to "predict" 1970-1976 Englewood municipal expenditures as well as 1970-1978 outlays for remaining mature New Jersey suburbs. The close correspondence between forecasted and actual marginal outlays is graphically shown in Exhibit 2-13, in this chapter.

In summary, the mathematical model appears to be reasonably valid, at least as indicated by testing it against known values. The strength of this confirmation should be viewed in the light that the projection equation was precisely custom tailored to "fit" the municipal spending patterns exhibited by Englewood and its sister mature suburbs. More important than the model's ability to predict, is the insight it lends to understand the considerable variations in suburban municipal spending.

Conceptual Analysis

Chapter one of this study documented that Englewood had much higher municipal expenditures than its sister communities. In 1978, its municipal functions cost \$10.383 million compared to an average of \$7.512 million for the average New Jersey mature suburb (see Exhibit 2-4). This spending gap cannot be explained by community size differences for Englewood's 24,000 population as of 1978 was about one-fifth smaller than the average number of residents (28,000) for the New Jersey older suburbs in this same year. In brief, Englewood, with a 20 percent lesser population than its peers, spends about 40 percent more for municipal services. The municipal expenditure model, by pointing to the determinants of local public outlays, suggests why Englewood's spending overage occurs.

Exhibit 2-4 lists the exogenous median voter-community profile variables associated with municipal costs. Municipal outlays will be high in instances of relatively low property tax share, high population (or accelerated population loss), considerable nonresidential employment, high public sector input costs, a generous intergovernmental allot-

EXHIBIT 2-4

Median Voter-Community Profile Traits: Englewood, New Jersey, Mature Suburbs and Growing Suburbs, 1970-1978

MEDIAN VOTER – COMMUNITY PROFILE TRAITS	1970			1978			1978 AS SHARE OF 1970 VALUES		
	ENGLEWOOD	MATURE SUBURBS @	NEWER SUBURBS @	ENGLEWOOD	MATURE SUBURBS @	NEWER SUBURBS @	ENGLEWOOD	MATURE SUBURBS	NEWER SUBURBS
Municipal Expenditures	$8,859,000	$6,251,000	$2,900,000	$10,383,00	$7,512,000	$3,903,000	1.17	1.20	1.35
Expenditure Determinants									
Property Tax Share (-.4201)@	.0114@	.0148@	.0149%@	.0126%@	.0136%@	.0295%@	1.10	.91	1.98
Population									
Growing (+.6383)@			21,000			22,000			1.05
Declining (+.1723)@	25,000	30,000		24,000	28,000		.96	.93	
Nonresidential Employment									
Service (+.1337)@	2,300	1,500	1,200	4,900	3,500	3,000	2.13	2.33	2.50
Industrial (+.0326)@	5,300	4,200	2,900	4,400	3,300	4,100	.83	.79	1.41
Commercial (-.0473)@	2,500	2,700	1,400	2,100	3,200	3,500	.84	1.19	2.50
Service Input Cost (+.9493)@	$17,300	$16,100	$15,700	$19,900	$18,700	$17,700	1.15	1.16	1.13
Intergovernmental Revenue									
Federal (+.0337)@	0	$16,000	$ 3,000	$978,000	$521,000	$119,000	Not indicated because of extremely small 1970 values		
Revenue Sharing (+.0327)@	0	0	0	$400,000	$324,000	$205,000			
"Urbanism"									
Utility tax revenue (+.5550)@	$870,000	$787,000	$640,000	$1,203,000	1,102,000	$928,000	1.38	1.40	1.45

Notes: @ Indicates coefficient strength for each variable in the older suburb expenditure equation; see Exhibit 2-3.
 @ All dollar terms expressed in constant 1978 dollars.
 @ See text for explanation.
 @ See chapter one for definition.

Source: See text and Appendix A.

ment and pronounced "urban" character. Englewood is characterized by almost all of these traits relative to the average, mature suburb profile (see Exhibit 2-4). Englewood's median voter has a .0126 percent property tax burden compared to .0136 percent share in the average older suburb. Since the tax "bite" is less, the Englewood voter is not as motivated to press for spending constraints relative to his/her counterpart in other communities. One of the reasons for the low property tax share is Englewood's considerable nonresidential base. As of 1978, Englewood's firms employed 4,900 service and 4,400 industrial workers compared to 3,500 and 3,300 employees respectively in these two sectors in the average mature New Jersey suburb. Besides their impact on property tax load, Englewood's extensive nonresidential uses are themselves responsible for generating police, fire, and other services. While Englewood has considerably fewer commercial employees relative to its peer localities (2,100 versus 3,200) this is an expenditure-inducing factor because of the inverse relationship between commercial employment (e.g., downtown retail health) and municipal costs.

Englewood's costs for providing services are slightly higher, at least as indicated by public sector employee salaries. These amount to about $20,000 in Englewood compared to an $18,500 average in its sister communities. Another final expenditure-driving force is intergovernmental revenues. Englewood receives about $1.4 million in federal aid compared to a $0.8 million average allotment in the mature suburbs. Finally, Englewood is granted a slightly more generous utility tax allotment, perhaps reflecting its more pronounced "urbanism" character and hence need or demand for public services.

A similar analysis can be performed to help explain the differences between municipal outlays in Englewood and individual members of the New Jersey mature suburb group. For purposes of illustration, we shall choose Bergenfield and Lodi -- two Bergen County neighbors about the same population as Englewood (Bergenfield has 26,000 residents, Lodi, 20,000). In 1978, Bergenfield and Lodi spent about $5,000,000 each for municipal purposes -- less than half Englewood's outlay. The mathematical model can help explain this disparity (see Exhibit 2-5). Lodi spends less relative to Englewood because its: tax price is higher, nonresidential sector is much less significant (as measured by employment), service factor costs are lower, and it is not as large a beneficiary of intergovernmental aid (See Exhibit 2-5). Bergenfield spends less than Englewood primarily because its nonresidential sector is far less significant and it receives considerably lower federal assistance (see Exhibit 2-5).

The mathematical model can also help explain why mature suburbs as a group have higher municipal expenditures than their newer suburban counterparts. Exhibit 2-4 indicates that on average the former communities expended $7.5 million each for municipal operating programs in 1978 compared to $3.9 million apiece for the latter jurisdictions. This variation again cannot be explained by community population distinctions for there is not that much difference in average size between the older suburbs (28,000 residents) and newer suburbs (22,000

EXHIBIT 2-5

**Median Voter and Community Profile Traits:
Englewood and Two Neighboring Communities,
Bergenfield and Lodi — 1978**

MEDIAN VOTER - COMMUNITY PROFILE TRAITS	ENGLEWOOD	BERGENFIELD	LODI
Municipal Expenditures	$10,383,000	$4,992,000	$5,183,000
Expenditure Determinants			
Property Tax Share (-.4201)[a]	.0125%[b]	.0125%[b]	.0147%[b]
Population (+.1723)[a]	24,000	24,000	26,000
Nonresidential Employment			
Service (+.1337)[a]	4,900	1,100	2,600
Industrial (+.0326)[a]	4,400	1,200	3,100
Commercial (-.0473)[a]	2,100	1,600	1,500
Service Input Costs (+.9493)[a]	$19,900	$23,500	$16,600
Intergovernmental Revenue			
Federal (+.0337)[a]	$978,000	$364,000	$170,000
Revenue Sharing (+.0327)[a]	$400,000	$246,000	$259,000
"Urbanism"			
Utility tax revenue (+.5550)[a]	$1,203,000	$669,000	$572,000

Notes: [a] Indicates coefficient strength for each variable in the older suburb expenditure equation; see Exhibit 2-3.
[b] See text for explanation.

Source: See text and Appendix A.

residents). In brief, while the former communities are 30 percent larger than the latter, they spend almost twice as much.

Why the mature suburb spending overage? The disparity can be traced to considerable differences in median voter-community profile traits identified by the expenditure model (see Exhibit 2-4). Compared to the older suburb group, newer suburbs: (1) have a considerably higher property tax share (.0295% versus .0135%) and, thus, homeowner-voter incentive to press for scaled-down public services expenditures; (2) benefit from lower service production costs as indicated by public employee salaries ($17,700 versus $18,700); and (3) receive considerably less generous intergovernmental revenues ($0.3 versus $0.8 million), thereby throwing the financial burden of paying for services more heavily on local resident-voters who in turn will be strongly inclined to press for reduced public spending.

Even larger distinctions are found in comparing the newer suburbs to Englewood (see Exhibit 2-4). These differences help explain why the latter spends $10.4 million for municipal services -- an amount almost three times greater than the former's $3.9 million outlay despite rough parity in population (24,000 for Englewood, 22,000 for the newer suburbs; see Exhibit 2-4). Compared to Englewood, the newer suburbs: (1) have lower service input costs as measured by public employee compensation ($17,600 versus $20,000); (2) are characterized by a much smaller service-industrial employment base (7,100 versus 9,300) and thus fewer demands for servicing the business sector; (3) receive significantly lower intergovernmental aid ($0.3 compared to $1.4 million), thereby increasing the local net price of public spending on local taxpayers; and (4) receive less generous utility tax revenues ($0.9 compared to $1.2 million) reflecting in part, the growing suburbs' less pronouned "urban" character relative to Englewood and hence a slighter demand/taste/need for public sector intervention.

The model can help interpret expenditure variations in other years besides 1978. To illustrate, in 1970, Englewood expended $8.7 million for municipal expenditure compared to $6.3 million for the average mature suburb and $2.9 million for the average growing suburb. These differences are linked to varying median voter-community traits much along the lines as that discussed for 1978 (see Exhibit 2-4). Thus Englewood has the lowest property tax share, newer suburbs, the highest; Englewood has the largest industrial service employment base; newer suburbs, the lowest; Englewood offers the highest public employee compensation, growing suburbs are the least generous; and Englewood receives the most intergovernmental aid, while growing suburbs are the least favored in this regard.

It is also instructive to consider how the median voter-community profile traits linked with municipal expenditures changed over time and how this shift, in turn, affected local outlays. Exhibit 2-4 shows these relationships for the 1970-78 period. Over this near decade span, Englewood increased its municipal outlays by 17 percent -- a figure almost identical to the 20 percent spending gain exhibited by the older suburbs. Expenditure-inducing factors in both cases are very similar. Englewood and the mature suburbs lost population and gained

service employment (Englewood lost commercial jobs) as well as additional intergovernmental aid. Interestingly, growing suburbs increased
their overall expenditures over 1970-78 by 35 percent -- almost twice
the rate of Englewood and the older suburbs. Exhibit 2-4 suggests that
the newer suburbs' relative spending spurt in the 1970's was largely a
function of their explosive growth of nonresidential uses as reflected
by nonresidential employment. Newer suburbs increased their industrial
job base by over 40 percent compared to a 20 percent loss in both Englewood and the older suburbs. Newer suburbs almost doubled their commercial employment in the 1970's while Englewood and the mature suburbs barely held their own. And while all three community groups experienced healthy increases in service employment, the newer suburbs
outdistanced the rest. Admittedly, newer suburbs garnered substantial
revenues from this nonresidential growth, however, they also paid a
price in spiraling municipal outlays. (See chapter three for discussion of fiscal impact techniques to compare the costs versus revenues
induced by nonresidential growth.)

Sensitivity Analysis

Our analysis, thus far, has been static -- focusing on spending
given fixed endogenous variables. It is also instructive to consider
expenditure projecting future municipal outlays under changing median
voter-community profile traits. For instance, we already know that
Englewood is a high-spending community and have linked this to high
factor costs, large nonresidential sector, etc. What will Englewood's
fiscal posture be in the near future, say 1985? The answer depends on
the disposition of the exogenous influences: what will happen to the
community's commercial center; how extensive will federal aid cutbacks
be; what compensation demands will be made by public employees and to
what extent will these be met, and so on. Since the future status of
these conditions themselves is uncertain, expenditure forecasts under
a range of possible scenarios will be examined (see Exhibits 2-6 and
2-7).

To illustrate, Englewood has been losing population over the 1970's
at a rate of about .69 percent annually. If this loss continues, then
over the eight years from 1978 to 1985, Englewood will therefore lose
about 5.5 percent (.0069 x 8) of its residents (from 23,700 to
22,400). This diminishment will shave the Englewood population value
entered into the municipal expenditure forecasting equation from
5.4680 to 5.4112 (logarithmic values of 23,700 and 22,400 respectively; see Exhibit 2-6). Given this change, with the other exogenous
variables frozen at their 1978 values, Englewood's 1985 municipal
expenditures will amount to $10.271 million in 1978 dollars -- an
$84,000 decrease from the 1978 $10.355 outlay (see Exhibit 2-7). In
other words, a declining population to service would offer some financial relief; however, the measure of relief (.9 percent) is much less
than the magnitude of population loss (6 percent). This "cost" is reflected in a rising per capita outlay from $440 in 1978 ($\frac{\$10,355,000}{23,700}$)

EXHIBIT 2-6

Calibration of Mature Suburb Municipal Expenditure Equation:
Englewood Current (1978 Base Case) and Projected 1985 Values

Equation Argument or Variable (see Exhibit 2-3)	1978-1985 Median Voter-Community Profile	Equation Constant or Coefficient (a)	Actual or Forecasted Value for Equation Variables (b)	Contribution to Total Municipal Function Expenditures (u)
Intercept		-5.4461		-5.44
Property Tax Share	·1978 base case (a)	-.4201	2.5244	-1.06
	·tax share increase, 1978-85 (b)	-.4201	2.6197	-1.1005
Population	·1978 base case (a)	.1722	5.4680	0.94
	·future population loss, 1978-85 -- current rate (c)	.1722	5.4112	0.93
	·future population loss, 1978-85 -- accelerated rate (d)	.1722	5.3510	0.92
	·future population gain, 1978-85 (e)	.1722	5.5073	0.95
Nonresidential Employment				
Commercial	·1978 base case (a)	-.0473	7.6686	-0.36
	·future employment loss, 1978-85 -- current rate (f)	-.0473	7.4942	-0.35
	·future employment loss, 1978-85 -- accelerated rate (g)	-.0473	7.2829	-0.34
	·future employment gain, 1978-85 (h)	-.0473	7.8170	-0.37
Industrial	·1978 base case (a)	+.0326	8.3972	0.30
	·future employment loss, 1978-85 -- current rate (i)	+.0326	8.2228	0.2977
	·future employment gain, 1978-85 (j)	+.0326	8.9851	0.33
Service	·1978 base case (a)	+.1337	8.4908	1.13
	·future employment loss, 1978-85 (k)	+.1337	7.9800	1.07
	·future employment gain, 1978-85 -- current rate (l)	+.1337	8.6042	1.15
Service Input Cost	·1978 base case (a)	+.9493	9.8991	9.39
	·future cost increase, 1978-85 -- moderate (m)	+.9493	10.0470	9.54
	·future cost increase, 1978-85 -- steep (n)	+.9493	10.2356	9.72
Intergovernmental Revenue				
Federal Aid	·1978 base case (a)	+.0337	6.8855	0.23
	·future aid increase, 1978-85 -- current rate (o)	+.0337	7.4733	0.25
	·future aid loss, 1978-85 (p)	+.0337	6.1913	0.21
Revenue Sharing	·1978 base case (a)	+.0327	5.9915	0.19
	·future aid loss, 1978-85 (q)	+.0327	5.4806	0.18
"Urbanism"				
Utility tax revenue	·1978 base case (a)	+.5550	7.0926	3.93
	·future aid loss, 1978-85 (r)	+.5550	6.5817	3.65
				TOTAL: (v) See Exhibit 2-7

Notes (a) - (v) : *See Page 2, Exhibit 2-6.*

EXHIBIT 2-6 (continued)

___

NOTES:

ⓐ 1978 Englewood median voter-community characteristics.

ⓑ Tax share increase, 10 percent cumulatively over the 1978-1985 period.

ⓒ Population decline over 1978-1985 period at current (1970-1978) loss rate (.69% annual decline).

ⓓ Population decline over 1978-1985 period at double the current (1970-1978) loss rate (1.38% annual decline).

ⓔ Population increase over 1978-1985 period at .05 percent annual increase.

ⓕ Commercial employment loss over 1978-1985 period at current (1970-1978) loss rate (2% annual decline).

ⓖ Commercial employment loss over 1978-1985 period at double the current (1970-1978) loss rate (4% annual decline).

ⓗ Commercial employment gain over 1978-1985 period at 2% annual rate.

ⓘ Industrial employment loss over 1978-1985 period at current (1970-1978) loss rate (2% annual decline).

ⓙ Industrial employment gain over 1978-1985 period at 5% annual rate.

ⓚ Service employment gain over 1978-1985 period at current (1970-1978) service job increase (14% annual increase).

ⓛ Service employment loss over 1978-1985 period at 5% annual loss.

ⓜ Factor costs increase over 1978-1985 period at 2% annual rate.

ⓝ Factor costs increase over 1978-1985 period at 5% annual rate.

ⓞ Federal aid increase over 1978-1985 period at 10% annual gain. *(Note: This rate is far less than the actual increases in federal assistance over the 1970-1978 period.)*

ⓟ Federal aid loss over 1978-1985 period at 5 percent annual rate.

ⓠ Revenue sharing loss over 1978-1985 period at 5% annual rate.

ⓡ Utility revenue loss over 1978-1985 period at 5% annual rate.

ⓢ Municipal expenditure equation coefficients expressed in logarithmic values (see Exhibit 2-2).

ⓣ Englewood values (1978 [base case] or future [1985]) expressed in logarithmic terms.

ⓤ Equals equation constant multiplied by actual/forecasted value.

ⓥ Equals sum of groupings of variables, e.g., 1978 base case, base case modified by population gain, base case modified by commercial employment gain, etc. To illustrate, the base case total equals the sum of -5.44, -1.06, .94, -.36, .30, 1.13, 9.39, .23, .19 and 3.93 or 9.24. The base case modified by population gain equals -5.44, -1.06, .95 (instead of .94 with the base case), -.36, .30, 1.13, 9.39, .23, .19 and 3.93 or 9.25. The remaining scenarios were calculated in the same fashion.

Source: See text and Appendix A.

EXHIBIT 2-7

**Current and Future Mature Suburb Municipal Expenditures
Given Changes to Median Voter-Community Profile Characteristics:
Englewood, New Jersey — 1978 and 1985**

Median Voter-Community Profile Traits	MUNICIPAL EXPENDITURES ESTIMATED BY EXPENDITURE EQUATION				
	Logarithmic Value ⓐ	Dollar Value (In $ Millions) ⓒ	Base Case Expenditure Dollar Value (In $ Millions) ⓤ	Difference from Base Case ⓥ ($ Thousands)	%
BASE CASE (1978) ⓐ	9.24526	$10.355 ⓤ	$10.355 ⓥ	$0	0.00%
FUTURE CASES (1978-1985)					
Property Tax Share					
Tax share increase ⓑ	9.20000	9.897	10.355	-458	-4.42
Population					
Population loss - current rate ⓒ	9.23706	10.271	10.355	- 84	-0.80
Population loss accelerated rate ⓓ	9.22666	10.164	10.355	-190	-1.83
Population gain ⓔ	9.25356	10.442	10.355	+ 87	+0.80
Nonresidential Employment					
Commercial job loss - current rate ⓕ	9.25056	10.410	10.355	+ 55	+0.50
Commercial job loss accelerated rate ⓖ	9.26076	10.517	10.355	+165	+1.57
Commercial job gain ⓗ	9.23552	10.255	10.355	-100	-1.00
Industrial job loss current rate ⓘ	9.24300	10.332	10.355	- 2	-0.00
Industrial job gain ⓙ	9.26654	10.578	10.355	+223	+2.15
Service job gain current rate ⓚ	9.26050	10.514	10.355	+159	+1.54
Service job loss ⓛ	8.11010	9.672	10.355	-683	-6.60
Service Input Cost					
Service cost increase - moderate ⓜ	9.41090	12.220	10.355	+1,865	+18.00
Service cost increase - steep ⓝ	9.71661	14.355	10.355	+4,000	+38.60
Intergovernmental Revenue					
Federal aid gain ⓞ	9.26510	10.562	10.355	+207	+2.00
Federal aid loss ⓟ	9.22391	10.137	10.355	-218	-2.10
Revenue sharing loss ⓠ	9.22860	10.184	10.355	-171	-1.65
"Urbanism"					
Public utility loss ⓡ	8.96180	7.799	10.355	-2,556	-24.68

Notes:

ⓐ 1978 Englewood median voter-community characteristics.

ⓑ Tax share increase, 10 percent cumulatively over the 1978-1985 period.

ⓒ Population decline over 1978-1985 period at current (1970-1978) loss rate (.69% annual decline).

ⓓ Population decline over 1978-1985 period at double the current (1970-1978) loss rate (1.38% annual decline).

ⓔ Population increase over 1978-1985 period at .05 percent annual increase.

EXHIBIT 2-7 (continued)

Notes (continued)

(f) Commercial employment loss over 1978-1985 period at current (1970-1978) loss rate (2% annual decline).

(g) Commercial employment loss over 1978-1985 period at double the current (1970-1978) loss rate (4% annual decline).

(h) Commercial employment gain over 1978-1985 period at 2% annual rate.

(i) Industrial employment loss over 1978-1985 period at current (1970-1978) loss rate (2% annual decline).

(j) Industrial employment gain over 1978-1985 period at 5% annual rate.

(k) Service employment gain over 1978-1985 period at current (1970-1978) service job increase (14% annual increase).

(l) Service employment loss over 1978-1985 period at 5% annual loss.

(m) Factor costs increase over 1978-1985 period at 2% annual rate.

(n) Factor costs increase over 1978-1985 period at 5% annual rate.

(o) Federal aid increase over 1978-1985 period at 10% annual gain. *(Note: This rate is far less than the automatic increases in federal assistance over the 1970-1978 period.)*

(p) Federal aid loss over 1978-1985 period at 5% annual rate.

(q) Revenue sharing loss over 1978-1985 period at 5% annual rate.

(r) Utility revenue loss over 1978-1985 period at 5% annual rate.

(s) Equals sum of groupings of variables, e.g., 1978 base case, base case modified by population gain, base case modified by commercial employment gain, etc. To illustrate, the base case total equals the sum of -5.44, -1.06, .94, -.36, .30, 1.13, 9.39, .23, .19 and 3.93 or 9.24. The base case modified by population gain equals -5.44, -1.06, .95 (instead of .94 with the base case), -.36, .30, 1.13, 9.39, .23, .19 and 3.93 or 9.25. The remaining scenarios were calculated in the same fashion.

(t) Converts indicated 1978 logarithmic value to 1978 dollar expenditure.

(u) See Exhibit 2-3.

(v) Equals future case less base expenditure expressed in dollar and percentage difference terms.

Source: See text and Appendix A.

to $459 in 1985 ($\frac{\$10,271,000}{22,400}$) -- an increase of 4 percent.

An acceleration in population loss from the 1970s' rate of .69 percent would yield a more pronounced "cost" effect. For instance, if the rate of population loss doubled to 1.38 percent a year so that between 1978 and 1985 Englewood would lose about 11 percent of its residents (.0138 x 8), then its population would drop from 23,700 to about 21,100. Its 1985 expenditures would then amount to $10.164 million (see Exhibit 2-7). This figure offers some spending relief of about $200,000 from the $10.355 million outlay in 1978. Again, however, the overall spending respite is small -- a 1.8 percent decline -- and has the practical effect of increasing per capita costs from $440 in 1978 ($\frac{\$10,355,000}{23,700}$ to almost $500 ($\frac{\$10,164,000}{21,100}$) in 1985 -- a rise of almost 14 percent. Population decline is thus costly in the sense that it offers negligible spending relief and demands that a still-large spending bill be borne by a noticeably smaller resident base.

The converse of population decline-associated costs is "economies" offered by growth. If Englewood increased its population by half of one percent annually between 1978 and 1985, then by 1985 its population would rise to about 25,000 and its municipal expenditures would increase to $10.442 million (see Exhibit 2-7). This spending gain of less than one percent from the 1978 outlay is more than matched by the fact that Englewood would have 4 percent additional residents over which to spread these costs. Per capita expenditures would thus decrease from $440 ($\frac{\$10,355,000}{23,700}$) in 1978 to $420 ($\frac{\$10,442,000}{25,000}$) in 1985.

There are further municipal expenditure penalties associated with decline. If Englewood's commercial employment base continued to drop at the rate of the late 1970's (about 2 percent a year), then by 1985 its municipal expenditures would increase by $55,000 (see Exhibit 2-7). A larger municipal spending bill would then have to be borne by a community tax base which likely would be shrinking in real dollars as commercial ratables atrophied and declined in value. Accelerated commercial decline would increase the fiscal crunch. A doubling of the commercial employment loss to about 4 percent annually would increase 1985 municipal outlays by almost $170,000 (see Exhibit 2-7). In contrast, a strengthened commercial sector would offer fiscal relief. For example, a small gain of the commercial job base, say by 2 percent yearly, would have the effect of reducing expenditures by about $100,000. This savings would be in addition to the added property tax revenues made possible by invigorated commercial ratables.

Growth in other business sectors will also likely be fiscally beneficial. If Englewood's industrial employment would increase by 5 percent a year, then by 1985 local municipal outlays would rise by only a little over $200,000 (see Exhibit 2-7) -- a spending increase which would likely be more than offset by the added revenues engendered by such nonresidential growth.

All of these projections point to the same underlying condition. Mature suburbs like Englewood, with their service infrastructure in

place, can accommodate growth with minimal added fiscal strain. In
fact, no growth or decline will many times be more expensive in its
own right.

Further Englewood fiscal scenarios are shown in Exhibits 2-6 and
2-7. Federal aid to older suburbs will likely be cut. Such shrinkage
will dampen local expenditures because diminished intergovernmental
support increases the local tax "bite" of municipal spending. Spending temperance, however, will often not be as significant as the
municipality's absolute loss in state/federal aid, so that on balance
the community's fiscal position will worsen.

Englewood is illustrative. As of 1978 it received approximately
$1,000,000 in federal grants (does not include CETA or Revenue Shar-
ing). If this stipend were cut by 5 percent annually, then by 1985,
federal aid would amount to about $600,000 -- a $400,000 loss. Such
retrenchment in federal assistance would also trigger spending temperance of about $200,000 by 1985. Thus, on a net basis, Englewood would
find itself at a 2:1 intergovernmental income-to-spending cut disadvantage.

Englewood's fiscal posture would be most severely affected by rising
public sector input or factor costs such as public employee salaries,
fringes, etc. If these increase by 5 percent a year in real terms, a
pace experienced in the early 1970's (albeit sharply reduced in the
past few years), then by 1985, Englewood's expenditure would increase
by a whopping $4,000,000 -- a 40 percent increment over the 1978 base
(see Exhibit 2-7). A more modest cost spiral of 2 percent yearly over
1978-1985 would also drastically increase spending by almost one-fifth
from the 1978 base year (see Exhibits 2-6 and 2-7). Statistically,
these large expenditure spirals are explained by the high equation coefficient (.9493) between municipal expenditures and factor costs -- a
constant at least 50 to 100 percent greater than any of the other
variables (see Exhibit 2-2). Conceptually, this finding conforms to
the common-sense perception that public employee salaries and support
costs strongly influence public sector expenditures: sharp increases
in the former significantly inflate the latter.

It is likely that many of the scenarios considered thus far will
occur simultaneously rather than separately. Fiscal implications for
Englewood and for that matter many sister older suburbs are chasten-
ing. If these communities continue to lose population, nonresidential
(especially retail sector) vigor, and intergovernmental aid, and in
addition do not constrain their service factor costs -- all conditions
which have been present in the past and may even be accentuated in
coming years -- then their fiscal future will be one of rising expenditures paid for by a declining population and ratable base.

Further insight into suburban municipal expenditures is provided by
the qualitative analysis below.

QUALITATIVE ANALYSIS OF MUNICIPAL EXPENDITURES

The discussion thus far has attempted to quantitatively explain the
relatively high level of municipal expenditures in mature suburbs in
general and Englewood in particular. Quantitative variables include

factor costs, business activity, tax burden and so on. This analysis assumed that there was a uniform entity entitled "municipal services" and that this common package had different price tags, depending on certain voter-community characteristics.

In reality, "municipal services" are not uniform. Herbert Simon's criticism of a half-century ago, that economists examining municipal cost variations were not sensitive to service output distinctions[17] (e.g., sanitation pickup at the curb versus rear yard), is still valid today. Can service output variations help explain the constrasts in municipal spending between Englewood, mature suburbs, and growing suburbs?

The answer is a qualified "yes." "Service output" encompasses numerous considerations, some of which are more measurable than others. To illustrate, service range and type -- what is being done and by whom -- can readily be identified, while service quality is more difficult to gauge. Survey of the service character as well as quality in Englewood and the older and newer suburbs suggests that the mature suburbs, and especially Englewood, provide a wide span of services and moreover these tend to be of superior quality.

Service Range-Type

Englewood has opted for a comprehensive local service system paid for by the municipal corporation and made available by full-time public employees. The older suburbs follow a similar strategy, however to a lesser extent than Englewood. Newer suburbs, in contrast, provide fewer services and/or rely more extensively on volunteers as opposed to a paid public work force.

Provision of fire protection is illustrative. This service can be made available by a: (1) fully-paid public force -- the most expensive public option as reflected by municipal government outlays; (2) unpaid volunteers -- an inexpensive approach; and (3) a mixture of the two strategies (e.g., paid dispatchers and volunteer firemen) displaying a similar "mid-range" price tag. Englewood has a fully-paid fire department. In this respect it is joined by most of its sister mature suburbs (see Exhibit 2-8). Remaining older suburbs have either a mixed public-private strategy (e.g., Millburn augments its 51 paid firemen with an additional 35 volunteers), or else a volunteer fire force. Growing New Jersey suburbs, in contrast, have universally adopted a volunteer fire protection arrangement -- none of the 20 communities in this group have any firemen on the public payroll.

These distinctions translate into sharp fire-protection cost implications. In 1978, older suburbs on average spent about $30 per capita for fire protection. Mature suburbs with a municipal fire department spend the most per capita ($39), those with a mixed strategy expended slightly less ($30), while communities with volunteer arrangements spend the least ($10) (see Exhibit 2-9). Newer suburbs, all of whom had volunteer departments, spent about $7 per capita. Differences in community outlays are also illustrative (see Exhibit 2-9). In 1978, Englewood expended $53 per capita for fire services. This amount was

EXHIBIT 2-8
New Jersey Mature Suburbs: Fire Protection Services/Strategies

MATURE SUBURB	TYPE OF FIRE COMPANY	STAFF SIZE PAID/VOLUNTEER	UNIONIZATION[1]	SALARY OF SENIOR FIREFIGHTER[1]	MUNICIPAL SUPPORT OFFERED TO ALL VOLUNTEER FIRE COMPANIES[2]	INSPECTION CYCLE (PAID AND PAID/VOLUNTEER COMPANIES)[3]	OTHER SERVICES RENDERED (PAID AND PAID/VOLUNTEER COMPANIES)[3]
Bergenfield	paid/volunteer	4/78	no	See Exhibit 6-4[1]	NA	1/year (comm.[5] + multi-fam.[6])	ambulance squad
Clifton	paid	154	FMBA[4]	Exhibit 6-4[1]	NA	1/year (comm.)	ambulance; night fire patrol
Cranford	paid/volunteer	30/26	FMBA	Exhibit 6-4[1]	NA	1/year (comm.)	rescue (motor vehicle extrication)
Dover	paid/volunteer	5/70	FMBA	Exhibit 6-4[1]	NA	1/year (comm.)	ambulance
Englewood	paid	46	FMBA	Exhibit 6-4[1]	NA	2/year (comm.) 1/year (ind.[7])	NA
Flemington	volunteer	52	NA	NA	vehicles, equipment, houses	NA	NA
Fort Lee	volunteer	160	NA	NA	vehicles, equipment,	NA	NA
Hackensack	paid	91	no	Exhibit 6-4[1]	NA	1/year	ambulance
Hillside	paid	52	FMBA	Exhibit 6-4[1]	NA	1/year (comm.) 1/2 year (multi-fam.)	ambulance on weekdays
Lodi	volunteer	100	NA	NA	vehicles, equipment, houses	NA	NA
Long Branch	paid/volunteer	21/150	FMBA	Exhibit 6-4[1]	NA	1/year (comm.) 2/year (rest.[8] & ind.)	ambulance
Lyndhurst	volunteer	55	NA	NA	vehicles, equipment	NA	NA
Maplewood	paid	47	FMBA	Exhibit 6-4[1]	NA	1/3 mos. (comm.)	NA
Millburn	paid/volunteer	51/35	FMBA	Exhibit 6-4[1]	NA	1/2 mos. (gas sts.[9]) 1/year (comm.)	rescue
Montclair	paid	84	FMBA	Exhibit 6-4[1]	NA	2/year (comm.)	NA
Morristown[1]	paid/volunteer	23/200	FMBA, FMBA, AFL-CIO	Exhibit 6-4[1] Exhibit 6-4[1]	NA	1/month (institutional) 1/month (comm.)	rescue squad
New Brunswick	paid	82			NA	1/year (comm.)	NA
Plainfield	paid	108	FMBA	Exhibit 6-4[1]	NA	1/year (comm.)	NA
Red Bank	volunteer	--	NA	NA	ment, houses vehicles, equipment, fire houses	NA	NA

EXHIBIT 2-8 (continued)

MATURE SUBURB	TYPE OF FIRE COMPANY	STAFF SIZE PAID/VOLUNTEER	UNIONIZATION[1]	SALARY OF SENIOR FIREFIGHTER[1]	MUNICIPAL SUPPORT OFFERED TO ALL VOLUNTEER FIRE COMPANIES[2]	INSPECTION CYCLE (PAID AND PAID/VOLUNTEER COMPANIES[3])	OTHER SERVICES RENDERED (PAID AND PAID/VOLUNTEER COMPANIES[3])
Ridgewood	paid/volunteer	46/65	FMBA	Exhibit 6-4[1]	NA	--	rescue
Roselle	paid/volunteer	26/25	FMBA	Exhibit 6-4[1]	NA	2/year (pub. assm.[10] ind. & comm.)	ambulance
Scotch Plains	volunteer	43	NA	NA	vehicles, equipment, firehouses	1/year (ind. & comm.) NA	NA
Summit	paid/volunteer	38/64	FMBA	Exhibit 6-4[1]	NA	4/year (comm.)	fire prevention patrols
Teaneck	paid	93	FMBA	Exhibit 6-4[1]	NA	1/year	NA
Wayne	volunteer	160	NA	NA	$15,000/year/ company, 5 companies	NA	NA

[1]Applicable only to paid professional firefighters.
[2]Applies only to volunteer fire companies.
[3]Applies only to paid and partially paid (paid and volunteer) fire companies.

Abbreviations

[4]FMBA	-	Firemen's Mutual Benevolent Association
[5]comm.	-	commercial
[6]ind.	-	industrial
[7]multi-fam.	-	multi-family dwellings
[8]rest.	-	restaurants
[9]gas sts.	-	gas stations
[10]pub. assm.	-	public assembly (i.e., social clubs, churches, synagogues, schools)

NA   - not applicable

Source: Rutgers University telephone survey of indicated municipalities, 1981-82.

EXHIBIT 2-9

Fire-Sanitation Service Strategies and Costs:
New Jersey Mature and Growing Suburbs, 1978

SUBURBAN COMMUNITIES	Fire Service Strategy	Per Capita Fire Cost (1978) Ⓣ	Sanitation Service Strategy	Per Capita Public Works Cost (1978) Ⓤ
OLDER SUBURBS				
Bergenfield	Mixed Ⓐ	$ 9	Municipal Ⓑ Ⓔ	$48
Clifton	Municipal	43	Private (M)	46
Cranford	Mixed	31	Private (I)	64
Dover	Mixed	9	Private (M)	49
Englewood	Municipal Ⓑ	53	Municipal	90
Flemington	Municipal	8	Private (M)	86
Fort Lee	Volunteer	10	Private (M)	52
Hackensack	Municipal	63	Municipal	71
Hillside	Municipal	67	Private (M)	64
Lodi	Volunteer	5	Private (M)	50
Long Branch	Mixed	15	Municipal	41
Lyndhurst	Municipal	26	Private (M)	47
Maplewood	Municipal	49	Private (I) Ⓓ	51
Millburn	Mixed	68	Municipal	76
Montclair	Municipal	42	Municipal	51
Morristown	Mixed	36	Municipal	67
New Brunswick	Municipal	44	Municipal	52
Plainfield	Municipal	52	Private (I)	41
Red Bank	Volunteer	9	Municipal	45
Ridgewood	Mixed	38	Municipal	67
Roselle	Mixed	29	Private (I)	55
Scotch Plains	Municipal	10	Private (I)	48
Summit	Mixed	39	Municipal	84
Teaneck	Municipal	48	Private (I)	61
Wayne	Municipal	5	Private (M)	59
	Average All :	*$32*	*Average All :*	*$59*
	Average Municipal:	*$39*	*Average Municipal :*	*$63*
	Average Mixed :	*$30*	*Average Private (M) :*	*$57*
	Average Volunteer:	*$ 8*	*Average Private (I) :*	*$53*
GROWING SUBURBS				
Bernards	Volunteer	$ 6	Private	$56
Cherry Hill	Volunteer	1	Municipal	33
East Brunswick	Volunteer	4	Municipal	50
East Hanover	Volunteer	5	Private	39
East Windsor	Volunteer	1	Municipal	21
Florham Park	Volunteer	4	Private Ⓔ	53
Holmdel	Volunteer	25	Private	44
Lawrence	Volunteer	5	Private	97
Montvale	Volunteer	13	Municipal	73
Moorestown	Volunteer	1	Municipal	51
Morris Township	Volunteer	24	Municipal	63
New Providence	Volunteer	6	Municipal	92
Parsippany-Troy	Volunteer	31	Municipal	26
Pennsauken	Volunteer	8	Municipal	40
Piscataway	Volunteer	1	Private	32
Rockaway	Volunteer	10	Private	50
Roseland	Volunteer	7	Municipal	44
South Brunswick	Volunteer	1	Private	50
Voorhees	Volunteer	1	Municipal	23
Warren	Volunteer	15	Private	42
	Average All:	*$ 8*	*Average All :*	*$49*
			Average Municipal:	*$47*
			Average Private :	*$51*

Ⓐ Mixed   = Fire protection provided by both volunteers and a paid force.
Ⓑ Municipal   = Fire protection or sanitation provided entirely by a municipal work force.
Ⓒ Private(M)= Municipally-contracted private scavenger service.
Ⓓ Private(I)= Individual households contract with private scavenger service.
Ⓔ Private   = Private(M) or Private(I) sanitation service.
Note: Expenditures below $1 per capita are shown as $1; differs slightly from figures in Exhibit 1-3 because of rounding.

Source: New Jersey Department of Community Affairs, Division of Local Government.

equivalent to the outlay in Maplewood ($49), Teaneck ($48) and numerous other older suburbs with a similar fully-paid fire force. Costs were lower in remaining mature suburbs with a mixed public-private fire protection strategy (e.g., $36 in Morristown, $31 in Cranford). The lowest charges were recorded by localities with a volunteer fire department such as Fort Lee ($10) and Red Bank ($9) and all of the newer suburbs who on average expended $7 per capita for fire protection. In short, examining service range-type helps explain threshold variations in municipal service costs.

Another example is provided by sanitation collection strategies. Garbage pickup may be handled in at least one of three ways: (1) the municipality may provide and pay for the service itself; (2) the municipality may contract with private companies; or (3) the private homeowner or business may contract directly with a private scavenger (see detailed discussion in chapter six).

In general, the public cost as indicated by a municipal government's budgetary expenditure will be highest with the first strategy and lowest with the third (see Exhibit 2-9). This distinction helps explain some of the expenditure variations pointed to in chapter one. Englewood and many of the older suburbs have opted for municipally-provided and paid-for public sanitation (see Exhibit 2-10). Newer suburbs, in contrast, have more readily turned to municipal or private homeowner contracting for services; about half of the New Jersey growing suburbs group have so acted. In part because of these decisions, Englewood and many of the mature suburbs spend more for public works — a service category in which sanitation is an important constituent member. In 1978, per capita public works expenditures were $90 in Englewood and about $60 on average in the older suburbs, compared to roughly $50 in the newer suburbs.

Intracommunity spending profiles amongst both the mature and growing suburb groups also reflect the service strategy type-expenditure linkage (see Exhibit 2-9). Older suburbs with municipally-provided and paid-for sanitation in general display higher per capita public works outlays (e.g., $90 in Englewood and $76 in Millburn) than their mature suburb counterparts with municipal/private-contract arrangements with scavengers (e.g., $46 in Clifton and $41 in Plainfield). Similarly, in the growing suburb group, per capita public works expenditures are highest amongst those communities directly providing sanitation pickup (e.g., $73 per capita in Montgomery and $63 in Morris Township) as opposed to the outlays in communities opting for contracting arrangements with private scavengers (e.g., $42 in Warren and $32 in Piscataway). Here again we see how attention to service range-type assists the interpretation of threshold differences in municipal service expenditures, albeit it leaves unexplained why communities nominally adhering to the same service approach differ so considerably in their spending (see Exhibit 2-9). For instance, while both Englewood and Bergenfield have municipally-provided sanitation, the former's per capita public works costs are almost double the latter's. To understand why such differences occur, we must turn to the expenditure model presented previously in this chapter.

Service Quality

   Service quality is yet another qualitative factor helping define
service output variations and attendant costs. "Quality," in turn, is
a very difficult criteria to define; it varies according to such factors as observer expectation, past performance, and so on. It is possible, however, to apply very crude indices of "quality" and by these
standards mature suburbs in general and Englewood in particular fare
well compared to growing suburbs. To illustrate, of all the older
suburbs, Englewood provides perhaps the most comprehensive garbage
collection service (see Exhibit 2-10). It offers rear-yard pickup at a
twice-weekly frequency for residences (an additional curbside collection is made weekly), and a five-time weekly cycle for commercial and
some industrial uses. In addition, Englewood provides collection of
"heavy items" (e.g., furniture, large appliances) once a week. In contrast, many of the older suburbs (Millburn, Morristown, Wayne) have
only curbside pickup and adhere to a less frequent service cycle (see
Exhibit 2-10). Summit, for example, provides commercial sanitation
service three times a week to Englewood's five; Morristown has "heavy"
pickup once a month as compared to Englewood's weekly cycle.
   These Englewood-to-older suburb differences should not make us lose
sight of the fact that both Englewood and the mature suburbs generally
provide higher quality services relative to the newer suburbs. Sanitation is again illustrative. None of the newer suburbs offers rear-
yard pickup. In addition, compared to the older suburbs, the newer
suburbs have less frequent pickup, especially of non-garbage items.
   "Quality" comes at a price -- extra manpower, capital equipment and
so on. Variations in the number of sanitation workers per 1,000 population are illustrative. Englewood's rate is 1.6 compared to 1.4 for
Montclair, 1.15 for Ridgewood and .8 for Bergenfield. In turn, these
figures are considerably higher than the public works staffing levels
found in growing suburbs. Such manpower declensions are, in part, a
product of the service quality distinctions described above.
   The combination of the qualitative factors discussed thus far --
service type-range and quality -- enhances our understanding of expenditure variations. To illustrate, this chapter previously referred to
the mathematical model to help explain why Englewood spent over $10
million for municipal services (1978) while two Bergen County neighbors, Bergenfield and Lodi, expended half as much. Service qualitative
factors also bear on this intracommunity distinction. While Englewood
spends the most relative to Bergenfield and Lodi it offers the widest
range of quality services. Englewood has a large paid fire department
(see Exhibit 2-8). Lodi has volunteers, and Bergenfield a paid/volun-
teer arrangement (4 paid members, 78 volunteers). Englewood has a
municipal sanitation department (see Exhibit 2-10). In this respect it
is joined by Bergenfield; however, Lodi contracts with a private scavenger. There are also quality differentiations, albeit these can only
be crudely measured. Bergenfield provides heavy pickup once every two
weeks compared to a weekly cycle in Englewood. Bergenfield and Lodi

EXHIBIT 2-10

New Jersey Mature Suburbs: Sanitation Services/Strategies

MATURE SUBURB	TYPE OF SANITATION COMPANY[1]	STAFF SIZE[4]	UNIONIZATION[4]	SALARY[4]	SERVICE LEVEL[5] TYPE	PICK-UP[16]	FREQUENCY[18]	FEES (OR CONTRACT)[6]	OTHER SERVICES[5]
Bergenfield	Municipal[1]	21	no	See Exhibit 6-2[4]	res. & comm.	curb[16]	2/wk.[18]	NA	heavy[21] 2/mo. leaves and grass
Clifton	Private (M)[2]	NA	NA	NA	res.	curb	2/wk.	$1,085,000[7]	Spring[20]
Cranford	Private (I)[3]	NA	NA	NA	NA	NA	NA	--	NA
Dover	Private (M)	NA	NA	NA	all	curb	2/wk.	$ 283,789[8]	heavy - 1/mo., snow
Englewood	Municipal	38	yes	Exhibit 6-2[4]	res.& comm.[10] some ind.	back-res.[9] curb	2/wk. (res.) 5/wk. (comm.)	NA	heavy- 1/wk. leaves, grass, snow
Flemington	Private (M)	NA	NA	NA	res.	curb	2/wk.	$ 44,675	none
Fort Lee	Private (M)	NA	NA	NA	all	curb	2/wk.	$ 264,355	none
Hackensack	Municipal	12	yes	Exhibit 6-2[4]	res., some comm.	back[17]	2/wk.	NA	leaves and grass, heavy
Hillside	Private (M)	NA	NA	NA	res.	curb	2/wk.	$ 152,000	none
Lodi	Private (M)	NA	NA	NA	all except ind. sup. mark[13] and auto body	curb	2/wk.	$ 371,088	leaves and grass, heavy
Long Branch	Municipal	17	yes	Exhibit 6-2[4]	all	curb	7/wk. (comm.) 2/wk. (res.)	NA	leaves and grass, heavy - 1/wk.
Lyndhurst	Private (M)	NA	NA	NA	res. & comm.	curb	2/wk.	$ 279,000	leaves and grass, heavy
Maplewood	Private (I)	NA	NA	NA	NA	NA	NA	$23.00/quarter	NA
Millburn	Municipal	11	yes	Exhibit 6-2[4]	res.	curb	2/wk.	NA	grass, spring; leaves, fall
Montclair	Municipal	39	yes	Exhibit 6-2[4]	all	back	2/wk.	NA	leaves, snow, grass, heavy
Morristown	Municipal	6	yes	Exhibit 6-2[4]	all	curb	2/wk.	NA	heavy - 1/mo.
Plainfield	Private (I)	NA	NA	NA	all	NA	NA	@$7.50/month	NA

EXHIBIT 2-10 (continued)

MATURE SUBURB	TYPE OF SANITATION COMPANY	STAFF SIZE[4]	UNIONIZATION[4]	SALARY[4]	SERVICE LEVEL[5] TYPE	PICK-UP	FREQUENCY	FEES (OR CONTRACT)[6]	OTHER SERVICES[5]
Ridgewood	Municipal	29	yes	Exhibit 6-2[4]	res., inst.[14]	back	2/wk.	NA	grass - 1/wk. heavy - 2/mo. leaves
Roselle	Private (M)	NA	NA	NA	all	back	2/wk.	$ 524,000	heavy - 1/wk. leaves and grass
Scotch Plains	Private (I)	NA	NA	NA	NA	NA	NA	NA	NA
Summit	Municipal	20	no	Exhibit 6-2[4]	res. & comm.	back	2/wk. (res.) 3/wk. (comm.)	NA	NA
Teaneck	Private (I)	NA	NA	NA	NA	NA	NA	$3.75-$8.25/mo.	NA
Wayne	Private (M)	NA	NA	NA	res. & multi-family.[15]	curb	2/wk.	$1,241,549	heavy, leaves and grass

1 Municipally provided sanitation service.
2 Municipally contracted private scavenger service.
3 Individually contracted scavenger service.
4 For municipally provided sanitation service.
5 For municipally provided and municipally contracted scavenger service.
6 For municipally contracted and privately contracted scavenger service.
7 Amount paid by municipality to private scavenger.
8 Amount paid by household to private scavenger.

Abbreviations

9 res.   - residential
10 comm.   - commercial
11 ind.   - industrial
12 apts.   - apartments
13 sup. mark. - supermarkets
14 inst.   - institutional
15 multi-fam. - multi-family
16 curb   - curbside
17 back   - backyard
18 wk.   - week
19 y.   - year(s)
20 Spring   - spring clean-up; fall; fall clean-up
21 heavy   - heavy items, i.e., furniture, large appliances
NA   - not applicable

Source: Rutgers University telephone survey of indicated municipalities, 1981-82.

have curb-side pickup compared to rear yard service in Englewood. The latter provides industrial service in contrast to the absence/limited nature of such pickup in both Bergenfield and Lodi. Thus, while Englewood outspends its two Bergen County neighbors by two to one, its municipal services are qualitatively superior.

In summary, the expenditure variations between Englewood, older suburbs, and newer suburbs reflect the quantitative median voter-community factors discussed previously and the service qualitative distinctions pointed to in this section.

POLICY IMPLICATIONS

Analysis of municipal spending suggests that the fiscal pressures confronting mature suburbs in general and Englewood in particular could be alleviated by the following actions:

1. Growth, both residential and nonresidential, should be encouraged. Mature suburbs have the ability to accommodate expansion with relatively minimal service outlays. They should capitalize on this capacity and garner the additional local revenues made available by growth.

2. Closely related is the commercial, predominantly retail, health of the older suburb. These communities must strive to restore the vigor of their once-strong business district activity. Commercial expansion should be encouraged both for the revenues it will realize and to stem the special municipal spending pressures incited by commercial decline.

3. Mature suburbs should pay careful attention to their municipal service factor costs. These are relatively high already and unless checked will continue to drive up municipal expenditures.

4. Older suburbs should carefully scrutinize the qualitative aspects of their municipal service systems. In an era of growing fiscal crunch, can they continue to provide the scope and quality of services they have traditionally offered? Additionally, the mode of service provision should be carefully reevaluated. Is the older suburb best off providing services directly as it traditionally has done? Should it instead contract with private firms? Perhaps even more radical surgery is appropriate such as reducing public sector involvement in "nonessential" areas (e.g., public tennis courts) in favor of residents making do on their own and reaping the benefit of reduced municipal expenditures-taxes.

These options provide the framework for section two of this study. The latter, consisting of chapters three through six, examines strategies for alleviating the fiscal pressures confronting mature suburbs. Using Englewood as a case study:

a. Chapter three examines the fiscal impact of new residential and nonresidential development.

b. Chapter four explores the dynamics of retail activity in the older suburb and considers how this important business sector can be invigorated.

c. Chapter five examines new uses for the older suburb downtown, specifically development of cultural facilities.

d. Chapter six considers municipal service strategy alternatives ranging from lowering service quality sights to rethinking traditional service delivery strategies.

Appendix A
A Municipal Expenditure Model:
Statistical and Technical Features

INTRODUCTION

This appendix discusses statistical and other technical aspects of the municipal expenditure model. It focuses first on the model's specification and then considers its calibration.

MODEL SPECIFICATION: DERIVATION OF
THE MUNICIPAL EXPENDITURE EQUATIONS

The expenditure determinant model focuses upon the market or choice behavior of the municipality's median voter.[18] From the point of view of the rational use of the median voter's income, Y, it must be divided between municipal goods, X_1^*, at unit price, p_1, and all other goods and services collectively annotated as X_2 at unit price p_2. (Note: the asterisk on the municipal goods term is part of its notation.) The budget constraint equation is:

$$1]\quad Y = X_1^* p_1 + X_2 p_2$$

In order to acquire the greatest benefit from income Y, this voter must find a way of consuming municipal and other goods such that the ratio of their marginal utilities on benefits equals the ratio of the marginal prices of these two classes of goods.[19]

$$2]\quad \frac{\partial U_1}{\partial U_2} = \frac{p_1}{p_2}$$

Equation 2 requires that the median voter consumes the two sets of goods at some point on the budget constraint line.

Next, recognizing that the price of a unit of public good charged the median voter through the local property tax is not necessarily the same as the cost per unit of goods faced by the municipality, this conceptual distinction must be incorporated into the concept of the price of municipal goods. Since the price to the taxpayer per unit of municipal goods is the ratio of that voter's property taxes to the total tax revenue acquired by the city, we can define total tax price p_1 as:

$$p_1 = \tau_i q,$$

where τ_i represents voter "i" share of the
              municipality's property taxes,

      q   represents the unit cost of municipal
            inputs or factors of production, and

      i   represents the median voter.

The next concern involves the concept of public goods versus market
goods. The former represents the phenomenon that the consumption of a
unit of public goods by one resident does not take away from the consumption of that good by another. On the other hand, a market good is
characterized by rivalness in consumption; when it is consumed by one
person, it cannot be drawn upon by another. This concept is intro-
duced into the equation by a crowding or rivalness indicator, "γ",
where perfect rivalness is represented by $\gamma = 1$ and perfect public
goods is $\gamma = 0$. The relationship between the municipal goods consumed
by the median voter $\left\{X_1^*\right\}$ and those produced in total $\left\{X_1\right\}$ is now:

$$3]\quad X_1^* = \quad X_1/n^\gamma \quad = \quad X_1 n^{-\gamma}$$

The budget constraint equation can now be reformulated to incorporate the concept of tax price and rivalness in consumption. This is
first done for the median voter's tax price term:

$$4]\quad Y_i = \tau_i q X_1^* + \quad p_2 X_2,$$

and completed by the combination of tax price and rivalness:

$$5]\quad Y_i = \tau_i q n^{-\gamma} X_1^* + p_2 X_2 \quad .$$

The demand for municipal goods can be formulated by solving the
identity in Equation 5 for the quantity X^*:

$$6]\quad X_1^* = \frac{Y_i - p_2 X_2}{\tau_i q n^{-\gamma}}$$

At this point several simplifying assumptions must be entered into
the model in order to fit it to the set of New Jersey older suburbs
under consideration. First, in order to transform the identity into a
behavioral equation, we shall assume that all market and demographic
variables in the expenditure equation enter with constant demand elasticities (that is, there is a constant percentage increase in demand
for each percentage increase in the value of an independent variable),
and second, that expenditures for private consumption enter as a constant fraction of income among the median voters of the communities in
the data base; that is,

$$7]\quad Y - p_2 X_2 = cY$$

The simplified demand model is now:

$$8] \quad X_1^* \propto cY^{\varepsilon} (\tau_i q n^{\gamma})^{\delta}$$

where ε = income elasticity of demand for municipal goods, and

δ = price elasticity of demand for municipal goods.

However, total municipal goods production is:

$$X_1 = X_1^* n^{\gamma} \quad ,$$

and equation 9 can be reformulated in terms of total goods production as:

$$9] \quad X_1 \propto n^{\gamma} cY^{\varepsilon} (\tau_i q n^{\gamma})^{\delta}$$

and total municipal expenditures (M) as:

$$10] \quad qX_1 \propto n^{\gamma} cY^{\varepsilon} (\tau_i q n^{\gamma})^{\delta} q.$$

Lastly, assuming that the factor cost elasticity approaches 1 and the tax price term approaches -1, by elimination of the q term and clustering of the n term, Equation 10 simplifies to:

$$11] \quad M = qX_1 = AY^{\varepsilon} \tau^{\delta} n^{\gamma(1+\delta)} = AY^{\varepsilon} \tau^{\delta} n^{\alpha}$$

where

$\alpha \equiv \gamma(1+\delta)$, and c has been incorporated into the equation constant: A.

In its logarithmic form to be used for estimation purposes, Equation 11 becomes:

$$12] \quad \ln M = \ln A + \varepsilon \ln Y + \delta \ln \tau + \alpha \ln n \ldots$$

Assuming that there are factors that influence the production of municipal goods that are independent of the median voter's decision-making process, the marginal expenditures required from these aggregative as opposed to individual factors (grants to the municipality, economic activity present in the municipality, etc.) will enter the logarithmic demand equation as additive terms with constant elasticities.

MODEL CALIBRATION: FITTING THE MUNICIPAL EXPENDITURE EQUATION

The preceding section has shown that a demand function for municipal goods and services can be derived based upon the concepts of median voter control over resident-population related service generation, budget constraint in relation to the individual's consumption of municipal and other goods, utility maximization on the median voter's part, and constant expenditure elasticities for all variables within the expenditure equation. This permits the analyst to place theoretical limits on the several coefficients found in the behavioral model and to justify the coefficient's use in forecasting on well-reasoned theory.

The equation used to estimate the elasticities in Equation 12 is:

$$\ln M = \ln A + \varepsilon \ln Y + \delta \ln \tau + \alpha \ln n + \beta_1 \ln z_i,$$

where (the terms in parentheses are the acronyms used in the computer printout to represent their corresponding theoretical terms.)

M   (LNTOTMUN) represents real municipal operating expenditures in 1978 dollars;

Y   (LNINC) is per capita income in 1978 dollars;

τ (LTAXP) is the median value homeowner's property tax share;

n   (LPOPGRO) (LPOPDEC) is municipal growing/ declining population; and

z_i represents a set of aggregate municipal characteristics.

z_i is included to ensure coverage of community variables which planners-economists[20] have recognized as influencing public outlays. The set of z_i expenditure determinants include the following:

S   (LNSERV) - employment in the service sector;

C   (LNCOMEMP) - employment in the commercial sector;

I   (LNIND) - employment in the industrial sector;

q   (LMEDSAL) - municipal factor cost index (average public employee salaries);

FA   (LNFDAIDR) - federal grants;

RS   (LNSLFIS) - revenue sharing; and

U   (LNUTTLT) - utility tax receipts.

The coefficients [ε, δ, α, β_1] represent the demand elasticities for each respective variable in the equation. Elasticities are statistically estimated from the New Jersey older suburb group (see chapter one) through the use of a pooled time series cross-sectional data base. That is, the 25 older suburbs have observations for each variable in the expenditure equation for the years 1970, 1974, 1976 and 1978. (A complete set of post 1978 data were not available.) In order to produce unbiased estimates of the elasticities, the regression procedure utilized is covariance analysis. This is essentially the solution of the normal equations using the ordinary least squares criteria with dummy variables included for (n-1) of the suburbs in the data base.[21] In other words, the equation parameters are simultaneously solved through the use of all the exogenous expenditure data available from the pooled suburban community set.

Relevant components of the municipal expenditure equation are displayed in Exhibit 2-11. The elasticities reported under the parameter estimates column are all in the expected direction. For instance, public expenditures rise as public employee salaries are raised. In terms of the theoretical discussion, it was suggested that the cost of municipal inputs should have an elasticity of 1.0. The estimated value of .94 is not significantly different from 1.0. Tax share elasticity τ is reported to be -.42, which is comparable to the values reported by Bergstrom and Goodman in their cross-sectional analysis. The rivalness index can be computed with the aid of the coefficients of the population term and that of the tax price term:

$$\alpha = \gamma(1+\delta)$$

Exhibit 2-12 displays the necessary calculations to estimate the structural parameter γ. It indicates that in growing population suburbs, the goods that are produced by municipal government are utilized by the resident population as private goods. In other words, the median voter views his/her consumption of a unit of public goods as thereby excluding the benefit of that good from others. In contrast, in mature suburbs with declining populations, much of the output is public in nature, indicating that efforts are being advanced to produce goods and services of value to the city as a whole as opposed to the benefit of its individual members. From the median voters' perspective, personal consumption of public goods is not seen as being mutually exclusive of others' enjoyment. This finding corresponds to earlier work by Beaton showing the relatively different expenditure determinants for declining versus growing communities.[22] The last term incorporated in the theoretical work was per capita income. This term failed to exhibit a significant coefficient and in addition was perversely signed; it was therefore excluded from further consideration.

Turning from median voter to community influences on the budget, two such sets were examined: local business development and non-property tax revenue. Business development has been thought to influence the municipal fisc through at least two separate forces: tax price effect and the costs of services rendered.[23] The tax price effect has been subsumed within the tax share term (γ) and explicitly specified. Cost consequences of business development include both direct service requirements recognized by the municipal staff, as well as costs correlated with voter perception of additional service requirements suf-

EXHIBIT 2-11

Municipal Expenditure Determinants Equation:
Mature New Jersey Suburbs

EQUATION FACTOR/STATISTICS	EQUATION SYMBOL	FACTOR/PARAMETER ESTIMATE	STANDARD ERROR
EQUATION FACTOR			
Constant/Intercept	a	-5.4460	4.9472
Property Tax Share	τ	-0.4200	.1436
Population			
Declining	n *(declining suburbs)*	0.1723	.3571
Growing	n *(growing suburbs)*	0.6383	.5610
Nonresidential Employment			
Commercial	C	-0.0472	.0391
Industrial	I	0.0326	.0396
Service	S	.1337	.0062
Service Input Cost	q	.9493	.6650
Intergovernmental Revenue			
Federal Aid	FA	0.0337	.00623
Revenue Sharing	RS	0.0327	.00626
"Urbanism"			
Utility Tax Revenue	U	0.5550	.0741

EQUATION STATISTICS	
Correlation	R^2 .98
Significance	F Ratio 180.9 [a]

[a] Significant at .001 level.

Source: See text.

ficient to maintain the community as a desirable place to reside in the face of business activity. Coefficients derived in the model indicate that the smallest expenditure effect is found with the industrial

EXHIBIT 2-12

Estimate of the Index of Rivalness

SUBURBAN GROUP	(a) α	(b) δ	(c) $\alpha/1+\delta$	(d) γ
Growing Suburbs	.64	-.42	.64/.58	1.1
Declining Suburbs	.17	-.42	.17/.58	.3

a. Coefficient of the population term.
b. Coefficient of the tax price term.
c. Rivalness value.
d. Equals division shown in c.

Source: See text.

sector (.032), that is, manufacturing and their related office activities. The negative commercial coefficient (-.047) is in this case largely influenced by the predominant loss of commercial activity among the older suburbs in the sample; this suggests to us that there are additional costs required of the municipality in the face of commercial decline and abandonment. Lastly, the newly emerging service sector (.13), consisting of personal, medical, and business services, is the most influential nonresidential factor generating municipal expenditures.

On the revenue side, it is found that non-property tax revenue can be viewed as an aggregate income factor in the municipal expenditure equation. This added "income" generates costs, an association indicated by the fact that all three terms included in the model (federal grants, revenue sharing and state assistance) are shown to be positive.

A computer output showing the statistical estimation of the equation's coefficients is shown in Exhibit 2-13. This graph has two axes: the vertical is the logarithmic value of the older suburbs' 1970-78 municipal expenditures; the horizontal displays the identification numbers of each municipality in the mature suburb sample (e.g., Englewood's identification code is 38, remaining community codes are shown in Exhibit 1-1). Actual expenditures (in logarithmic terms) of each older suburb in the 1970-78 period is indicated by a capital "A" on the graph. Outlays projected by the expenditure equations are shown by an asterisk. To illustrate, in 1978 Englewood expended $10.3 million for municipal operating purposes or 9.2 in natural log terms. The

EXHIBIT 2-13

**Correspondence Between Actual ^{c} and Equation-Forecasted Municipal
Expenditures ^{d} of Mature New Jersey Suburbs, 1970–1978**

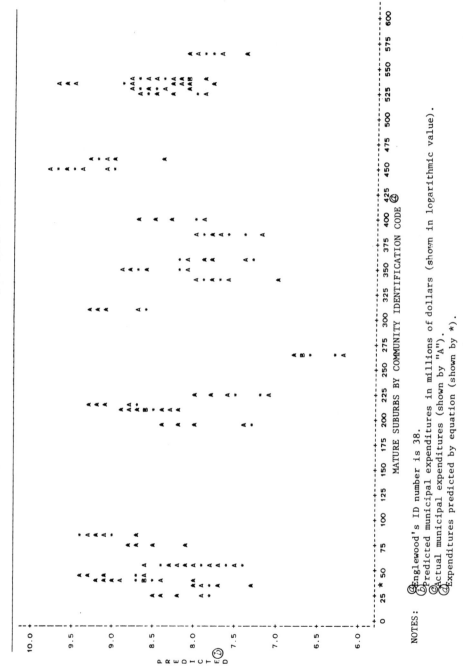

NOTES: ^{a}Englewood's ID number is 38.
        ^{b}Predicted municipal expenditures in millions of dollars (shown in logarithmic value).
        ^{c}Actual municipal expenditures (shown by "A").
        ^{d}Expenditures predicted by equation (shown by *).

expenditure equation predicts a very close value -- a correspondence shown by the proximity of the equation's asterisk to the actual "A" value. A similar tight fit exists for the 1970-1976 predicted versus actual Englewood expenditures as well as for the 1970-1978 pre-dicted-actual outlays of the remaining older suburbs. The tight clustering of "asterisks" to "A"s, graphically indicates the equa-tion's strong backcasting performance.

NOTES

1. Harvey Brazer, City Expenditures in the United States (Ann Arbor: University of Michigan Institute of Public Administration, 1959).

2. See Robert Burchell and David Listokin (editors), Cities Under Stress (New Brunswick: Rutgers University, Center for Urban Policy Research, 1980).

3. William J. Baumol, "Urban Services: Interactions of Public and Private Decisions," in Howard Schaller (editor), Public Expenditure Decisions in the Urban Community (Washington, D.C.: Resources for the Future, 1963).

4. Woo Sik Kee, "Central City Expenditures and Metropolitan Areas," National Tax Journal Vol. 18 (1965), p. 337.

5. Seymour Sacks and Robert Harris, "The Determinants of State and Local Government Expenditures and Intergovernmental Flow of Funds," National Tax Journal Vol. 17 (1964), p. 75.

6. Jack Osman, "The Dual Impact of Federal Aid on State and Local Government Expenditures," National Tax Journal Vol. 19 (December, 1966), pp. 362-372.

7. John C. Weicher, "Determinants of Central City Expenditures: Some Overlooked Factors and Problems," National Tax Journal Vol. 23 (1970), pp. 379-396.

8. Emile M. Sunley, Jr., "Some Determinants of Government Expendi-tures Within Metropolitan Areas," The American Journal of Economics and Sociology Vol. 30 (1971), pp. 345-64.

9. L. R. Gabler, "Population Size as a Determinant of City Expendi-ture and Employment: Some Further Evidence," Land Economics Vol. 47, No. 2 (May 1971), pp. 130-138.

10. Teh-wei Hu, and Bernard Booms, "A Simultaneous Equation Model of Public Expenditure Decisions in Large Cities," The Annals of Regional Science Vol. 5 (1971), pp. 73-85.

11. George Sternlieb, et al. Housing Development and Municipal Costs (New Brunswick, NJ: Rutgers University, Center for Urban Policy Re-search, 1972).

12. Helen F. Ladd, Local Public Expenditures and the Composition of the Tax Base. Unpublished Ph.D. Dissertation, June 1974, Harvard Uni-versity.

13. Patrick Beaton, "The Determinants of Police Protection Expendi-ture," National Tax Journal Vol. 29 (1975), pp. 328-335. See also, J. J. Carroll and S. Sacks, "Influence of Industry on the Property Tax Base and the Pattern of Local Government Expenditures." Paper pre-sented at Conference of Regional Science Association, December 27,

1961; Alan K. Campbell, "Taxes and Industrial Location in the New York Metropolitan Region," National Tax Journal, Vol. 11 (September 1978). See also Roy W. Bahl, "The Determinants of Local Government Police Expenditures: A Public Employment Approach," National Tax Journal, Vol. 31 (March 1978), p. 67; Seymour Sacks and Robert Harris, "The Determinants of State and Local Government Expenditures and Inter-governmental Flows of Funds," National Tax Association Papers and Proceedings 1969, pp. 569-593; J. Weicher, "Aid Expenditures and Local Government Structures," National Tax Journal, Vol. 25 (1972), pp. 573-584; Advisory Commission on Intergovernmental Relations, Federal Grants: Their Effects on State-Local Expenditure, Employment Levels, Wage Rates (Washington, D.C.: ACIR, 1977).

14. See for example, Theodore C. Bergstrom and Robert Goodman, "Private Demands for Public Goods," The American Economic Review, Vol. 63, No. 3 (June 1975) pp. 280-296.

15. Herbert A. Simon, Fiscal Aspects of Metropolitan Consolidation (Berkeley: University of California, Bureau of Public Administration, 1943).

16. Bergstrom and Goodman, "Private Demands for Public Goods."

17. Simon, Fiscal Aspects of Metropolitan Consolidation.

18. Bergstrom and Goodman, "Private Demands for Goods."

19. C. E. Ferguson, Microeconomic Theory (Homewood, Illinois: Richard D. Irwin, Inc., 1972).

20. Wallace E. Oates, "On Local Finance and the Tiebout Model," American Economic Review, Vol. 71, No. 2, Papers and Proceedings, 93-98, (May 1981).

21. G. S. Maddala, "The Use of Variance Components Models in Pooling Cross Section and Time Series Data," Econometrica, 39, No. 2, pp. 341-58 (1976).

22. W. Patrick Beaton, "The Determinants of Police Protection Expenditures," National Tax Journal, Vol. XXVII, June 1974.

23. Helen F. Ladd, "Municipal Expenditures and the Composition of the Local Property Tax Base," in Property Taxation, Land Use and Public Policy, edited by Arthur D. Lynn, Jr. (Madison, Wisconsin: Committee on Taxation Resources and Economic Development, University of Wisconsin Press, 1976).

SECTION TWO
Responding to the Fiscal Challenge

Chapter Three
New Development in
the Older Suburbs

INTRODUCTION

The future scenario analysis of chapter two suggested that new development in a mature suburb such as Englewood would induce relatively minor increments of municipal spending. Since the service infrastructure of such communities is in place, they can accommodate new growth without major additions of manpower, capital facilities, and supplies. While new residential/nonresidential construction would not be costless to the host community, the revenues thereby engendered would likely exceed the relatively low level of consequent municipal expenditures. Thus, one strategy for older suburbs seeking fiscal relief is to permit new residential/nonresidential ratables.

This chapter considers how new development fiscally affects mature suburbs. It first considers the range of new construction likely to occur in such localities. It then turns to the case study community, Englewood, and examines how development of its largest remaining vacant site would impact local public costs versus revenues. The emphasis of the analysis is to provide a sound methodological approach to ascertain the fiscal effects of growth in mature suburbs, one superior to the often crude accounting techniques utilized to date.

BACKGROUND TO THE FISCAL IMPACT ANALYSIS

New Development in Older Suburbs

For much of the post-World War II era, many mature suburbs saw little new residential construction other than infilling with single or two-family homes and scattered low density, multifamily configurations such as garden apartments. Englewood is illustrative. In the 1920's, Englewood "made its first and only experiment with large scale apartment construction."[1] Three high-rise buildings, together containing about 300 units, were built in this period. The first garden apartment was constructed in the late 1930's.[2] It was followed by a few similar projects in the war years and immediately afterwards. Resistance to multifamily development arose however:[3]

> By 1947, the number of garden apartment projects being approved were causing some concern in the city. In March, the local press

predicted that Englewood would soon be dotted with apartment
houses....

...Resistance towards this type of development was beginning to
show itself...Homeowners...claimed it would be a public nuisance
....A delegation of over 100 homeowners met with the Mayor and
Council to protest the proposed construction of yet another...
project....Over 150 residents of the Third Ward left no doubt
about their sentiments...no more garden apartments.

The opinions voiced in the other wards were similar....The business community on the other hand, felt that Englewood was des-
tined to grow and garden apartments were a benefit...superior
ratables.

Homeowner sentiments were largely heeded. In 1949, Englewood's Planning Board severely restricted apartment zones in a revised zoning
code.[4] This change constrained, but did not stop, multifamily construction for the next few decades. Numerous garden apartment complexes were built as were subsidized projects sponsored by such groups
as the Englewood Housing Authority, Greater Englewood Housing Corporation, and the Mt. Carmel Guild. By 1970, about 40 percent of Englewood's housing units were renter occupied -- a very high figure for a
New Jersey suburb. Much of the multifamily stock, however, was built
prior to 1939. In the post-World War II era, Englewood was characterized predominantly by single-family residential development.
    Englewood's single-family emphasis was shared by many other mature
suburbs, albeit less so than the near universal single-family imprint
of outer ring, developing suburban areas. Recently, however, Englewood
and its sister suburbs, both old and new, have become more receptive
to townhouse and other attached forms of residential construction.
This shift reflects new demographic, environmental, and financial
realities. Townhouse and kindred construction is well suited to
smaller households, both old and young, not always able to afford nor
universally attracted to standard fare, single-family dwellings. Attached housing also lends itself to a clustering arrangement so as to
better preserve remaining open space. These and other advantages have
made suburbs more amenable to non-traditional housing configurations
-- townhouses, garden condominiums, patio homes, and so on.
    Even more dramatic are commercial incursions into suburbia. Hotel
and conference centers are being built. Office space is also being
constructed on a scale never before witnessed outside of cities. As
summarized in a 1982 report:[5]

During the past few years, the Central Business District (CBD)
office market has experienced a healthy growth rate of approximately 8 percent annually. Yet a 14 percent annual growth rate
has catapulted the suburban market into a position virtually
equivalent to the CBD in size. In the major cities surveyed, 49.7
percent of the total office market is in the suburbs, while the

CBD market represents 50.3 percent. Only four years ago the CBD accounted for 55 percent of the total market.

During the past four years, construction and absorption of new space have added more than 146 million square feet to the suburban market, compared to less than 89 million square feet added to the CBD....A number of factors contribute to suburban growth. Costs for both land and construction are lower outside the CBD ....And in many cases, developers also find it easier to purchase land and obtain financing for projects in the suburbs.

In considering the impact of new growth in mature suburbs such as Englewood, it is thus important not to limit the analysis to single-family construction but rather to include the full range of development which may occur -- conventional and emerging residential varieties as well as various nonresidential complexes.

New Development in Englewood: A Detailed
Look at the Englewood Golf Course

The case study community, Englewood, affords an excellent opportunity to examine the fiscal effects of a range of new development options. The Englewood golf course has attracted strong interest from developers seeking to build single-family homes, townhouses, and various nonresidential projects. The site is prime for many reasons. At 35 acres, it is the single largest assembled vacant tract available in Englewood. It currently lies fallow as the golf course has been closed for many years. Further pluses are its location (five miles from the George Washington Bridge and about 20 minutes from mid-town Manhattan), transportation access (abutting Interstate 95 and state route 4), and utility advantages (already serviced by sewer, water, gas and electric).

One of the major controversies concerning whether and how the golf course should be opened for development is the question of financial consequences -- what public costs versus revenues will be produced? This issue is not unique to Englewood. It is raised in sister communities similarly facing a fiscal crunch, and thus sensitive to the economic bottom line of new construction.

Methodological considerations and procedures for determining the fiscal effect of development in an older suburb can be illustrated by considering the impact of a range of residential and nonresidential alternatives for the Englewood golf course including:

Development Type	Size	1982 Selling Price (approximate)
1. Single-family	75 units	$200,000-$250,000
2a. Lower density townhouses	160 units	$150,000-$200,000
2b. Higher density townhouses	240 units	$100,000-$150,000

Development Type	Size	1982 Selling Price (approximate)
3. Office building	300,000 ft^2	not applicable
4. Office building	400,000 ft^2	not applicable
5. Office building	500,000 ft^2	not applicable
6. Office-hotel	350,000 ft^2 300 rooms	not applicable

The six development scenarios span the range of possible residential and nonresidential uses. The first is low density, expensive, single-family homes. The second includes two alternative townhouse complexes -- lower density (160 units) very expensive houses ($150,000-$200,000), or higher density (240 units) slightly less expensive ($100,000-$150,000) dwellings. Remaining development possibilities are nonresidential uses ranging in size (300,000 to 500,000 ft^2) and type (office or combined office-hotel).

FISCAL IMPACT ANALYSIS: METHODOLOGY

Comparing the induced local costs versus the generated local revenues of new development is referred to as fiscal impact analysis. Such projections are by no means a new phenomenon. As suggested by Ruth Mace in a now-classic summary of the literature, fiscal impact analyses have been a part of the planning profession for over forty years.[6] Planners first employed this type of evaluation in the early 1930s' public housing efforts to justify the replacement of deteriorated housing due to negative local fiscal effects.[7] In the early 1940's, it was used in the urban renewal process to demonstrate the local fiscal advantages of the new land use which would replace the old.[8] During the 1950's, it was employed during the massive suburbanization movement to gauge the impact of single-family homes on the local school district.[9] In the 1960's, supported by HUD 701 planning assistance funding, it was used to evaluate the economic effects of the master plan.[10] During the 1970's, the technique emerged as an almost universal large-scale development accompaniment -- either volunteered by the developer or required by the municipality.[11]

While fiscal impact analysis has a long history of application, it has a less proud record of achievement. For many years, most cost revenue projections largely ignored municipal expenditures and merely estimated the revenue side of the fiscal equation. Even the latter was not always calculated correctly. To illustrate, equalized (full value) property values were multipled by nominal tax rates instead of equalized tax rates, thus yielding an overestimate of generated property revenues. In other instances, one-time income sources such as project application fees would be counted erroneously as a recurring revenue.

In the last decade, fiscal impact analysis has emerged from a "dark age" of ignorance and misapplication. Major research efforts conducted

by Rutgers University, the Urban Institute, and others[12] have produced standardized estimation techniques. Most of these: 1) project
the population induced by a residential development and then "convert"
the incremental population change to added local public service spending; and 2) assume average costing -- costs are attributed to development according to the average cost per unit, e.g., per capita municipal expenditures and per pupil school district outlays.

The per capita multiplier approach, the most common modern technique
applied by planners, is illustrative. This approach relies on average
municipal costs per person, average costs per pupil, and the number of
persons/pupils generated by various housing types to project future
municipal/school district costs. To illustrate, if single-family homes
contain, on average, 4.5 residents and 1.5 school children, and if
local municipal/school costs are $300 per person and $3,000 per pupil
respectively, the per capita multiplier technique will project that an
incoming single-family unit would generate $1,350 in municipal outlays
($300 x 4.5) and $4,500 in school costs ($3,000 x 1.5) for a total of
$5,850 in local public service expenditures. This cost estimate would
then be matched against the revenues generated by the single-family
home, thereby yielding a fiscal surplus or deficit.

Traditional fiscal impact analysis, typified by the per capita
multiplier method, assumes a direct relationship between growth and
costs; development brings in new residents who in turn linearly increase local service outlays. Such a cost assumption is at best sim-
plistic for it does not include many variables which likely influence
municipal spending decisions, e.g., the extant local tax burden and
intergovernmental assistance flows (see chapter two). In certain instances, the assumption of a linear causal fiscal effect may be totally inapplicable. To illustrate, a mature suburb, with its service infrastructure in place, is often able to accommodate new growth with
minor additional public expenditure. In this instance, application of
a per capita multiplier approach, incorporating the high per capita-
pupil expenditures characteristic of older suburbs, would significantly overstate true costs.

Fiscal impact techniques are even more wanting in nonresidential
situations. For many years only revenues, not costs, were counted.
More recently, costs have been projected but in a very crude fashion,
for instance via a simple, proportional valuation technique. It assigns a share of municipal costs to an incoming nonresidential facility based on the facility's proportion of total local real property
value. To illustrate, a $10 million shopping center built in a com-
munity with a $100 million property tax base and $5 million in annual
municipal expenditures would be apportioned one-tenth of all municipal
costs or $500,000; a luncheonette valued at $100,000 would be assigned
a one-thousandth share of extant municipal outlays or $5,000. This
method tends, however, to overestimate the true municipal servicing
obligations for very large nonresidential facilities (e.g., shopping
center) and understate them for small nonresidential uses (e.g.,
luncheonette).

To correct the frequent inaccurate costing of the simple proportional valuation approach, refinement coefficients have been developed. These scale-down projected municipal expenditures when entering nonresidential facilities are significantly larger than the average extant local ratable, and scale-up projected impact when they are significantly smaller than the average. Application of the "refined" proportional valuation method will be detailed shortly.

While the "refined" approach improves on its predecessors, it too often falls short in truly gauging the fiscal effects of nonresidential development. Is property value and impact on the municipal service system truly synonymous? Even were the value-effect translation correct, the proportional valuation technique is not sensitive to the complicated influences on municipal expenditures. For instance, the mathematical model discussed in chapter two of this study indicates that varying nonresidential uses (service, industrial, commercial) differently affect municipal outlays, at least in the case of older suburbs. Such differentiation is not incorporated in the proportional valuation technique. Further deficiencies are discussed later in this chapter.

Given the mathematical model's inclusion of the many factors influencing municipal spending, it would be desirable to utilize it in a fiscal impact analysis of new development in a mature suburb. As we shall see shortly, such an application of the model can be achieved. This chapter therefore examines the financial consequences of developing the Englewood golf course via both traditional fiscal impact techniques (per capita multiplier method and proportional valuation) and the mathematical model. The per capita technique is applied to the two of six golf course development scenarios which are residential in nature (single-family and townhouse), while the proportional valuation approach is used to determine the municipal costs engendered by the four remaining nonresidential development possibilities. Applicable to both residential and nonresidential situations, the mathematical model is utilized to examine all six golf course cases.

One final note concerns the time frame of the analysis. Since the mathematical model of municipal expenditures was presented in chapter two in terms of 1978 data, the fiscal impact projections discussed here are similarly expressed in 1978 dollars. For the sake of consistency, the 1978 time frame is applied when not only the model is used but also in the case of the fiscal calculations using the "traditional" approaches.

Fiscal effects of the six Englewood golf course developments, expressed in 1978 dollars, are summarized in Exhibit 3-1. Their derivation and implication to the community are highlighted below.

APPLICATION OF TRADITIONAL FISCAL IMPACT ANALYSIS

Per Capita Multiplier Technique

As of 1978, municipal per capita property taxes in Englewood were approximately $350.[13] Local school property taxes per pupil were

EXHIBIT 3-1

Fiscal Impact of New Development in a Mature Suburb:
Englewood Golf Course

Golf Course Development	Size	Estimated Assessed Value[b] (In $ Millions)	Estimated Local (Municipal and School) Property Tax Revenue[b] (In $ Millions)	ESTIMATED LOCAL COSTS[c] (In $ Thousands)							ESTIMATED LOCAL FISCAL IMPACT[f] (In $ Thousands)		
				Per Capita Multiplier			Proportional Valuation	Model			Per Capita Multiplier	Proportional Valuation	Model
				Municipal	School	Total	Municipal	Municipal	School	Total			
1. Single family	75 units	$ 6.600	$413	118.3	128.8	247.1	NA[d]	19.0	128.8	147.8	+165.9	NA[d]	+265.2
2a. Townhouse	160 units	$14.100	$883	162.4	92.0	254.4	NA	26.0	92.0	118.0	+628.6	NA	+765.0
2b. Townhouse	240 units	$14.100	$883	243.6	138.0	381.6	NA	42.0	138.0	180.0	+501.4	NA	+703.0
3. Office building	300,000 ft.[2]	$ 8.100	$507	NA[d]	NA	NA	90.0	100.0[e]	NA	100.0	NA	+417.0	+407.0
4. Office building	400,000 ft.[2]	$10.500	$657	NA	NA	NA	96.0	129.0[e]	NA	129.0	NA	+561.0	+528.0
5. Office building	500,000 ft.[2]	$12.900	$808	NA	NA	NA	101.0	156.0[e]	NA	156.0	NA	+707.0	+652.0
6. Office/hotel	350,000 ft.[2]/ 300 rooms	$13.700	$858	NA	NA	NA	108.0	182.0[e]	NA	182.0	NA	+750.0	+676.0

Notes:
[a] Higher estimated parameters are used for the development scenarios.
[b] At $6.26 local (municipal and school) tax rate; rounded to nearest thousand.
[c] Utilizes average of impacts at one employee per 200 ft.[2] and 250 ft.[2] of office space.
[d] NA = Not applicable.
[e] See Exhibits 3-3, 3-4 and 3-5 for derivation.
[f] Equals project revenue less project-induced public cost.

approximately $2,300. The $350 cost per capita and $2,300 cost per pu-
pil are the basic expenditure parameters for average residents (see
Exhibit 3-2).

To obtain the local property tax-supported cost per entering dwell-
ing, these parameters are multiplied by the number of persons and pu-
pils found in the unit under review. To illustrate, if single-family
homes contain on average 4.5 people and .75 public school children,
and if municipal expenditures per capita amount to $350 while school
costs are $2,300 per pupil, then the single-family home would generate
$3,300 in local costs:

$$
\begin{array}{rclcl}
4.5 & x & \$ \ 350 & = & \$1,575 \\
.75 & x & \$2,300 & = & \underline{\$1,725} \\
     &   &   &   & \$3,300
\end{array}
$$

To obtain the local fiscal impact, local costs are matched against
local (municipal and school) property tax revenue. A single-family
Englewood home assessed at about $100,000 per unit (1978) would yield
over $6,000 in local (municipal and school) property taxes. It would
therefore generate a local fiscal surplus of approximately $2,700
($6,000-$3,300).

This methodology was employed to project the fiscal impact of the
single-family and townhouse unit development alternatives for the
Englewood golf course site. All the calculations are shown in Exhibit
3-3.   It reveals that the single-family option would generate an
annual fiscal surplus of about $170,000. Townhouses would be more
profitable to Englewood. Constructing 160 of the more expensive
townhouses would result in an annual fiscal surplus of about $630,000;
building 240 of the less expensive townhouses would yield an annual
fiscal gain of about $500,000 (see Exhibit 3-3). These different
effects result from the following cost-revenue relationships:

1. On a per-unit basis, single-family homes are more costly to service because they generate a relatively large number of persons/pu-
pils. Townhouses, in contrast, are much less expensive because of
their low population/student counts (see Exhibit 3-2). Each single-
family unit, housing about 4.5 people and .75 public school children,
induces about $3,300 in combined Englewood municipal and school costs
(4.5 x $350 = $1,575; .75 x $2,300 = $1,725; $1,575 + $1,725 =
$3,300). Each townhouse, generating 2.9 residents and .25 public
school children, costs $1,600 (2.9 x $350 = $1,015; .25 x $2,300 =
$575; $1,015 + $575 = $1,590). Townhouses thus cost half as much to
service as single-family homes.

2. On a per-unit basis, single-family homes typically generate relatively bountiful property tax revenues. Single-family units on the Englewood golf course produce about $5,500 apiece in combined municipal
and school property taxes (see Exhibit 3-3). Expensive townhouses,
however, approach this income or else have a more beneficial cost-

EXHIBIT 3-2

**Basic Community Parameters for Calculating
Fiscal Impact of Development
Englewood, 1978**

(1)	Municipal property taxes	:	$7,800,000
(2)	Englewood population	:	23,000
(3)	Per capita municipal costs[b]	:	$350. (1÷2)
(4)	School property taxes	:	$7,900,000
(5)	School population (students)	:	3,500
(6)	Per pupil educational costs[b]	:	$2,300 (4÷5)
(7)	Household size parameters[c]		
	Single family	:	4.5
	Townhouse	:	2.9
(8)	School-age children parameters		
	Single family	:	1.5
	Townhouse	:	.5
(9)	Public school attendance ratio[d]	:	.5
(10)	Public school-age children parameters (8 x 9)		
	Single family	:	.75
	Townhouse	:	.25
(11)	Englewood municipal and school property tax rate	:	$6.26
	Municipal[a]	:	3.10
	School	:	3.16

Notes:
[a] Includes Type I district school debt service.
[b] Property-tax supported.
[c] *Source:* 1977 Annual Housing Survey; discussions with Englewood Planning Department.
[d] *Source:* Discussions with Englewood Planning and other departments.
Note: This figure is unusually high and reflects the tendency of many upper-middle and upper- income Englewood households to send their children to non-public schools.

EXHIBIT 3-3

Fiscal Impact Analysis of New Development in a Mature Suburb
(Englewood Golf Course)
Utilizing the Per Capita Multiplier Approach

FISCAL IMPACT PARAMETERS	Single Family		Low-Density (160-unit) Townhouses		High-Density (240-unit) Townhouses	
LOCAL COSTS						
1. Number of units	75		160		240	
2. Household size per unit	4.5		2.9		2.9	
3. Project-generated population	338	(1x2)	464	(1x2)	696	(1x2)
4. Public school-age children per unit	.75		.25		.25	
5. Project-generated public school pupils	56	(1x4)	40	(1x4)	60	(1x4)
6. Local cost per capita	$ 350.		$ 350.		$ 350.	
7. Project-generated municipal cost	$118,300.	(3x6)	$162,400.	(3x6)	$243,600.	(3x6)
8. Local cost per pupil	$ 2,300.		$ 2,300.		$ 2,300.	
9. Project-generated school cost	$128,800.	(5x8)	$ 92,000.	(5x8)	$138,000.	(5x8)
10. Total local public cost	$247,100.	(7+9)	$254,400.	(7+9)	$381,600.	(7+9)
LOCAL REVENUES						
11. Estimated project assessed value	$6,600,000. ⓐ		$14,100,000. ⓐ		$14,100,000. ⓐ	
12. Municipal property tax rate	$3.10		$3.10		$3.10	
13. School property tax rate	$3.16		$3.16		$3.16	
14. Total local property tax rate	$6.26		$6.26		$6.26	
15. Project-generated municipal property taxes	$204,600.	(11x12)	$437,100.	(11x12)	$437,100.	(11x12)
16. Project-generated school property taxes	$208,560.	(11x13)	$445,560.	(11x13)	$445,560.	(11x13)
17. Project-generated total local property taxes	$413,160.	(15+16)	$882,660.	(15+16)	$882,660.	(15+16)
LOCAL FISCAL IMPACT						
18. Municipal fiscal impact	+$86,300.	(15-7)	+$274,700.	(15-7)	+$193,500.	(15-7)
19. School fiscal impact	+$79,760.	(16-9)	+$353,560.	(16-9)	+$307,560.	(16-9)
20. Total local fiscal impact	+$166,060.	(18+19)	+$628,260.	(18+19)	+$501,060.	(18+19)

ⓒ Includes Type I district school debt service.
ⓐ *Source:* Englewood Assessment Department and Finance Department.

revenue ratio. Each townhouse in the lower density golf course project yields about $5,500 in local property taxes (see Exhibit 3-3) -- an amount identical to that generated by single-family units. Admittedly, the latter's income exceeds the $3,700 per unit revenue yielded by the higher density townhouses (see Exhibit 3-5), however, this revenue advantage is much less than the townhouse's two-to-one service cost benefit cited previously. The Englewood golf course townhouses are therefore a more desirable ratable than single-family units built on the site.

3. Lower density townhouses are fiscally more advantageous than a higher density equivalent because of their differing cost-revenue posture alluded to above: lower and higher density units both cost the same to service (about $1,600 apiece; see Exhibit 3-3); however, the former generate far more revenue than the latter ($5,500 versus $3,700).

In summary, application of the per capita multiplier method suggests that all of the alternative residential developments which could be built on the Englewood golf course would be fiscally desirable. The low density townhouse complex would generate the largest surplus, while the single-family complex would yield the smallest gain. These findings will shortly be compared to the results suggested by mathematical model.

Proportional Valuation Technique

A basic assumption of the proportional valuation method is that municipal costs increase with the intensity of land use, and change in real property value is a reasonable proxy for measuring the change in intensity of use. Further, as nonresidential real property value departs significantly from the average local real property value, the direct proportional relationship must be refined to avoid either overstating or understating costs. A third assumption is that the aggregate impacts of different nonresidential land uses on municipal services are sufficiently similar to treat them as a single category. Finally, it is assumed that nonresidential development primarily affects municipal functions rather than school district services, which may thus be ignored.

Procedurally, the proportional valuation approach is applied in the following two step manner:

Step 1. Assign a Share of Existing Municipal Expenditures
to Total Local Nonresidential Uses

Both nonresidential and residential land uses generate municipal costs. To pinpoint the share of expenditures that a nonresidential facility will generate, it is important to first determine the proportion of municipal outlays assignable to the nonresidential sector

of the community. The proportional valuation method assumes that these
costs can be allocated based on the proportion of nonresidential to
total local real property value. Since the relationship is nonlinear,
it must be scaled to reflect this deviation through the application of
a refinement coefficient. This process yields the dollar share of
existing municipal expenditures attributable to local nonresidential
uses. Expressed in formula terms:

```
Total Existing
Municipal                                Proportion of
Expenditures                             Nonresidential
Attributable      Total                  Value to
to Nonresi-    =  Municipal     x        Total Local Real   x   Refinement
dential Uses      Expenditures           Property Value         Coefficient
```

As of 1978, Englewood expended $10.4 million for municipal operating
services, and nonresidential ratables, valued at roughly $69 million,
amounted to 28.5 percent of the total $242.5 million property tax
base. The $10.4 million and 28.5 percent figures constitute two of the
three data elements needed for determining the share of community
municipal expenditures induced by nonresidential uses. Derivation of
the remaining equation input, the refinement coefficient, is accomplished from the following calculations:

```
         (A)                                      (B)
Nonresidential Property Value           Total Property Value
_____           _____
Number of Residential Land              Total Number of Land Parcels
Parcels

$69,000,000   =   $115,000              $242,500,000   =   $42,000
   600                                     5,774

         (C)                                      (D)
Average Nonresidential                  Refinement Coefficient Given
Property Value                          2.7 Nonresidential to Resi-
                                        dential Value Ratio
_____           _____
Average Local Property Value

$115,000    =   2.7                                1.5
$ 42,000
```

In brief, the average Englewood nonresidential property is valued at
2.7 times the average local property. At such a ratio, empirical evidence[14] suggests that an insufficient share of nonresidential-in-
duced local costs would be assigned via the simple proportion of aggregate real property value, in Englewood's case 28.5 percent. The
cost allocation should therefore be increased -- an adjustment accom-

plished by the refinement coefficient. At a 2.7 ratio of nonresidential-to-average-local-property value, empirical evidence suggests that a 1.50 refinement factor be utilized.[15] Applying the 1.5 refinement coefficient to Englewood's 28.5 percent simple proportion of nonresidential-to-residential value yields a product of 42.8 percent. In other words, Englewood's nonresidential uses are responsible for slightly over 40 percent of the community's $10.4 million municipal expenditure or roughly $4.5 million (see Exhibit 3-4).

Step 2. Project the Future Total Municipal Operating Costs
        Induced by the Incoming Nonresidential Use

Having isolated extant total municipal expenditures assignable to existing nonresidential development, the second and final step is to project the share of this amount that will be added to by an incoming nonresidential facility. The procedure is analogous to the one described above. First, the market value of the entering nonresidential ratable is divided by the extant nonresidential property tax base to determine a simple proportion of value. This figure is then multiplied by a refinement coefficient. The product of this multiplication carves out, from total local nonresidential expenditures, a share of cost to be assigned to the new nonresidential facility. In formula terms:

| Total Existing Municipal Expenditures Attributable to an Incoming Nonresidential Facility | = | Total Existing Municipal Expenditures Attributable to Nonresidential Uses | x | Proportion of Incoming Non-Residential Value to Total Local Non-Residential Value | x | Refinement Coefficient |

To illustrate, the 300,000 ft^2 Englewood golf course office building has an estimated $8.1 million assessed value (1978; see Exhibit 3-1). It is therefore equal to 11.7 percent of Englewood's 69 million total nonresidential property tax base (see Exhibit 3-4). At an $8.1 million assessment, this office complex has a property value roughly 70 times the $115,000 average Englewood nonresidential parcel assessment. At such a level of relative overvaluation, empirical evidence suggests a refinement coefficient of .17. Applying the .17 percent refinement factor to the 11.7 value ratio (incoming-nonresidential-facility value to total-local-nonresidential-property value) derived earlier, yields a product of 1.99 percent. The 300,000 ft^2 office building is therefore assigned 1.99 percent of Englewood's extant nonresidential-induced municipal expenditures (estimated earlier at $4.5 million) or about $90,000 ($4,500,000 x .0199).

Exhibit 3-4 indicates the municipal costs assigned by the proportional valuation method to all the nonresidential development possibilities for the Englewood golf course. The 300,000 ft^2 office generates roughly $90,000 in local expenditures; the 400,000 ft^2 office, $96,000; the 500,000 ft^2 office, $100,000; and the office-

EXHIBIT 3-4

Fiscal Impact Analysis of New Development
(Englewood Golf Course, Nonresidential Cases)
In a Mature Suburb Utilizing the Proportional Valuation Approach

LOCAL NONRESIDENTIAL USE COST PROJECTION: ENGLEWOOD 1978

Total Existing Municipal Expenditures Attributable to Nonresidential Uses	=	Total Municipal Expenditures	x	Proportion of Nonresidential Value to Total Local Property Value	x	Refinement Coefficient[1]
				$\frac{(\$69,000,000)}{\$242,500,000}$	x	1.50
$4,500,000		$10,400,000	x	(.285)	x	1.50)

INCOMING NONRESIDENTIAL USE COST PROJECTION: ENGLEWOOD 1978

Municipal Costs Allocated to the Incoming Nonresidential Facility	=	Total Existing Municipal Expenditures Attributable to Nonresidential Uses	x	Proportion of Facility to Total Local Nonresidential Real Property Value	x	Refinement Coefficient[1]

1. *OFFICE BUILDING, 300,000 ft.²*

				$\frac{\$ 8,100,000}{\$69,000,000}$		
		$4,500,000	x		x	.17
$90,000	=	$4,500,000	x	.117		.17

2. *OFFICE BUILDING, 400,000 ft.²*

				$\frac{\$10,500,000}{\$69,000,000}$		
		$4,500,000	x		x	.14
$96,000	=	$4,500,000	x	.152	x	.14

3. *OFFICE BUILDING, 500,000 ft.²*

				$\frac{\$12,900,000}{\$69,000,000}$		
		$4,500,000	x		x	.12
$101,000	=	$4,500,000	x	.187	x	.12

4. *OFFICE BUILDING/HOTEL*

				$\frac{\$13,700,000}{\$69,000,000}$		
		$4,500,000	x		x	.12
$108,000	=	$4,500,000	x	.199	x	.12

[1]See text and Robert W. Burchell and David Listokin, The Fiscal Impact Handbook (New Brunswick, Rutgers University Center for Urban Policy Research, 1978).

Note: Assessed rather than equalized values are used in these correlations.

hotel complex, $110,000. Matching these figures to the revenues generated by each project (see Exhibit 3-1) indicates that all non-residential projects produce a large fiscal gain. The 300,000 ft^2 office yields roughly a $420,000 annual surplus; the 400,000 ft^2 office, a $560,000 surplus; the 500,000 ft^2 office, a $700,000 surplus; and the office-hotel combination a $750,000 gain.

Application of the per capita multiplier and proportional valuation methodologies represents "conventional" fiscal impact analysis. We now turn to a different cost-revenue approach, one suggested by the mathematical model of municipal expenditures.

APPLICATION OF THE MATHEMATICAL
MODEL FISCAL IMPACT METHOD

The mathematical model discussed in chapter two was constructed to show the relationship between municipal spending and certain median voter-community variables. In formula terms (for cities with declining populations):

Total Municipal
Functions Operating
Expenditures   =   −5.4461

− .4021 x Median Voter Property Tax Share   + .1723 x Population x 100 Declining Cities

+ .1337 x Municipal Service Employment   + .0326 x Municipal Industrial Employment

+ .0473 x Municipal Commercial Employment   + .9493 x Municipal Factor of Production Cost Index

+ .0337 x Federal Aid Revenues   + .0327 x Revenue Sharing Revenues

+ .5551 x Local Utility Tax Receipts

The model can be applied for fiscal impact projection purposes in both residential and nonresidential contexts. New residential growth is accompanied by incoming households. Their entry will alter the population independent variable in the estimation equation and the ensuing change in the dependent municipal expenditure variable will constitute the municipal service cost attributed to the incoming

development. In an analogous fashion, the model also permits examination of the municipal spending engendered by nonresidential growth.
Such development bears directly on the local employment independent
variables in the estimation equation. A shift in these factors will,
in turn, affect the dependent municipal spending measure. The resulting changes in municipal outlays are the local public costs induced by
the incoming nonresidential facilities.

To illustrate, the single-family development scenario for the Englewood golf course would add 338 new residents (see Exhibit 3-3) and
would thus increase the community's population from 23,700 to about
24,000. In logarithmic values, Englewood's population will rise from
5.4680 to 5.4840 (see Exhibit 3-5). Entering the 5.4840 instead of
5.4680 value into the estimation equation indicates that Englewood's
1978 municipal expenditures would increase from $10.355 to $10.374
million -- a minor gain of $19,000 (see Exhibit 3-6).

This exercise yields the municipal expenditures generated by the
single-family development. As the mathematical model does not deal
with school costs, we shall use the same educational expenditures
projected by the per capita multiplier approach. In the case of the
single-family project, we would therefore assign a school spending
figure of $129,000 (see Exhibit 3-3). Total public service costs
induced by the 160 single-family homes would therefore amount to
$148,000 ($19,000 + $129,000). Matching this figure against estimated
revenues of $413,000 generated by the single-family project yields a
fiscal impact surplus of $265,000 ($413,000-$148,000; see Exhibit
3-1). Fiscal impacts of the remaining residential alternatives were
calculated in a similar fashion. The lower density (160 unit) townhouse project would induce $26,000 in municipal costs and $92,000 in
school outlays for a total of $118,000. Subtracting this sum from the
project's $883,000 revenues leaves an annual surplus of $765,000 (see
Exhibit 3-1). The higher density (240 unit) townhouse project generates slightly higher public costs ($180,0000) and a slightly lower
annual fiscal surplus of about $700,000 (see Exhibit 3-1).

The mathematical model was similarly applied to examine the fiscal
effects of the golf course's nonresidential development cases. To
illustrate, a 500,000 ft^2 office building, employing roughly 2,500
workers, would increase Englewood's industrial employment from 4,435
to 6,935. (Office workers are classified as "industrial" under the
Standard Industrial Code [SIC].) In logarithmic values, Englewood's
industrial employment would go from 8.3972 to 8.8443 (see Exhibit
3-5). Entering the latter instead of the former figure into the municipal expenditure equation suggests that Englewood's 1978 municipal
outlay would rise from $10.355 to $10.525 million -- an increase of
about $170,000 (see Exhibit 3-6). Subtracting the $170,000 cost from
the roughly $800,000 in revenues generated by the 500,000 ft^2 office
facility leaves an annual surplus of over $600,000 (see Exhibit 3-1).

Remaining nonresidential cases were analyzed in a similar fashion.
The smaller office complexes, 300,000 and 400,000 ft^2, induce both
fewer costs and less generous revenues, and therefore yield smaller

EXHIBIT 3-5

**Calibration of Mature Suburb Municipal Expenditure Equation
Given Various Development Options: Englewood, 1978**

Equation Argument or Variable (see Exhibit 2-3)	Development Scenario	Equation Constant or Coefficient	Actual or Forecasted Value for Equation Arguments	Contribution to Total Municipal Functions -- Expenditures
Intercept Ⓒ	Base case Ⓒ	5.4461		-5.44
Property Tax Share Ⓒ	Base case Ⓒ	.4201	2.5244	-1.06
Population	Base case Ⓒ	.1722	5.4680	0.94
	Growth - single family ⓓ	.1722	5.4840	0.9443
	Growth - 160 townhouses ⓓ	.1722	5.4877	0.9450
	Growth - 240 townhouses ⓓ	.1722	5.4969	0.9466
Nonresidential Employment				
Commercial	Base case	-.0473	7.6686	-0.36
Industrial	Base case	.0362	8.3972	0.30
	Growth - 300,000 ⓓ ft.^{2} office ⓐ	.0362	8.6886	0.3145
	Growth - 300,000 ⓓ ft.^{2} office ⓑ	.0362	8.6367	0.3126
	Growth - 400,000 ⓓ ft.^{2} office ⓐ	.0362	8.7694	0.3175
	Growth - 400,000 ⓓ ft.^{2} office ⓑ	.0362	8.7053	0.3151
	Growth - 500,000 ⓓ ft.^{2} office ⓐ	.0362	8.8443	0.3202
	Growth - 500,000 ⓓ ft.^{2} office ⓑ	.0362	8.7694	0.3175
	Growth - Office ⓐ/hotel	.0362	8.7298	0.3160
Service	Base case	.1337	8.4908	1.13
	Growth - Office/hotel ⓓ	.1337	8.5301	1.1405
Service Input Cost	Base case	.9493	9.8991	9.39
Intergovernmental Revenue				
Federal Aid	Base case	.0337	6.8855	0.23
Revenue Sharing	Base case	.0327	5.9915	0.19
"Urbanism"				
Utility tax revenue	Base case	.5550	7.09257	3.73
			TOTALⓒ:	See Exhibit 3-6.

ⓐ At one employee per every 200 ft.^{2} office space.
ⓑ At one employee per every 250 ft.^{2} office space.
ⓒ Englewood absent golf course development; in other words, as it "stood" in 1978 (see Exhibit 2-2).
ⓓ See text and Exhibit 3-1.
ⓔ Equals sum of groupings of variables, e.g., 1978 base case, base case as modified by single-family development, base case modified by townhouse construction, etc. To illustrate, the base case total (in logarithmic values) equals the sum of -5.44, -1.06, .94, .30, 1.13, -.36, 9.39, .23, .19 and 3.73. or 9.24. The base case modified by single-family construction on the golf course equals 5.44, -1.06, .9443 (instead of .94), .30, 1.13, -.36, 9.39, .23, .19 and 3.73, or 9.2457 (instead of 9.24). The remaining development scenarios were calculated in the same fashion.

Source: See text.

EXHIBIT 3-6

Fiscal Impact Analysis of New Development
(Englewood Golf Course Residential and Nonresidential Cases)
In a Mature Suburb Utilizing the Mathematical Model Approach

Growth Strategy	Logarithmic Value	Dollar Value	Base Case Expenditure Dollar Value	Growth-Induced Municipal Expenditure Dollar Value	Growth-Induced School Expenditure	Growth-Induced Total Municipal and School Expenditures
Base Case (1978)	9.24526	$10,355,000	NA	NA	NA	NA
Growth Cases						
Residential						
Single family - 75 units	9.2456	$10,374,000	$10,355,000	+$ 19,000	+$128,800	+$147,800
Townhouses - 160 units	9.2478	$10,381,000	$10,355,000	+$ 26,000	+$ 92,000	+$118,000
Townhouses - 240 units	9.2494	$10,397,000	$10,355,000	+$ 42,000	+$138,000	+$180,000
Nonresidential						
Office - 300,000 ft.^{2}	9.2559	$10,465,000	$10,355,000	+$110,000	NA	+$110,000
Office - 300,000 ft.^{2}	9.2540	$10,445,000	$10,355,000	+$ 90,000	NA	+$ 90,000
Office - 400,000 ft.^{2}	9.2589	$10,497,000	$10,355,000	+$142,000	NA	+$142,000
Office - 400,000 ft.^{2}	9.2565	$10,471,000	$10,355,000	+$116,000	NA	+$116,000
Office - 500,000 ft.^{2}	9.2616	$10,525,000	$10,355,000	+$170,000	NA	+$170,000
Office - 500,000 ft.^{2}	9.2589	$10,497,000	$10,355,000	+$142,000	NA	+$142,000
Office/hotel	9.2627	$10,537,000	$10,355,000	+$182,000	NA	+$182,000

Notes: At 1 employee per every 200 ft.^{2} office space.

At 1 employee per every 250 ft.^{2} office space.

Equals sum of groupings of variables, e.g., 1978 base case, base case as modified by single-family development, base case modified by townhouse construction, etc. To illustrate, the base case total (in logarithmic values) equals the sum of -5.44, -1.06, .94, .30, 1.13, -.36, 9.39, .23, .19 and 3.73 or 9.24. The base case modified by single-family construction on the golf course equals 5.44, -1.06, .9443 (instead of .94), .30, 1.13, -.36, 9.39, .23, .19 and 3.73, or 9.2457 (instead of 9.24). The remaining development scenarios were calculated in the same fashion.

Expresses indicated logarithmic value in 1978 dollars.

See Exhibit 2-3.

Equals the municipal expenditures post-growth less municipal expenditures pre-growth.

As indicated by the per capita multiplier method (see Exhibit 3-3). The reader should realize that average, linear school costs are being added to the marginal municipal expenditures suggested by the expenditure equation.

Not applicable.

See text and Exhibit 3-5 for details.

surpluses of about $400,000 and $500,000 respectively (see Exhibit 3-1). The office-hotel combination generates the highest revenue and the greatest surplus, approximately $700,000 annually (see Exhibit 3-1).

COMPARISON OF TRADITIONAL FISCAL IMPACT
ANALYSIS TO THE MUNICIPAL EXPENDITURE MODEL

At least six development alternatives are possible for the Englewood golf course: 1) single-family; 2a) townhouses - 160 units; 2b) townhouses - 240 units; 3) office building - 300,000 ft^2; 4) office building - 400,000 ft^2; 5) office building - 500,000 ft^2; and, 6) office-hotel complex. Traditional fiscal impact techniques (per capita multiplier and proportional valuation) and the municipal expenditure model both yield similar fiscal declinations with respect to the six course development cases:

1. All six generate a surplus of public revenues compared to public costs.

2. The smallest fiscal gain is provided by the single-family option.

3. The largest fiscal benefits are offered by the townhouse developments and the most intensive nonresidential complexes (e.g. 500,000 ft^2 office and office-hotel combination).

4. The smaller nonresidential projects (e.g. 300,000 - 400,000 ft^2 offices) generate a fiscal surplus larger than the one offered by the single-family development yet smaller than the fiscal advantage of the more intensive nonresidential cases.

While the traditional and model fiscal impact approaches yield similar findings with respect to the financial order of magnitude summarized above, they differ in the specific cost-revenue figures determined for each of the golf course developments. To illustrate, the per capita multiplier approach projects that the 240 unit townhouse project would produce a surplus of $500,000 while the model estimates a $700,000 gain. The proportional valuation technique assigns a $750,000 surplus to the office-hotel project -- about $100,000 more than the gain indicated by the municipal expenditure model (see Exhibit 3-1).

Why these differences? As both the traditional and model techniques utilized identical revenue estimates, their fiscal impact variations arise from diverging public service cost assignments, specifically with respect to municipal outlays. The per capita multiplier approach projects much higher municipal service expenditures induced by residential growth than the model. While the former assigns municipal costs of $118,000, $162,000, and $244,000 to the golf course single-family, low density townhouse, and high density townhouse projects respectively, the latter projects expenditures of $19,000, $26,000, and $42,000 respectively -- a variance of about 600 percent. These divergent expenditure findings reflect contrasting methodological approaches. The per capita technique assumes that each entering resident increases costs by the average expenditure per capita. Since Englewood's per capita outlays are quite high, considerable total service costs are assessed. The mathematical model, in contrast, projects much lower outlays for it is sensitive to the ability of mature suburbs to readily accommodate new residential development. Englewood is illustrative. Building single-family or townhouse units on this community's golf course will not necessitate new school and other public buildings, massive hiring of teachers and other public staff, much additional equipment, supply purchases, and so on. In short, older suburbs pay a high price for their generous service structure, yet once this system is in place, they are well prepared to handle incoming residents. The per capita multiplier approach, developed in the 1960's-1970's as a tool to gauge economic impacts in rapidly growing suburbs, is simply not sensitive to the differing growth fiscal dynamic in mature suburbs.

Traditional and model approaches also display varying municipal service cost assignments with respect to nonresidential growth, albeit, this difference nowhere approaches that characterizing residential development. Relative to the model, the proportional valuation approach projects lower municipal outlays. The latter estimates costs of about $90,000 to $110,000 for the varying office and office-hotel complexes compared to $100,000 to $180,000 for the former (see Exhibit 3-1). These differences also reflect alternate methodological approaches and derivations. The proportional valuation approach accords municipal expenditures on the basis of property value under the assumption that value measures intensity of use and therefore the demand placed on the municipality. Translation of value to use to municipal cost has certain logical appeal yet often falls short in the particulars. Do all difficult-to-accommodate facilities from a public service perspective have relatively high property values? Conversely, do all high value uses make significant demands on public services? The answer is clearly no. For instance, a relatively low value, fast food restaurant may impose severe traffic, sanitation and other demands to the municipal service system while a high value, nuclear or other utility plant often can practically be ignored by local officials. A better measure of municipal service demand must be sought. The employment factors of the municipal expenditure model, themselves based on empirical analysis of actual public outlays in communities with varying levels of nonresidential development, are likely a better gauge of nonresidential expenditure effects.

Even were there a sounder translation of property value to local spending pressures, the proportional valuation technique would suffer from a further drawback, namely how accurate are the refinement coefficients? The latter represent an advance over a simple proportional assignment of cost which as discussed earlier, often bordered on the ludicrous. While constituting an improvement, the refinement coefficients themselves sometimes yield results which are dubious. In the Englewood case, for instance, it increased the share of municipal expenditures induced by extant nonresidential facilities from 29 percent to 43 percent, a figure which seems suspiciously high. A slight change in some of the relevant ratios could have yielded even more suspicious results. For instance, if the average Englewood non-residential property would have been only 2.0 instead of 2.7 times more valuable than the average local parcel, then the coefficient would have been about 1.7 (instead of 1.5), thereby suggesting that about half (.299 x 1.7, see page 114) of Englewood's municipal outlays were caused by local nonresidential uses -- a finding further straining credibility.

This discussion points to the rather crude nature of fiscal impact analysis, especially when nonresidential uses are examined via traditional methodologies. The expenditure model, based on a more rigorous empirical underpinning (e.g., regression analysis of 1970-1980 local spending in 25 communities as opposed to a few case studies from which the refinement coefficients were derived), hopefully represents an advance, albeit one which also must be improved upon.

CONCLUSION

Chapter two of this study hinted that new development in older suburbs such as Englewood would likely often be financially desirable. Our analysis confirms this benefit at least for the type of residential and nonresidential uses which could be constructed on Englewood's golf course. Application of both traditional fiscal impact analysis as well as a model of municipal expenditures indicates the following:

. Construction of single-family units would generate an annual surplus of about $200,000.

. Townhouse development would yield a surplus of about $500,000 to $750,000.

. Nonresidential development would generate an annual surplus of $400,000 to $750,000 depending on the level of intensity.

From a purely fiscal perspective, the townhouses and more intensive nonresidential options would be most favorable, the single-family development least desirable, and the remaining nonresidential uses falling somewhat in between. This conclusion should be viewed with the following perspective:

1. Fiscal impact analysis gives only one measure of impact -- economic. Other effects, such as environmental, social and physical, clearly must be considered as well.

2. The projections are rough estimates of impact. Fiscal impact analysis, whether utilizing traditional techniques or a more comprehensive mathematical model, is a rather new analytical tool. The figures cited above are estimates based on emerging state-of-the-art techniques and should be viewed accordingly.

3. The fiscal impact projections do not incorporate site-specific considerations which pertain to the golf course development, e.g., traffic impact on surrounding roads, depreciation/appreciation of adjacent property values, etc.

4. The fiscal impact projections do incorporate numerous community-wide characteristics. To illustrate, a relatively large share of upper-middle and upper-income Englewood households do not send their children to the local public schools. Instead, parochial and other private educational institutions are turned to. It is for this reason that we assumed that only one-half of the public school-age children generated by the golf course residential units would attend public schools (see Exhibit 3-2). If this ratio were to rise from .5 to say .75, the costs induced by residential development would also increase (e.g. by $60,000 for the single-family complex, $46,000 from the lower density, and $69,000 from the higher density townhouses). These increases would not, however, change our overall finding that the single-family development is relatively the least fiscally desirable and the townhouses roughly comparable to the economic benefits engendered by the more intensive nonresidential complexes.

5. The analysis in this chapter assumed that all six golf course development scenarios could physically be built and that all shared equal market demand and developer interest. These assumptions must be carefully checked. While townhouses yield a higher fiscal benefit than either the single-family or many of the nonresidential alternatives, the practical economic benefit of townhouses to Englewood may be chimerical if there is a soft market for such units. Conversely, the single-family alternative may be the most desirable if this is the only construction demanded by the market. In short, a development probability matrix must be applied to the predicted fiscal impacts in order to determine the likelihood of the estimated economic gains being realized.

6. The surpluses indicated in Exhibit 3-1, all expressed in 1978 dollars, should be viewed with the perspective of how they match against Englewood's total fiscal parameters for that year. In 1978, Englewood spent about $23,000,000 for municipal and school purposes and imposed about $18,000,000 in total property taxes. Matched against these figures, the cost-revenue differences between the six golf course developments, already small especially with respect to the townhouse versus nonresidential alternatives, become insignificant. Moreover, the fiscal surpluses of about $200,000 to $800,000 provided by the range of golf course developments are clearly only a fraction of Englewood's overall public spending/revenue totals. Thus, while new construction would offer needed financial relief, the level of fiscal respite is relatively minor. This finding is not unexpected. By definition, mature suburbs such as Englewood are largely developed. New development opportunities are thus limited in number and scale and it would be unrealistic to expect such activity to markedly affect the

fiscal environment already in place. It is, therefore, important to consider additional meliorative actions to lessen the older suburbs' fiscal pressures -- a strategy explored in the next three chapters.

NOTES

1. D. Bennett Mazur, People, Politics, and Planning: The Comparative History of Three Suburban Communities. Ph.D. dissertation, Rutgers University, May 1981, p. 147.
2. Ibid., p. 519.
3. Ibid., p. 541-545.
4. Ibid., p. 546.
5. The Office Network Inc. "National Office Market Report." Fall-Winter 1982 (Houston: Office Network, 1982), p. 2.
6. Ruth L. Mace, Municipal Cost-Revenue Research in the United States (Chapel Hill: University of North Carolina Press, 1961), p. 1. See Robert W. Burchell and David Listokin, The Fiscal Impact Handbook (New Brunswick, Rutgers University, Center for Urban Policy Research, 1980).
7. Boston City Planning Board, Report on the Income and Cost of Six Districts in the City of Boston (Boston: Boston City Planning Board, 1934).
8. Burchell and Listokin, The Fiscal Impact Handbook.
9. Scott Bagby, A Comprehensive Plan for the Borough of Morris Plains, N.J. (Montclair, NJ: Bagby Associates, 1948): Morrow Planning Associates, The Master Plan of Florham Park (Ridgewood, NJ: Morrow Planning Associates, 1965); Homer Hoyt Associates, Economic Survey of Land Uses of Evanston (Larchmont, NY: Homer Hoyt Associates, 1949); Walter Isard and Robert E. Coughlin, Municipal Costs and Revenues Resulting from Community Growth (Wellesley, MA: Chandler Davis, 1955); William Wheaton and Morton J. Schussheim, The Cost of Municipal Services in Residential Areas (Washington, D.C.: Government Printing Office, 1955).
10. See U.S. Department of Housing and Urban Development, 701 Comprehensive Planning Assistance Statutes, Regulations and Pertinent Excerpts from Selected House and Senate Reports (Washington, D.C.: Government Printing Office, 1975).
11. For further discussion of the fiscal impact analysis context, see Thomas Muller, Fiscal Impacts of Land Development (Washington, D.C.: The Urban Institute, 1973); John F. Kain, "Urban Form and the Cost of Services," Program on Regional and Urban Economics, Discussion Paper No. 6 (Cambridge: Harvard University, 1967); Thomas Muller and Grace Dawson, The Fiscal Impact of Residential and Commercial Development: A Case Study (Washington, D.C.: Urban Institute, 1972); Robert W. Burchell, Planned Unit Development: New Communities American Style (New Brunswick, NJ: Rutgers University, Center for Urban Policy Research, 1972): Sternlieb et al., Housing Development and Municipal Costs; (New Brunswick, N.J.: Rutgers University, Center for Urban Policy Research, 1972); Connecticut Development Group, Inc., Cost-Revenue Impact Analysis for Residential Developments (Hartford, Conn.: Connecticut Development Group, 1972).

12. See footnotes 6 and 11 in this chapter.

13. For the sake of brevity, the analysis focuses on property tax revenues and property tax-supported costs only. In Englewood's case, the property tax dominates. To illustrate, the $350 municipal property tax-supported cost per capita (1978) is about 80 percent of the 1978 $438 total municipal operating expenditure per person (see Exhibit 1-3). In addition, non-property tax supported expenditures (e.g. $88 [$438-$350] in 1978) will likely be somewhat matched by non-property tax revenue. This "wash" transaction is a further reason permitting focus on property tax costs-revenues only.

14. Burchell and Listokin, The Fiscal Impact Handbook, chapter six.

15. Ibid.

16. Ibid.

Chapter Four
Strengthening the Retail Sector
of the Older Suburbs

INTRODUCTION

A strong retail sector is a key ingredient for the fiscal health of
the older suburb. Chapter two indicated that commercial decline exerts
special municipal spending pressure. The importance of commercial vig-
or goes beyond municipal outlays, however. Commercial ratables are
often an important component of local property wealth. Englewood's
commercial properties, for instance, constitute about one-eighth of
its ratable base. Fiscal solvency demands that the commercial property
contribution must be protected if not enhanced. There is also an important psychological consideration. Commercial buildings, for the
most part, consisting of central business district (CBD) retail establishments, define the older suburb's downtown. A thriving CBD
creates a positive ambiance and sense of community while a deterio-
rating image has a deleterious effect.

This chapter examines the role, vigor, and future of the retail
sector in mature suburbs in general and Englewood in particular. The
discussion is divided into three sections:

1. Section one considers the retail state-of-health of Englewood and
sister older suburbs. It does this in an analogous fashion to the comparative community analysis of chapters one and two. Englewood's retail performance is compared to that exhibited by urban areas, older
suburbs, and shopping centers.

2. Section two extends the analysis of the retail dynamic by examining shopper and retailer profiles/perceptions in the older suburb.
This discussion is based on surveys of retailers and shoppers conducted in Englewood as well as numerous other comparable communities.

3. Section three examines various strategies for invigorating the
retail sector in mature suburbs in general and Englewood in particular.

OLDER SUBURB RETAIL PATTERNS

Deurbanization of Retail Trade

To understand older suburb retail patterns, it is important to
briefly sketch the broader spatial-retail shifts which have occurred

in the United States. A half a century ago, Americans shopped in
cities; today they shop where they predominantly live, in suburbia.
The urban-to-suburban retail shift has been commented on by numerous
observers over the past few decades.[1] In the early 1960's, George
Sternlieb examined the future of downtown retailing and concluded
that:[2]

> The decline of retailing downtown is a concomitant of deep-
> seated changes in residential and transportation patterns that
> are not likely to be reversed by attempts to revitalize the
> central business district....New suburban outlets, well suited
> to the demand for easy auto access and quick shopping, consti-
> tute formidable competition for downtown. Measures to bolster
> the retail core should aim at positive adjustment to a reduced
> value of business....

A decade later, in 1970, a study of retail patterns in 30 large
metropolitan areas summarized:[3]

> The downtown of the big city has given way to the shopping center
> of the suburbs.
>
> Between the 1958 and 1967 retail trade censuses, the nation's
> retail business grew by over 50 percent. Sales by stores located
> in the suburbs of the sample areas increased at twice that rate,
> but sales by stores doing business in the central cities in-
> creased by only half that rate.

Numerous studies conducted in the late 1970's-early 1980's have
documented the continued suburbanization of retail trade.[4] Thomas
Muller, for example, concluded that:[5]

> Retail sales in the Central Business District (CBDs) declined
> between 1967 and 1972 and their decline accelerated between 1972
> and 1977. Recent losses appear unaffected by size or region....
> CBD sales in nominal terms declined by 2 percent in large SMSAs,
> or about 46 percent when adjusted for inflation.

The catastrophic position of urban retail is evident from the summary data shown in Exhibits 4-1 and 4-2. Prior to the great Depression, about three-quarters of the retail trade (as indicated by retail
employment) in "frostbelt" (northeast and midwest) standard metropolitan statistical areas (SMSAs) was clustered in the central city.[6]
Urban retail hegemony was largely maintained until the post-war era,
but then slipped significantly. By the end of the 1950's "frostbelt"
metropolitan retail trade was split between city and suburb; two decades later, only a third was still to be found in urban centers (see
Exhibit 4-1).

EXHIBIT 4-1
"FROSTBELT" Central Cities[a] **Proportion of**
Metropolitan Retail Trade Employment

	YEAR					
CITY	1929	1939	1948	1958	1967	1977
Baltimore	95%[a]	91%[a]	88%[a]	73%[a]	54%[a]	33%[a]
Boston[b]	61	55	52	43	34	NA[c]
Buffalo	79	73	70	57	42	29
Chicago	82	78	76	68	NA	36
Cincinnati	80	77	74	68	49	35
Cleveland	88	83	81	68	45	29
Detroit	82	78	73	55	72	NA
New York	80	76	75	53	51	39
Philadelphia	79	70	68	56	44	30
Average	81	76	73	60	49	33

Notes: a) Central cities' retail employment as percentage of corresponding standard metropolitan area total retail employment.
b) After 1948 includes Boston only, not Lowell, Lawrence.
c) Information not available.

Source: 1929-1958 data from Raymond Vernon, The Changing Economic
Function of the Central City (New York: Committee for Eco-
nomic Development, 1959); 1967-1977 data from U.S. Census of
Retail Trade for indicated areas.

Flight of urban retailing has been most dramatic in "frostbelt" locations where urban distress is most rampant. "Sunbelt" cities have
not been immune, however. In the late 1950's about three-quarters of
the retail trade in "sunbelt" SMSAs was urban; two decades later the
"sunbelt" city retail share dropped to about half. Interestingly, the
pace of "sunbelt" urban retail decline -- a near halving of market
share from 1958 to 1977 -- is not so different from the market share
loss exhibited by "frostbelt" areas in the same time period (compare
Exhibit 4-1 and 4-2). Thus, while the former's retail trade has not
plummeted to the same dismal level as the latter's, this differentiation is perhaps just a lag function, a respite which may not last.

EXHIBIT 4-2

**"SUNBELT" Central Cities'[a] Proportion of
Metropolitan Retail Trade Employment**

	YEAR		
CITY	1958	1967	1977
Atlanta	67%[a]	57%	51%[a]
Dallas	80	73	40
Denver	74	57	38
Houston	95	77	72
Los Angeles	45	43	41
Miami	55	38	24
Phoenix	70	70	55
San Antonio	95	89	83
San Diego	67	57	51
Seattle	73	60	45
Average	72	62	50

Note: a) Central cities' retail employment as percentage of corresponding standard metropolitan area total retail employment.

Source: U.S. Census of Retail for indicated areas.

Retail Dynamic of the Older Suburb:
Englewood Historical Overview

   The deurbanization of retail trade has presented both opportunities
and problems for older suburb retail. These communities are near areas
of population and business vigor yet face the formidable competition
of newer, free-standing shopping centers. A glimpse of this dynamic is
afforded by examining retail patterns in Englewood. This community has
a "classic" downtown shopping area -- a potpourri of small, long-established retail establishments are clustered on a main shopping strip
(Palisade Avenue) and intersecting side streets.
   The development of Englewood's central business district parallels
the growth and decline of many downtowns in older suburbs and small
cities similarly settled in the nineteenth century. Scattered commercial establishments first arose in these communities to serve
mainly local residents and travelers passing through. With the development of the trolley car, railroad, and other means of transportation
facilitating access to and from older suburbs-smaller cities, they
expanded in population and developed CBDs of regional importance. The
national prosperity spanning the late nineteenth century to the great
Depression of the twentieth, fueled the golden era of these downtowns.
Retail complacency was shattered by the 1930's Depression but returned
in the early post-World War II era. It did not last long. Competition
from free-standing shopping centers was first felt in the 1950's, and

grew more severe in the years to come. By the 1970's, most older downtowns had lost their former unquestioned regional retail dominance.

We are fortunate in Englewood's case to be able to present a more
exact historical accounting of its CBD. The following historical syn-
opsis is derived from a dissertation by Bennett Mazur tracing the
history of Englewood and two sister Bergen County communities.[7]

When Englewood was first founded as a separate community in 1860,
"there was only one grocery store a mile away and most shopping was
done in New York by commuters who brought provisions home in a bas-
ket."[8] In-town commercial growth soon followed:[9]

> As the years passed, a downtown shopping district emerged to pro-
> vide the goods and services the wealthy required....Palisade Ave-
> nue was the axis of this shopping district and commercial build-
> ings spread out from the railroad in each direction. It was com-
> prised of office buildings for professionals, merchants, livery
> stables, carriage makers, a bank organized by the Village Im-
> provement Society, Western Union Office, and a Post Office....

By 1870, there were about 35 businesses in Englewood including
Lander's Peoples' Market, Palisade General Market, Green's Boot and
Shoe Store, De Mott's Dry Goods, and Gruber's Hair Cutter and Lager
Beer Saloon.[10]

In the post Civil War period, Englewood's retail sector flourished:[11]

> Englewood quickly grew into the regional shopping center of the
> Northern Valley. The activities present were not only more numer-
> ous, but also of a higher order than those of the communities
> around it, with the exception of Hackensack, the county seat.

> Palisade had been widened into a spacious main street 70 feet
> wide....English Neighborhood Road was renamed Grand Avenue by the
> legislators and the new road was called Broad Avenue (names that
> some residents felt were quite parvenu). Both new roads ap-
> proached Englewood from the South and aided in the development of
> the downtown area by increasing accessibility from that more
> densely populated direction....

Englewood's commercial functions were aided by further access-
transportation improvements. Numerous trolley lines to and from the
community were opened in the late 19th-early 20th centuries. Comprehensive bus service was also inaugurated; by the 1920's, Englewood was
served by three bus companies, by the 1930's, five lines:[12]

> Englewood's commercial expansion continued with this increased
> accessibility for residents of other communities who could now
> travel there via the greatly expanded public transportation
> system. Two theatres were constructed, 18 automobile dealers
> appeared, banks, and a variety of specialty stores could be
> found....

According to older residents, Englewood had become known as "the shopping hub of the Northern Valley." It was an era of great prosperity for Englewood merchants. According to Joseph Carney, former City Clerk, "The twenties were great."

During the Great Depression, Englewood's CBD suffered as did all of the community's economic sectors. Better times returned in the post-war period. The 1948 Census of Business reported that Englewood was second only to Hackensack, the county seat, in Bergen County retail sales. Prosperity was accompanied by some problems, however:[13]

Parking was becoming a vexing difficulty as the commercial district spread further north along Van Brunt, West and Dean Streets and westerly along Palisade Avenue.[14]

Englewood's business district was initially created along the trolley car route and stores were built in as compact an area and fashion as feasible so as to reduce walking distance from convenient transportation to each retail establishment. Now those firms found themselves at a disadvantage since their potential customers lived a distance and used autos to shop.

Some of the retail establishments (the chain food stores) which could afford to do so, had accommodated this change by moving to new quarters where they could provide adequate on-site parking. Grand Union had done so on Hudson Avenue and Grand Avenue, there was a new Safeway Store just south of the Monument, and a new A & P on Tallman and West Streets. The other merchants were clamoring for more municipal parking.

By the early 1950's, a greater outside menace to Englewood's retail health arose:[15]

On the horizon was the shadow of more frightening developments, greater competition in the form of highway-oriented shopping centers designed for autoborne shoppers. At the intersection of Routes 4 and 17 just a few miles west of Paramus, a major shopping center initiated by Bamberger's Department Store was under construction....

The launching of a second major shopping center on Route 4 in Paramus -- the Bergen Mall -- brought a renewed concern for the future of retail activities in Englewood.

In an interview at a national appraisers' conference in Atlantic City, real estate tycoon William Zeckendorf, president of Webb and Knapp, predicted that a second major shopping center would "murder Bergen's established business districts."

A succession of Paramus malls did not "murder" Englewood's downtown. Palisade Avenue and surrounding streets still contained a multitude of stores and physically the downtown looked remarkably the same as it had in years past. Emerging shopping centers did take their economic toll, however. While the number of Englewood retail establishments grew slightly in the 1950's (e.g., from 317 in 1948 to 340 in 1954), Englewood's retail dominance slipped:[16]

> In the 1948 to 1954 period, the city, once known as the shopping hub of Bergen, was not holding its own with the rest of Bergen County. Its sales, 8 percent of the county total in 1948, had slipped to 6.2 percent in 1954, and by 1958, the number of firms would decline to 327 and its sales to 5.4 percent of the total.

The modern era retail record of Englewood and its sister older suburbs is explored below.

Retail Dynamic of the Older Suburb:
The Performance Record

Englewood's retail profile can best be examined on a relative basis. The grounds for comparison will be similar as that referred to in chapters one and two with some modification for the specific analysis at hand. Englewood's retail activity will therefore be compared to patterns in:

a) Urban areas -- New Jersey's largest cities and the borough of Manhattan (New York City). The latter is included because of its proximity as a significant retail center.

b) Older suburbs -- Including the more important retail centers of the New Jersey mature suburb group delineated in this study.

c) Newer suburbs/shopping centers -- New Jersey shopping centers, located for the most part in the newer suburb cohort.

Retail activity in these different locations will be examined from data contained in the 1958, 1967, and 1977 U.S. Census of Retail Trade reports. This source offers the advantages of acceptance and comprehensiveness. Retail activity is shown for communities, major retail centers, and so on. In addition, retail sales are differentiated by category -- shopper, convenience, other, etc. The principal disadvantages of the Census of Retail Trade are its dating -- the most recent information for our purposes is about five years old -- and the suppression of information in relatively small retail locations (e.g. shopping centers) to protect confidentiality.

The comparative retail sales analysis reveals the following:

Englewood and its sister older suburbs still are important retail concentrations. They each contain 200 to 300 retail establishments (see Exhibit 4-3). The 1977 retail store count was 353 in Montclair, 289 in Morristown, 271 in Teaneck, 266 in Englewood, and 215 in Bergenfield. While these figures are but a fraction of those found in nearby urban centers (e.g. 2,000 establishments in Newark, 20,000 in

EXHIBIT 4-3

**Retail Establishments Over Time: New Jersey Cities,
Mature Suburbs, and Shopping Centers**

Area	Total Retail Establishments		Percentage Change, 1958–1977
	1958	1977	
Cities			
Newark	6,055	2,304	-62
Jersey City	3,345	1,719	-49
Paterson	2,163	1,015	-53
Trenton	2,388	818	-66
Manhattan	30,643	19,852	-35
Mature Suburbs			
Bergenfield	220	215	- 2
Englewood	327	266	-19
Fort Lee	194	285	+47
Montclair	456	353	-23
Morristown	338	289	-14
New Brunswick	713	380	-47
Plainfield	616	293	-52
Teaneck	276	271	- 2
Shopping Centers			
Bergen	NA@	99	NA
Fashion Plaza	NA	84	NA
Garden State	NA	95	NA
Livingston	NA	107	NA
Menlo	NA	67	NA
Riverside	NA	76	NA
Willowbrook	NA	164	NA

Note: @Information not applicable or available.

Source: U.S. Census of Retail Trade for indicated years/areas.

Manhattan), they are comparable and often exceed the number of stores clustered in nearby shopping centers. Admittedly, the latter contain huge department stores thereby making it difficult to ascertain relative retail significance by comparing numbers of retail establishments. By other measures, however, mature suburbs would still be counted as important retail areas. For instance, there is approximately 500,000 square feet of retail space located along Englewood's Palisade Avenue.[17] A retail concentration of such size is defined by the Urban Land Institute as a regional center.[18] Englewood is thus roughly comparable to such New Jersey regional shopping centers as Hackensack's Riverside Square (617,000 ft^2), Paramus's Fashion Center (542,000 ft^2), and Lawrence's Lawrenceville Mall (400,000 ft^2).

Sales figures also attest to the lingering importance of the older suburb as a retail hub. As of 1977, retail sales in these communities amounted to $50 to $100 million apiece (in 1967 dollars, see Exhibit 4-4). To cite some examples, sales were about $90 million in Morristown, $80 million in both Englewood and New Brunswick, $60-$70 million in Plainfield and Montclair, and in the $40-$50 million range in Teaneck and Bergenfield. The $50 to $100 million sales achievement was not that dissimilar from that recorded in such urban areas as Trenton ($97 million) and Paterson ($129 million), albeit it was considerably below the sales volume of the remaining urban locations (e.g. $300 million in Newark and Jersey City, $4 billion in Manhattan). Shopping centers provide a closer sales comparison. The older suburbs' $50-$100 million sales range achieved in 1977, is very similar to the 1977 sales record in such free-standing shopping centers as Riverside Square ($34 million), Bergen Plaza ($57 million), Fashion Plaza ($70 million), and Livingston Mall ($70 million). Only huge super regional malls such as Willowbrook Center with a 1977 sales volume of $125 million, significantly exceeded the mature suburbs' retail achievement. Many older suburbs and shopping centers, while surely differing in physical guise, thus provide a comparable clustering of retail sales activity.

How has the mature suburbs' retail performance fared over time, say over the last two decades? While it is difficult to generalize, analysis of data provided by the 1958 and 1977 <u>Censuses of Retail Trade</u> suggests that older suburbs have experienced:

. a contraction in the number of retail establishments;

. small gains or losses in sales volume (measured in constant dollars);

. a change in sales focus -- deemphasizing traditional "shoppers" goods and emphasizing "other" goods, especially automotive sales.

The 1958 to 1977 review also reveals that overall the older suburbs displayed a mid-range record -- their retail performance is better than the sorry urban retail plight, yet not as robust as the sales record of many suburban shopping centers.

EXHIBIT 4-4

**Real Changes in Retail Sales Over Time for New Jersey Cities,
Mature Suburbs, and Shopping Centers
(Retail Sales Expressed in $000s of 1967 Dollars)**

Area	Retail Sales			Annual Percentage Increase in Sales		
	1958	1967	1977	1958-67	1967-77	1958-77
Cities						
Newark	$ 778,397	$ 643,596	$ 354,505	-1.73%	-4.49%	-2.72%
Jersey City	314,997	335,596	276,752	+0.65	-1.75	-0.61
Paterson	244,242	221,782	128,859	-0.92	-4.19	-2.36
Trenton	255,552	213,177	96,810	-1.66	-5.46	-3.11
Manhattan	5,010,154	5,045,725	3,917,874	+0.07	-2.24	-1.09
Mature Suburbs						
Bergenfield	35,271	45,844	51,269	+3.00	+1.18	+2.27
Englewood	56,537	69,090	82,339	+2.22	+1.92	+2.28
Fort Lee	27,115	50,356	61,187	+8.57	+2.15	+6.29
Montclair	79,366	87,918	72,141	+1.08	-1.79	-0.46
Morristown	73,387	89,550	88,912	+2.20	-0.07	+1.06
New Brunswick	95,854	121,738	82,151	+2.70	-3.25	-0.71
Plainfield	131,008	125,460	66,686	-0.42	-4.68	-2.45
Teaneck	37,633	49,755	43,141	+3.22	-1.33	+0.73
Shopping Centers						
Bergen	NA	71,442	57,108	NA	-2.00	NA
Fashion Plaza	NA	59,684	69,712	NA	+1.68	NA
Garden State	NA	141,567@	113,489	NA	-1.98	NA
Livingston	NA	54,846@	70,352	NA	+5.64@	NA
Menlo	NA	74,259@	55,045	NA	-5.17@	NA
Riverside	NA	NA	33,836	NA	NA	NA
Willowbrook	NA	NA	124,333	NA	NA	NA

Note: @1972 data and 1972 to 1977 change (1967 data was not available).
NA=Information not available or not applicable.

Over the past few decades, consolidations, strenuous demands on
retail proprietors, and other factors have led to a decline in the
number of retail establishments. The New York SMSA, for example, lost
30 percent of its retail outlets from 1958 to 1977. This trend is evident in older suburbs as well (see Exhibit 4-3). In certain cases
there has been a precipitous drop. Plainfield had 600 retail stores in
1958 and just shy of 300 in 1977. More common is a more moderate yet
relentless shrinkage. In 1958, Englewood contained about 330 retail
establishments; two decades later, 266, a decline of about one-fifth.
Similar contraction was exhibited by many sister suburbs such as Montclair (23 percent loss) and Morristown (14 percent loss). This rate of
decline is far less than the 30 to 60 percent drop in urban retail establishments betwen 1958 and 1977. Even Manhattan, considered an
island of retail vigor, lost 35 percent of its retail purveyors. It is
important to bear in mind, however, that while mature suburbs may have
fared relatively better than urban centers as far as 1958 to 1977 retailer contraction is concerned, the former's loss stands in contrast
to the gains recorded at free-standing shopping centers which were
built and/or were growing in this period.

This urban-older suburb-shopping center relative performance is
roughly repeated when changes in total retail sales are examined. From
1958 to 1967, mature suburbs exhibited moderate sales gains of about 2
to 3 percent annually in real (inflation-adjusted) dollars (see Exhibit 4-4). While some fared worse, such as Plainfield losing sales at a
.4 percent yearly pace, more typical was Englewood's 2.2 percent annual sales gain between 1958 and 1967. Over the late 1960's to late
1970's, the older suburb sales record worsened (see Exhibit 4-4).
Certain communities had a disastrous performance. Plainfield lost 5
percent of its sales annually and losses were recorded in Montclair,
Morristown, and Teaneck. When sales gains were achieved, they tended
to be modest -- one to two percent yearly in Bergenfield, Englewood,
and Fort Lee.

The older suburbs' record is again "mid-range" when matched against
New Jersey urban centers and then shopping centers. City retail performance has been very weak. From 1958 to 1967, their sales dropped by
one to two percent yearly; city sales fell even more precipitously between 1967 to 1977, declining at a 2 to 5 percent annual clip. Older
suburbs have clearly outperformed this sorry sales picture, but have
not done so well relative to many shopping centers, especially some of
the newer facilities. To illustrate, in the 1970's, real sales grew by
6 percent yearly in the Livingston mall compared to flat performance
(1 to 2 percent gains) or even small losses in the older suburbs (see
Exhibit 4-4).

The older suburb to shopping center comparison is even more telling
when only non-automotive sales are counted. This factoring is necessary because while car-related transactions (automobile and gasoline
purchases, and car repairs) are important constitutent members of mature suburb retail sales, they are largely absent in shopping centers.
Factoring automotive-oriented transactions is thus important to avoid
an "apples to oranges" comparison of retail activity at mature suburbs

versus shopping centers. Such refinement is particularly compelling since the nature of automotive sales (high ticket items experiencing sharp price increases in recent years) may "unnaturally" enhance the retail sales record at older suburban locations. Such "sales inflation" is evident in the New Jersey mature suburbs since their sales performance sharply deteriorates when automotive transactions are excluded (see Exhibit 4-5). To illustrate, Englewood's total retail sales grew by 2 percent yearly from 1967 to 1977. This overall record masks the following distinctions. Over the 1967 to 1977 span, Englewood's automotive-related sales increased by almost 5 percent yearly in real terms while non-automotive sales declined by 1 percent a year (see Exhibit 4-5). A similar disparity is evident in sister communities. The mature-suburb's non-automotive performance is especially anemic when compared to the comparable record at shopping centers. (In the New Jersey centers studied total sales are equivalent to non-automotive transactions since these facilities contained neither car dealers nor garage stations.) In short, shopping centers typically outperform older suburbs when a common retail base, non-automotive sales, is compared.

Further analysis of the composition of older suburb retail sales reveals that these communities are experiencing a deemphasis on traditional "shoppers" goods and a growing emphasis on "other" goods. These terms deserve definition.

a) Shoppers goods are typically higher-priced merchandise which are "shopped" for and purchased relatively infrequently. As used here, shoppers goods include furniture (items for furnishing the home, e.g. furniture, floor coverings, draperies, etc.), appliances, and general merchandise (e.g, dry goods, apparel and accessories).

b) Convenience goods are lower-priced merchandise which are purchased relatively frequently as needed. This category includes items sold by food establishments (offering food for home preparation and consumption), eating and drinking places (selling prepared food and drinks for consumption on the premises), and drug stores (selling prescription and patent medicines, and related lines such as cosmetics, toiletries, tobacco, and novelty merchandise).

c) Other goods are items not enumerated above including goods sold by building material establishments (lumber, hardware, lawn/garden stores), automotive dealers (selling new and used automobiles, motorcycles, etc.), gasoline service stations (selling gasoline and lubricating oils and performing minor repair work and services), and miscellaneous retail stores (offering a range of merchandise, e.g. liquor, sporting goods, books, stationery, luggage and so on).

In the 1950's one went to cities and older suburbs for shoppers goods. A relatively large share of sales in these areas consisted of general merchandise, appliances, and furniture items. In 1958, shoppers goods constituted between 30 and 40 percent of total sales in

EXHIBIT 4-5

**Real Changes in Retail Sales Over Time by Total
And Non-Automotive Sales Categories:
New Jersey Mature Suburbs, 1967–1977
(Retail Sales Expressed in $000s of 1967 Dollars)**

| | SALES CATEGORY | | | | | | 1967-77 Annual Percentage Increase in Sales | | |
| | Total Sales | | Automotive-Related Sales[a] | | Non-Automotive Sales[b] | | | | |
Area	1967	1977	1967	1977	1967	1977	Total Sales	Automotive Sales	Non-Automotive Sales
Mature Suburbs [c]									
Bergenfield	$ 45,844	$51,269	$12,378	$15,894	$33,466	$35,375	+1.18	+2.84	+0.57
Englewood	69,090	82,339	35,236	51,874	33,854	30,465	+1.92	+4.72	-1.00
Montclair	87,918	72,141	28,134	20,921	59,784	51,220	-1.79	-2.56	-1.43
Morristown	89,550	88,912	22,387	32,898	67,163	56,014	-0.07	+4.70	-1.66
New Brunswick	121,738	82,151	29,217	22,181	92,521	59,970	-3.25	-2.41	-3.52
Plainfield	125,460	66,686	28,856	21,340	96,604	45,346	-4.68	-2.60	-5.31

Notes: [a] Includes automotive dealer and gas station sales.
[b] Equals total sales less automotive-related sales.
[c] Fort Lee and Teaneck are not shown because requisite data for calculations were lacking.

Source: U.S. Census of Retail Trade for indicated periods/years.

Newark, Morristown, New Brunswick, and Plainfield (see Exhibit 4-6). Over the 1960's and 1970's, the shopping goods loci shifted from urban and older suburbs to suburban free-standing centers. The latter locations were devoted almost exclusively (50 to 90 percent of sales) to shoppers goods (see Exhibit 4-6). The converse of the mall's focus on shoppers goods was a severe decline of this retail sector in cities and older suburbs. By 1977, shoppers goods constituted about 10 to 25 percent of total retail sales in Newark, Morristown, New Brunswick, and Plainfield compared to the 30 to 40 share twenty years earlier.

While shoppers goods have declined in importance in cities and mature suburbs, other retail sales activity has become more significant. (Convenience sales have roughly held their own as is evident in Exhibit 4-6.) In 1958, other goods constituted about one-third of total sales in Morristown and Plainfield; in 1977 they comprised more than one-half of the retail activity in these two communities. Increasingly, one comes to an older suburb to buy a car, have it fixed, or the tank filled and to purchase "miscellaneous" goods (e.g. sports equipment, books, stationery, jewelry, cameras, luggage, sewing-piece goods, and gifts-novelties) rather than for clothes, appliances, or furniture (see Exhibit 4-6).

The emphasis on other goods is especially pronounced in Englewood. In 1958 this category comprised about 40 percent of total sales. Most of the other retail activity in Englewood, in turn, is automotive related -- in 1958 automotive purchasers were 30 percent and gas/car service items, 9 percent of total sales. In contrast, all shoppers retail sales combined constituted only roughly 15 percent of Englewood's total sales. Two decades later, in 1977, Englewood's shopper's transactions dropped to 10 percent of total sales while other retail activity rose to 76 percent. Most of the latter continued to be automotive related (automobile purchases were 54 percent and gas-car service transactions, 9 percent of total sales; see Exhibit 4-6).

The older suburbs' emphasis on other retail activity makes them vulnerable to downturns in the housing and especially automotive markets. Englewood is especially vulnerable to soft car sales because this one category comprises more than half of its total retail volume.

Further insight into the retail dynamics of mature suburbs in general and Englewood in particular is provided by the following survey.

OLDER SUBURB RETAILERS AND SHOPPERS:
THE ENGLEWOOD SURVEY

Methodology

As part of its older suburb analysis, the Rutgers University Center for Urban Policy Research (CUPR) conducted a survey of downtown Englewood shopkeepers and shoppers. This effort was assisted by the Englewood Chamber of Commerce and Englewood League of Women Voters. In the spring of 1982, CUPR distributed approximately 200 survey forms to retailers located on or near Englewood's main shopping strip, Palisade Avenue. The survey elicited information on retailer characteristics

EXHIBIT 4-6
Composition of Retail Sales, 1958-1977: New Jersey Cities, Mature Suburbs, and Shopping Centers

RETAIL SALES CATEGORY 1968-1977	URBAN					MATURE SUBURBS								SHOPPING CENTER AVERAGE [a]
	Newark	Jersey City	Paterson	Trenton	Manhattan	Bergenfield	Englewood	Fort Lee	Montclair	Morris-town	New Brunswick	Plainfield	Teaneck	
1958														
Shoppers [a]														
General Merch.	21.7%	3.5%	12.3%	15.0%	15.7%	0.2%	NA	6.1%	9.4%	21.9%	11.2%	16.1%	1.4%	NA [a]
Apparel	10.1	10.8	10.3	10.6	16.5	11.3	8.1%	1.1	6.4	8.6	18.6	10.3	4.2	NA
Furniture	6.6	6.6	8.0	8.1	6.6	4.7	5.1	3.3	4.3	4.7	8.5	8.0	5.8	NA
Total	38.3	20.9	30.6	33.7	38.8	16.2	NA	10.5	20.1	35.3	37.3	34.4	11.4	NA
Convenience [a]														
Food	19.6	30.9	23.6	21.9	15.9	27.4	24.4	25.9	23.6	22.1	18.2	26.0	48.0	NA
Eat/drink	11.7	11.7	8.5	9.3	19.0	4.3	5.2	11.7	3.4	3.4	8.8	2.7	7.1	NA
Drug	2.6	3.1	2.8	2.4	2.7	2.9	2.2	2.4	2.9	2.4	2.7	2.3	4.0	NA
Total	33.9	45.7	34.9	33.6	37.6	34.6	31.8	40.0	29.8	27.9	29.7	31.0	59.1	NA
Other [a]														
Building	3.0	3.4	3.8	4.1	1.6	7.0	2.7	NA	3.4	6.8	3.6	6.0	4.1	NA
Automotive	6.6	10.0	15.1	9.1	3.5	25.9	29.7	17.4	22.7	16.9	14.1	16.6	2.3	NA
Gas Station	3.5	5.7	4.2	5.2	1.1	4.5	8.6	22.7	4.8	3.0	3.9	2.7	8.6	NA
Miscellaneous	14.4	14.3	11.3	14.3	17.4	11.5	NA	NA	19.3	10.1	11.4	9.3	14.6	NA
Total	27.5	33.4	34.5	32.7	23.6	48.9	41.0	40.2	50.1	36.8	33.0	34.5	29.5	NA
TOTAL ALL CATEGORIES	100.0	100.0	100.0	100.0	100.0	100.0	88.2	90.7	100.0	100.0	100.0	100.0	100.0	NA

EXHIBIT 4-6 (continued)

| | AREA | | | | | | | | | | | | | | SHOPPING CENTER AVERAGE[c] |
| | URBAN | | | | | MATURE SUBURBS | | | | | | | | | |
1958–1977 1977	Newark	Jersey City	Paterson	Trenton	Manhattan	Bergenfield	Englewood	Fort Lee	Montclair	Morristown	New Brunswick	Plainfield	Teaneck	
Shoppers[a]														
General Merchandise	14.2	10.2	8.3	10.4	16.4	3.3	0.5	NA	NA	16.8	NA	15.5	NA	NA
Apparel	8.4	9.3	5.3	7.2	13.5	8.7	4.3	3.8	8.5	4.6	3.5	6.3	4.1	NA
Furniture	6.9	4.2	8.9	5.3	6.0	2.6	5.7	2.1	4.6	2.9	9.9	7.8	2.8	NA
Total	30.2	23.7	22.5	22.9	35.9	14.5	10.5	NA	NA	24.4	NA	29.5	NA	69.8[b]
Convenience[a]														
Food	21.8	25.9	21.6	17.5	16.5	23.3	8.7	41.3	21.7	12.5	7.7	12.9	45.0	NA
Eat/Drink	13.1	10.3	8.4	14.6	18.7	4.4	3.2	11.2	5.1	6.7	9.2	5.3	9.8	NA
Drug	3.5	3.6	NA	NA	2.9	4.9	1.6	4.0	2.5	1.3	1.1	1.9	2.9	NA
Total	38.3	39.8	30.0	32.1	38.1	32.6	13.5	56.6	29.3	20.5	18.1	20.0	57.7	6.4
Other[a]														
Building	1.8	2.5	2.3	4.2	1.1	1.4	2.0	0.4	1.4	4.2	3.0	2.3	1.6	NA
Automotive	8.8	14.4	16.8	6.9	3.1	27.3	54.2	4.5	24.8	31.3	21.0	26.0	5.1	NA
Gas Stations	6.8	6.7	7.0	8.4	0.9	4.2	8.5	21.3	4.4	5.9	5.6	5.6	11.8	NA
Miscellaneous	15.1	12.7	12.7	17.1	20.9	20.0	11.2	NA	NA	13.6	NA	16.5	NA	NA
Total	31.4	36.3	38.8	36.6	26.0	52.9	76.0	NA	NA	55.1	NA	50.4	NA	NA
TOTAL ALL CATEGORIES	100.0	100.0	91.3	91.6	100.0	100.0	100.0	88.6	76.0	100.0	88.0	100.0	83.1	

EXHIBIT 4-6 (continued)

| RETAIL SALES CATEGORY 1958-1977 | URBAN | | | | | MATURE SUBURBS | | | | | | | | SHOPPING CENTER AVERAGE (a) |
	Newark	Jersey City	Paterson	Trenton	Manhattan	Bergenfield	Englewood	Fort Lee	Montclair	Morristown	New Brunswick	Plainfield	Teaneck	
1977 AS SHARE OF 1958 SALES COMPOSITION														
Shoppers	.79	1.13	.74	.68	.93	.90	NA	NA	NA	.69	NA	.86	NA	NA
Convenience	1.13	.87	.86	.96	1.01	.94	.42	1.42	.98	.73	.61	.64	.98	NA
Other	1.05	.89	1.12	1.19	1.10	1.08	1.85	NA	NA	1.50	NA	1.46	NA	NA

Notes:
(a) Average value for seven shopping centers shown in Exhibit 4-7.
(b) Includes miscellaneous as well as shoppers goods.
(c) Not applicable or information not available.
(d) See text for definitions.

(e.g. number of years in business, number of employees, type of merchandise sold and so on), retailer evaluation of the strengths or
weaknesses of the Englewood CBD, and retailer recommendations to address downtown problems and enhance advantages. A total of 105 questionnaires were returned; five were mostly incomplete leaving 100
replies.

Englewood's retailers have been in the community for a substantial
period of time -- about one-half for 20 years or more, one-third for
30 or more years. While the community has witnessed a reduction in
retail establishments in the past two decades, few of the surviving
retailers have plans to leave. Only 15 percent of the respondents to
the CUPR questionnaire mentioned that they planned to relocate from
their present Englewood facility and of this group about half planned
to move to another location in Englewood.

While remaining within the community, Englewood's retailers are for
the most part, thinking consolidation -- holding their own -- rather
than expansion. Only one in four has plans to make significant improvements to their facilities in the next five years. The overwhelming majority, over 70 percent, forsee they will decrease employment
over the next five years. Even those planning improvements or staff
additions often predicated these changes on "business or the economy
improving."

Englewood retailers offer a potpourri of merchandise as is evident
from the following roster of stores: Sahadi's University Shop (boys
and mens wear), La Puerta Del Sol East (boutique clothing and jewelry), Herbert's Camera House, Pottery International, Carl's House of
Silver, Benzel-Bush (Mercedes), UDO's Automotive (Mercedes service-
restoration), Jewel Spiegel Custom Framing, Audio Guild, Craftworks,
Blue Ribbon Custom Kitchens, Colony Antiques, Parke Art, Livingston
Stationery, Lebson's Jewelers, Schneider Pharmacy, Englewood Florist,
State News, Down Beat Records, Jean's Luggage, Engle Sports Center,
Sneaker Stadium, Rugs of the Orient, York Lighting, Michele Decorat-
ing, Evelyn Furs, Smokers World, The Bagel Place, and the Railroad
Cafe.

A large share of Englewood's retail merchandise is sold to a local
clientele (see Exhibit 4-7). About two-thirds of the CBD merchants
estimated that roughly half or more of their 1981 sales came from
Englewood residents or businesses. (This figure is only an approxi-
mation for retailers are often unaware where their customers reside.)
Englewood's shallow geographical pull as a retail center is further
evident when we examine where Englewood shoppers, who are not local
residents/businesses, came from. For the most part, these individuals
live or work in communities either immediately adjacent or very close
to Englewood such as Tenafly, Englewood Cliffs, or Teaneck (see
Exhibit I-2).

Further insight into the profile of the Englewood customer is provided by the CUPR survey of this group. Whenever possible our findings
will be compared to the results from previous market research-shopper
surveys conducted in Englewood, most notably, the 1973 Lawrence Alexander study, 1974 Urban Land Institute Panel Report, 1977 Virginia

EXHIBIT 4-7

Mature Suburb Retailer and Shopper Profile: Englewood, New Jersey — 1982

Retailer Characteristics[c]	Responses to CUPR Englewood Retailer Survey n=100[a]	*Shopper Characteristics*[c]	Responses to CUPR Englewood Shopper Survey n=100[a]
Years Located in Englewood		*Residence*	
Under 5 years	30.0%	In Englewood	60.0%
5-9	14.0	Outside Englewood	40.0
10-19	14.0	Total	100.0%
20-29	12.0		
30+	30.0	*Age*	
Total	100.0%		
		Under 25	14.0%
Store Size (in sq. ft.)		25-40	23.0
		41-65	30.0
Under 500	13.5%	Over 65	33.0
500-999	28.1	Total	100.0%
1,000-1,499	13.5		
1,500-1,999	14.6		
2,000 or more	30.3	*Number of Years Shopping in Englewood*	
Total	100.0%		
Own Store		10 or less	14.3%
		10-15	49.5
Yes	17.9%	15-20	27.5
No	82.1	20+	8.8
Total	100.0%	Total	100.0%
Full-Time Employees[b]			
2 or less	48.4%	*Household Income*	
3-4	28.6		
5+	23.1	Less than $10,000	24.0%
Total	100.0%	$10,000-$19,999	16.0
		$20,000-$29,999	28.0
Estimated % of Sales from Englewood residents/businesses		$30,000-$50,000	13.0
		$70,000+	19.1
20% or less	11.0%	Total	100.0%
20%-39%	20.0		
40%-59%	35.0	*Sex*	
60%+	33.0		
Total	100.0%	Male	30.9%
		Female	69.1
Plan to Relocate from Englewood		Total	100.0%
Yes	15.0%		
No	63.0	*Race*	
No plans/other	22.0		
Total	100.0%	White	67.7%
		Non-white	32.3
		Total	100.0%
		Travel to Shop	
		Automobile	76.8%
		Other	23.2
		Total	100.0%

Notes: [a] Number of actual respondents to individual questions may be less than 100.
[b] Excluding proprietor.
[c] Response cohorts have been collapsed from those used in original survey.

Source: Rutgers University Center for Urban Policy Research, Survey of Englewood Retailers and Shoppers, Spring 1982.

Miles analysis, and 1978 Stadtmauer proposal.[20] In brief, the CUPR
survey of Englewood shoppers reveals that these individuals are typically (see Exhibit 4-7):

- Englewood residents or live in nearby communities;

- middle-aged;

- on the average middle-income yet display a wide range of
  affluence;

- white, however there is a substantial minority presence;

- predominantly female;

- longtime patrons of the Englewood CBD yet frequently patronize
  nearby retail areas, typically shopping centers.

Sixty of the shoppers responding to the CUPR survey were Englewood
residents. The remainder came from numerous nearby Bergen County communities including Englewood Cliffs, Tenafly, Teaneck, Cresskill,
Alpine, Leonia, and Fort Lee (see Exhibit I-2). This profile is very
slightly different from the results of the 1973 shopper survey conducted by Lawrence Alexander.[21] Alexander found that "45 percent of
those interviewed in Englewood lived there with the remainder coming
from numerous, and for the most part, Bergen County communities."[22]
Thus, over a decade the Englewood CBD has become slightly more localized as far as shopper draw is concerned.
    Englewood customers typically have been long-term patrons. When
asked "How many years have you been buying in Englewood?", only
one-eighth replied 10 years or less while about 40 percent indicated
they had frequented the Englewood downtown for at least 15 years (see
Exhibit 4-7). There is then a parallelism of long established Englewood merchants serving long-term customers.
    Young, middle-aged, and older individuals patronize the Englewood
CBD. Englewood shoppers are typically middle-aged however, with the
median being about 40 to 45 years old. This age profile corresponds to
the Alexander finding that 56 percent of Englewood's customers were
middle-aged, 29 percent were young, while 15 percent were elderly.[23]
    Englewood shoppers display a range of affluence; a quarter, mainly
elderly shoppers, earn less than $10,000 annually (household income)
while almost one-fifth enjoy a $70,000 or greater income (see Exhibit
4-7). Typically, however, those patronizing the Englewood downtown are
middle-income with median household yearly earnings of very roughly
$25,000.
    The CUPR survey reveals that the CBD shopper is usually white yet a
strong minority presence is evident. About two-thirds were Caucasian,
the remainder minority. This profile is very similar to that indicated
by Alexander in 1973 that 72 percent of Englewood's shoppers were
white, 28 percent nonwhite.[24]

Considerably more women than men patronize the Englewood CBD. Sixty-nine percent of those interviewed by CUPR were female, 31 percent male. Again this finding is nearly identical to the Alexander shopper profile of 76 percent women, 24 percent men.[25]

Approximately three out of four Englewood customers come to the downtown by car while the remainder either use a bus, taxi, or other means of conveyance (e.g. bicycle) and sometime walk. Shopper reliance on the automobile appears to have increased slightly over time for the 1973 Alexander survey indicated that only 6 out of 10 Englewood shoppers relied on the automobile.[26] While this change to enhanced auto-dependence may have occurred, it is noteworthy that even today those coming to the Englewood CBD use a car less often than when shopping in other areas where a car is almost universally utilized (97 percent of the time) as a means of transportation.

"Other" retail areas frequented by the Englewood shoppers are typically nearby shopping centers including Hackensack's Riverside Square (patronized by 80 percent of those interviewed) and the Paramus malls such as the Paramus Park, Paramus Fashion Center, Bergen Mall, Garden State Plaza, and Alexanders (visited by 50-70 percent of those surveyed). Retail areas of nearby communities are patronized including those of Teaneck, Leonia, and Bergenfield. Manhattan's proximity and its potpourri of retail establishments also lures many Englewood customers; 65 percent of those interviewed shop Manhattan stores. These myriad areas are visited quite frequently: Englewood 3 times or more a month, and Riverside Square, Paramus Park, and Bergen Mall, about one to two times monthly.

Englewood shoppers thus have access to and patronize nearby shopping centers. What characteristics draw these individuals to malls; what features attract them to Englewood? To ascertain the strength/weaknesses of the older suburb retail sector, CUPR asked Englewood shoppers and retailers to evaluate various features of the Englewood CBD including: appearance, traffic, parking facilities, and merchandising, customer relations (see Exhibit 4-8). Respondents could rank these downtown characteristics on a five-point scale:

1. critical problem
2. slight problem
3. neutral (neither problem nor advantage)
4. slight advantage
5. major advantage

Their rankings are shown in Exhibit 4-8. The discussion below draws on this evaluation as well as interviews conducted in prior studies of the Englewood CBD (Lawrence Alexander 1973, and Virginia Miles, 1977).[27]

The ills of the older suburb downtown are legion especially relative to free standing shopping centers. Traveling to shop is a first hurdle. While it may be physically farther to a shopping center than to a mature suburb CBD, the fact that the latter is typically located off fast-moving, limited access roads makes the trip less burdensome than

EXHIBIT 4-8

**Mature Suburb Retailer-Shopper Ratings of
CBD Characteristics: Englewood, New Jersey — 1982**

CBD CHARACTERISTIC		Retailer(R)-Shopper(S) Quality Ratings					
		Critical Problem	Slight Problem	Neutral	Slight Advantage	Major Advantage	TOTAL
ENGLEWOOD CBD		Percentage Responding (n=100) [a]					
Appearance							
Design	R [b] [c]	9.5%	29.8%	53.6%	6.0%	1.2%	100.0%
	S	13.2	30.8	45.1	6.6	4.4	100.0
Cleanliness	R	23.3	44.4	15.6	12.2	4.4	100.0
	S	12.6	37.9	24.2	18.9	6.3	100.0
Sign Quality	R	9.5	33.3	46.4	10.7	0.0	100.0
	S	5.7	34.5	47.1	6.9	5.7	100.0
Sign Maintenance	R	4.9	37.8	48.8	7.3	1.2	100.0
	S	5.1	32.1	47.4	10.3	5.1	100.0
CBD Traffic							
Access to CBD	R	29.5	17.0	22.7	18.2	12.5	100.0
	S	22.1	35.8	22.1	6.3	13.7	100.0
Traffic Movement Within CBD	R	36.0	30.9	16.9	12.4	4.5	100.0
	S	43.6	45.7	5.3	2.1	3.2	100.0
CBD Parking							
Number of Spaces	R	49.4	30.3	6.7	11.2	2.2	100.0
	S	21.3	51.1	17.0	7.4	3.2	100.0
Parking Location	R	37.9	23.0	14.9	16.1	8.0	100.0
	S	23.5	41.8	16.3	9.2	9.2	100.0
Parking Cost	R	17.1	24.4	45.1	8.5	4.9	100.0
	S	4.2	14.7	62.1	8.4	10.5	100.0
CBD Facilities							
Pedestrian-Auto Conflict	R	20.7	26.8	47.6	3.7	1.2	100.0
	S	16.5	39.2	36.1	4.1	4.1	100.0
Eating Establishments	R	17.9	31.0	22.6	21.4	7.1	100.0
	S	24.2	31.9	27.5	13.2	3.3	100.0
Other Convenience [b]	R	29.5	25.6	33.3	5.1	6.4	100.0
	S	28.9	48.5	17.5	4.1	0.0	100.0
Lighting	R	20.2	23.8	28.6	20.2	7.1	100.0
	S	7.5	21.5	47.3	20.4	3.2	100.0
Security	R	55.8	29.1	10.5	3.5	1.2	100.0
	S	31.2	26.9	30.1	9.7	2.2	100.0
CBD Merchandising-Customer Relations							
Product Selection Variety	R	5.0	12.5	35.0	23.7	23.7	100.0
	S	16.3	12.0	26.1	32.6	13.0	100.0
Product Quality	R	4.9	4.9	33.3	39.5	17.3	100.0
	S	3.3	21.1	21.1	32.2	22.2	100.0
Product Pricing	R	4.9	14.6	50.0	23.2	7.3	100.0
	S	13.2	25.3	29.7	28.6	3.3	100.0
Product Display	R	6.1	13.4	45.1	26.8	8.5	100.0
	S	2.2	12.1	49.5	27.5	8.8	100.0
Customer Servicing	R	3.7	9.8	46.3	19.5	20.7	100.0
	S	4.5	10.1	22.5	27.0	36.0	100.0
Store Hours	R	13.1	15.5	45.2	19.0	7.1	100.0
	S	14.9	21.3	50.0	10.6	3.2	100.0
Absence of Department Store	R	14.1	23.1	43.6	10.3	9.0	100.0
	S	30.4	35.9	23.9	5.4	4.3	100.0
Competition from Other Shopping Districts	R	31.1	35.1	28.4	4.1	1.4	100.0
	S	54.0	24.1	19.5	0.0	2.3	100.0
CBD Community-Public Attitude							
Overall Community Concern	R	28.9	26.3	19.7	19.7	5.3	100.0
	S	29.6	19.8	34.6	11.1	4.9	100.0
Downtown Businesses' Concern	R	24.7	19.5	23.4	23.4	9.1	100.0
	S	22.4	21.1	36.8	11.8	7.9	100.0

Notes: [a] Actual number of respondents to individual questions may be less than 100.
[b] Such as benches, fountains, restrooms.
[c] R = Retailer responses.
[d] S = Shopper responses.

Source: Rutgers University Center for Urban Policy Research survey of Englewood retailers and shoppers, Spring 1982.

fighting the former's local traffic. About three-quarters of the Englewood retailers-shoppers felt that traffic access to and traffic movement within this community's retail area was problematical (see Exhibit 4-8). The following shopper comments are illustrative:[28]

> Trucks and angle parking on Palisade Avenue bring (movement) to a crawl. Wastes too much time.

> Riverside Square is so much easier to get to.

Once having reached the mature suburb, a shopper is confronted with parking problems. Parking in such areas typically involves some cost, frequently for meters. Meters are not expensive in an absolute sense; however, they represent an inconvenience -- they must be "fed" and offer the "danger" that a prolonged shopper sojourn will result in a parking ticket. As expressed by one retailer:[29]

> Metered parking causes a major problem. And these meter maids; although they are only doing their job, are an uncomfortable thing for shoppers -- too much tension to shop.

Besides the issue of cost, the number and location of parking spaces also can be problematical in the older suburban CBD. About three-quarters of the Englewood retailers-shoppers felt these parking characteristics were a slight to critical problem (see Exhibit 4-8). Respondents complained that the most desirable spaces -- those directly in front of retail establishments -- were often unavailable because of abuses by store employees and office workers who parked there all day. While adequate parking could be found in municipal lots just off the main shopping street, Palisade Avenue, this resource was often not drawn upon because shoppers were not aware of this parking, viewed it as inconvenient, and/or were fearful for their security in the off-street lots.

Myriad older suburb parking woes stand in contrast to the parking advantages at shopping centers:[30]

> Parking at malls is free. There are no meters to feed and no overtime parking tickets. One can always find a parking space and can stay until one has finished shopping, without having to watch the time. This is an important reason why, when women want to make "a shopping trip" in which they will shop for several items, they tend to go to a mall.

> Parking in Englewood is considered to be a hassle, "a pain in the neck," a significant deterrent to shopping there, an important reason for doing only one-item shopping there (as opposed to making "shopping trips" for multi-items to malls). One often has to go around and around the block to find a parking space, which is made difficult by the one-way streets, depending on the direction one is coming from. For some women, after going around the

block looking for a parking space, it is easier to just keep going to Route 4 and a mall, or up Engle Street to Tenafly or Closter.

Women do not like to have to watch the time and feed the meter. They are very emotional about this. Further, getting an overtime parking ticket is regarded as adding insult to injury. One ticket can cause a woman to swear she will never shop in Englewood again! Meters make lingering in Englewood to make a shopping trip difficult, if not impossible. People also dislike angle parking, because each person pulling out holds up traffic on the whole block.

Some women were not aware of private parking lots belonging to certain stores, nor of off-Palisade Avenue parking lots.

Once having secured parking, the shopper in the older suburb is confronted by certain less-than-desirable CBD characteristics. The overall appearance is often unattractive. Stores are typically old and sometimes shabby. Signs, window displays, facade treatments, etc. are often disparate to the point of distraction, are sometimes in poor taste, and in addition are not always adequately maintained. Streetscape quality is further eroded by litter and a crumbling infrastructure (e.g. cracked sidewalks, curbs, streetlights, etc.). These drawbacks are illustrated by the following Englewood retailer-shopper comments:[31]

sidewalks are always littered with soda bottles and cans and cigarette butts. Signs protrude.

"honky-tonk" appearance

no harmony with signs

sidewalks all too old

many buildings need face lift, litter in front of fast food places is a major contribution to unclean streets and sidewalks.

Older suburb CBD ambiance is made worse by the absence of certain facilities and amenities (see Exhibit 4-7). Englewood retailers-shoppers bemoaned the scarcity of eating establishments; food and luncheonettes were to be found; however, there were inadequate restaurants with the exception of the upscale Railroad Cafe and that was considered by many to be too expensive. Creature comforts such as public benches, fountains, restrooms, etc. were lacking. There was also fear for personal safety. Retailers and shoppers complained of dangerous pedestrian-automobile conflicts especially at two major intersections (Palisade and Engle, Palisade and Dean). Apprehensions concerning bodily harm from crime were also voiced. About three-quarters of those interviewed felt downtown security was a problem. Shoppers were fearful of loiterers, purse snatching, etc.; retailers feared break-ins and harassment of their customers. The following comments are telling:[32]

> Fear (for safety) of walking sidewalks particularly west of railroad tracks.

> During busy hours I feel safe along Palisade Avenue, but I hang on to my handbag tightly during "off hours" on the side streets.

> Downtown not as garish as used to be [however], hate huge billboards on intersection of Palisade and Grand.

> Loitering around McDonalds menacing and unsightly.

> People always coming into my store to use the restrooms.

Patronizing shopping centers, in contrast, is viewed as being easier, safer, and more entertaining in its own right. Malls provide the shopping and in many cases the recreational and cultural excitement once found in cities and older suburbs alike:[33]

> There is more fun and excitement at malls. Shopping at malls is more of a treat, shopping as entertainment. At malls there is much to look at: lots of people, stores, windows, displays, plantings, action.

> A mall gives a woman a kind of day off, when she wants to spend several hours shopping -- a break from the usual.

> It is not fun or exciting to shop in Englewood. It is not fun to walk around -- Palisade Avenue has no glamour, is a little tacky, is not pretty, is not elegant, is purely utilitarian. The present ambiance cannot compare to most malls. Far from a treat, shopping in Englewood takes endurance.

> Part of the fun of a mall is a choice of restaurants to eat in. Often two women go shopping together, and lunch is a pleasant break....Englewood does not have a pleasant place to have lunch.

> Palisade Avenue doesn't even look like the suburbs. Rather, it looks like part of a city that is maybe over the hill -- "the kind I moved to get away from."

> [It] is difficult to cross the street, especially at the corners on red and green. Younger women who shop with young children or babies in strollers are particularly fearful.

Despite these many drawbacks, mature suburbs are still important retail centers. Englewood is illustrative. It is surrounded by a sea of nearby shopping facilities; half a dozen suburban shopping centers as well as Manhattan's retail clustering lie within a 15-minute drive. Notwithstanding such stiff competition, Englewood shows a respectable retail performance. What draws customers to such an older suburb?

Convenience is surely a factor. The Englewood CBD serves a local market -- residents of Englewood and nearby communities -- and for this audience the Englewood stores are right at hand. As expressed by one shopper, "it is near to my home and office -- gives an easy, quick shopping ability, why go to the highway?"[34] Englewood shopping is not only convenient, it is one's own; numerous respondents stated they shopped in town specifically to support local merchants. Local boosterism was expressed in such terms as "they're our stores," "why support Bergenfield," "we sink or swim together," and "I support all good things in my town."[35]

Convenience and town fidelity alone cannot explain Englewood's current (1982) roughly $200 million sales volume. Shoppers come to this community for a retail experience unavailable at free-standing centers. Personal service and interest is a prime attraction of the older suburb. The shopping center's large scale, in part a virtue for the variety and anonymity it offers, disallows much personal attention. Customers are not known by name, their health and good fortune are not inquired after, previous purchases are not remembered, personal likes and dislikes are forgotten, etc. Frequent shopping center understaffing and high turnover also means that salespersons are often not readily available nor very knowledgeable.

The smaller scale, long tenure, and owner involvement of older suburb retail offers the potential, if not always the reality, of more personal, knowledgeable service. About two-thirds of the Englewood shoppers interviewed felt that superior service was an important downtown advantage. The following responses to "Why do you shop in Englewood?" are revealing:[36]

> Better service, better relationship with store which knows one as a regular customer, deals with any problems effectively. I do not like department stores -- mass confusion -- shopping more personal in Englewood.

> Malls allow people anonymity, privacy. However, women say that at the malls, many times sales clerks (particularly in department stores) couldn't care less. Some women complain about this, want better and more caring service.[37]

In addition to service, another retail advantage of the older suburb is superior product quality and merchandising. This is not to say that quality is absent at better department stores or that low quality goods are not found in mature suburbs. The quality we are referring to here encompasses the taste, display, and range of goods found in some of the better specialized, older suburb retail establishments. Comments regarding two Englewood stores are illustrative.[38]

I purchase all my children's clothes at Sahadi's because they have the best fashion quality goods. Alexanders has junk, Bambergers is better, yet uneven. Bloomingdales and Saks at Riverside Square are fine (but) Sahadi makes its money only selling (clothes) and it shows.

Carl's House of Silver has the best selection in New Jersey.

It would be overstating the case that Englewood is a customer's paradise, offering uniformly superior service and products. Numerous Englewood shoppers interviewed by CUPR voiced personal gripes such as: "shoddy merchandise especially on West Palisade," "inadequate snow removal by store owners," "overt racism -- including following minority group customers around the store," "bemoans the passage of some better stores such as Cloth and Clothes," "pushy salespeople -- I want to browse, not always buy," and "returns are easier (and) surely less personal at department stores."[39] Despite these complaints, it is still the image if not always the reality of better retail service, products, and merchandising that draws many consumers to Englewood.

Many Englewood retailers interviewed by CUPR recognized the importance of maintaining service product and merchandising quality and perhaps even more important, an overall upscale image of the downtown. This sentiment was reflected in their recommendations that the CBD would be enhanced by such additions as a "first-rate, French-style bakery," "classy food store such as Zabars in Manhattan," and "more boutique establishments such as those found on Engle Street."[40]

The service, product, and merchandising characteristics mentioned thus far surely have an impact on prices: quality stores cannot offer steep discounts. About a third of the Englewood shoppers interviewed by CUPR complained that downtown prices were too high. (Interestingly, this was the only CBD trait for which shopper evaluations differed significantly from retailer perceptions.) The overwhelming majority of respondents, however, accepted the price consequences of Englewood's retail advantages.

Englewood Retailer-Shopper Profile: Summary
and Comparison to Other Older Suburbs

While it is difficult to define the "average" Englewood retail establishment or customer, CUPR's survey of downtown merchants and shoppers reveals the following profile. Englewood's downtown consists of a collection of small, diverse, long-established stores catering predominantly to a local market and selling largely what are classified as "other" goods. Englewood shoppers are typically middle-aged, middle-income, white (with a strong minority presence), women who have been long-time patrons of the CBD yet frequently shop other areas as well, especially nearby shopping centers. Englewood shoppers dislike such CBD characteristics as traffic and parking difficulties, shabby and/or confusing physical appearance, scarcity of certain amenities

(e.g. better restaurants, benches, fountains, restrooms), and incipient personal safety problems. Shoppers are drawn to the CBD because
of convenience, loyalty and the image, if not always the realization,
of superior service, products, and merchandising.

Many of the above features also likely characterize other mature
suburban retail areas. Concrete evidence of such similarity is shown
in Exhibit 4-9 which compares Englewood retailer-shopper profiles to
those of older Long Island suburban retail centers (e.g. Hempstead,
Babylon, Cedarhurst, etc.).[41] Englewood is far from unique. About
two-thirds of its shoppers are local residents -- a share almost
identical to that found in the mature Long Island suburbs. A similar
close match is found when shopper race, sex, and age traits are
examined (see Exhibit 4-9). Englewood customers complain of parking,
CBD appearance, and security problems. Similar gripes are voiced by
the Long Island shoppers.[42] There are also parallelisms in retailer
profiles: both Englewood and the mature Long Island suburban downtowns
are characterized by long-established merchants offering mostly
"other" as opposed to "shoppers" goods.

Exhibit 4-9 also lists selected shopper profiles at a New Jersey
shopping center (Paramus Park) and urban downtown (Jersey City).
Shoppers are oldest in urban areas, youngest in shopping centers;
predominantly female in urban areas, while a rough male-female parity
is evident at centers; and are overwhelmingly local residents in the
urban case, while the converse is evident with respect to center customers. Interestingly, older suburb shopper traits stand roughly mid-
way between those at shopping centers and cities. Mature suburb customers are: younger than in urban areas yet older than the center
profile; disproportionately female compared to centers yet less so
than in urban locations; and are more often local residents than at
centers yet not to the same extent as in cities.

The older suburb retail profile points to both strengths and weaknesses. A loyal, local customer emphasis suggests a strong almost
captive retail base yet also augurs a limited potential for future
sales expansion. The middle-aged accentuation of the mature suburb
shopper promises a relatively more affluent customer, however, also
indicates that not many new patrons have been attracted. Similarly,
older suburb retailer longevity is both a sign of stability and one of
weakness, reflecting the limited number of new merchants coming to the
CBD.

The advantages and disadvantages of the mature suburb commercial
environment also place it in a vulnerable position. Attractions of
older suburb retail -- superior service, products, and merchandising -- are difficult and expensive to continue. An error in restock-
ing, a discourteous sales clerk, some resistance to returned goods,
etc. can quickly lose a customer forever. Moreover, the downside of
mature downtown -- traffic congestion, shabbiness, security apprehensions -- often has its own self-building, destructive momentum, which
is difficult to correct. It is therefore particularly important to
consider how the older suburbs' retail sector can be bolstered.

EXHIBIT 4-9

Shopper Profile: Mature Suburbs, Shopping Center, and Urban Center

	SHOPPER CHARACTERISTICS									
	Age[a]				Sex		Race		Residence	
AREA	Under 25	25-40	41-65	Over 65	M[b]	F[c]	C[d]	M[e]	Local[f]	Non-Local[g]
MATURE SUBURBS										
New Jersey [h]										
Englewood	14%	36%	39%	11%	31%	69%	68%	32%	60%	40%
Long Island [i] *(New York)*										
Babylon [f]	11	40	32	17	43	57	NA [l]	NA	49	51
Bay Shore	24	34	26	16	NA	NA	70	30	NA	NA
Cedarhurst	0	77	19	4	NA	NA	NA	NA	53	47
Freeport	19	29	32	20	22	78	71	20	67	33
Garden City	9	35	46	10	4	96	NA	NA	NA	NA
Glen Cove	12	38	35	15	25	75	93	5	70	30
Great Neck	13	38	32	17	17	83	NA	NA	52	48
Hempstead	32	42	18	8	30	62	42	50	NA	NA
Huntington	24	50	22	4	37	54	NA	NA	NA	NA
Long Beach	14	37	31	18	48	48	76	22	56	44
Manhasset	25	35	25	15	27	73	NA	NA	58	42
Port Washington	16	40	32	12	28	67	86	6	NA	NA
Smithtown	12	65	23	0	36	55	98	1	NA	NA
Valley Stream	9	60	26	5	16	84	NA	NA	96	4
Average	16	44	29	11	28	69	76	21	62	38
SHOPPING CENTER [j]										
Paramus Park [l]	Median 32				58	42	NA	NA	5	95
URBAN CENTER										
Jersey City [k]	Median 44				80	20	52	38	77	23

Notes:
[a] Approximate; age cohorts have been collapsed in some cases.
[b] Male
[c] Female
[d] Caucasian
[e] Minority
[f] Shopper lives in indicated local community.
[g] Shopper does not live in indicated local community.
[h] *Source:* Rutgers University Center for Urban Policy Research survey, 1982.
[i] *Source:* Barry Berman (editor), An Evaluation of Selected Business Districts in Nassau, Suffolk and Queens, Hofstra University Yearbook of Business, Series 15, Vol. 5 (Hempstead, Hofstra University, 1980).
[j] Rouse Corporation, Department of Market Research, "Attitudinal Shoppers Survey, Paramus Park" (1975) and Summary of Findings, Paramus Park Survey, 1979.
[k] Survey conducted by National Center for Telephone Research for Hartz Industries (1979).
[l] NA=Information not available.

STRENGTHENING OLDER SUBURB RETAIL TRADE:
ENGLEWOOD CASE STUDY ANALYSIS

Englewood displays many of the strengths and weaknesses of the mature suburb retail environment. Strategies to revitalize Englewood's CBD point the way to how these communities as a group can stem further retail erosion.

The Conceptual Frame:
Needed -- A Dose of Realism

Realism concerning metropolitan retail shifts and private-public revitalization resources is essential. Englewood and many sister localities have had plans for grandiose CBD schemes which in effect try to recreate suburban shopping centers in the older suburb. Examples include attracting department stores to act as downtown anchors, closing streets and building pedestrian-only malls, enclosing portions of the CBD, and so on. Mature suburbs can learn from the suburban shopping center retail approach; however, it is misguided to clone the latter in the former. Shopping centers are shopping goods dynamos, concentrating on general merchandise, apparel for the family, household items, furniture, and so on. These retail categories are no longer handled with any significance in older suburbs. It is fighting retail history to bring back department store shopping to these communities.

Retailer economics are a related consideration. Department store construction costs are so high that such development makes sense only when significant shopper volume can be envisioned -- an unlikely situation in most older suburbs. Competitive pressures are a further hurdle. Mature suburbs are typically located in close-in locations to urban centers. This retail belt is already well serviced by a near saturation of existing, free-standing suburban shopping centers as well as in some cases by a newly-invigorated urban retail core. Englewood is illustrative. It is surrounded by older shopping centers (e.g., Paramus malls), new center entrants (e.g., Riverside Square), and a fabulous Manhattan retail revitalization. Given such competition will a department store locate in Englewood?

Realism regarding the resources and attitudes of older suburb retailers is also important. If the Englewood survey is indicative, these individuals are wary about the future. Englewood retailers are thinking consolidation -- holding their current position -- rather than expanding. Some were even apprehensive they could hold "their own" as is evident from the following comments: "Why invest if business continues to be bad?" or "Another mall like Riverside could be devastating." There was also far-from-uniform confidence in the future of the Englewood CBD. When asked their opinion on this issue, Englewood retailers were equally divided -- half gave positive responses, the remainder negative.

Private hesitation in investing in mature suburb downtown revitalization efforts could, in part, be offset if public monies were avail-

able. Such support in significant amounts is not forthcoming. Older
suburb municipal governments are often fiscally hard pressed themselves and are thus unable to make major financial commitments to improve their downtowns. Major public capital improvements for roads,
malls, sidewalks, parking lots, etc., are especially unlikely. Prospects for extralocal public assistance from the state and federal governments are also not good. These governmental bodies, confronting
financial hard times themselves, have substantially cut back their
economic development assistance. Furthermore, remaining subsidies are
often slotted to the most needy localities, a targeting which typically puts older suburbs at a disadvantage relative to cities. To illustrate, all of the New Jersey urban communities referred to in chapter
one are eligible for Urban Development Action Grants (UDAG), the most
significant current federal downtown revitalization subsidy. In contrast, only a handful of the mature suburbs (Plainfield, Montclair,
and New Brunswick) qualify for UDAG. Englewood and many sister communities are ineligible. In short, retail renewal strategies for older
suburbs must be cognizant of the very real retail shifts which have
occurred in the metropolitan area and the current realities of limited
merchant and public financial resources.

Retail Revitalization Specifics:
A Proposed Englewood Agenda

Given these limitations what can be done? An overall strategy would
address the drawbacks and enhance the strengths of the older mature
suburb retail environment.[43] The following agenda, designed for Englewood, is applicable in many sister communities as well.

Parking in downtown Englewood is one of the prime annoyances of
shopping there especially when compared to the ease of this task at
nearby, freestanding centers. Improving the parking situation is thus
a first item of importance. This problem fortunately lends itself to
correction because Englewood, as many older suburbs, has expanded its
parking resources. Numerous previous studies[44] have indicated that
Englewood has sufficient parking spaces for its retail size. Parking
woes can thus be alleviated by better utilization of existing resources. Prime parking spots in front of Palisade Avenue stores are
often occupied for long periods of time by Englewood merchants, their
workers, and others (e.g., bank and office employees). This practice
forces shoppers to cruise Palisade Avenue or park off this street --
both currently unpleasant alternatives. The remedy for extended re-
tailer-employee parking and attendant meter feeding should not be
merely one of enforcing current parking time limitations on Palisade
Avenue. Such a "ticket" approach in general should be reconsidered
given the frustration it adds to shopping downtown Englewood. A self-
education-enforcement policy on the part of Englewood merchants, main
street financial institutions, and other employers is far preferable
to curb parking abuses. Their economic prosperity rests with improved
shopper and other downtown user access. Should they not then abstain
from taking for their own use the most convenient CBD parking?

Instead of parking on the main street, the Englewood business community should utilize the many off-Palisade Avenue lots. Shoppers too should be encouraged to take similar advantage of this relatively bountiful resource. Such customer utilization would be facilitated if: 1) these lots would be patrolled more frequently by the Englewood police so as to forestall security apprehensions; 2) better information concerning the location of the off-street lots would be provided through such means as a give-away booklet, flyer, or map, and public directional signs; 3) parking meters in off-Palisade Avenue lots would be removed so as to make these locations a "best-buy and worry free" parking resource; and 4) direct access from stores to off-lot parking would be provided. This last feature, already available in such nearby sister communities as Bergenfield, was commented on favorably by numerous Englewood shoppers.

Overall appearances also demand improvement. A decade ago the prescription for this particular CBD malady was a full blown store facade-sidewalk-street mall transformation. This remedy is now being questioned. It is expensive in an era when retailer and even public resources are strained. It sometimes compounds other problems such as becoming a magnet for loiterers, posing public safety difficulties by offering concealed vantage points, eliminating main-street automobile access to stores, and so on. The conceptual underpinning of the mall approach -- provision of shopping center-like amenities -- has also been called into question. Mature suburb malls are a poor physical substitute for the fully enclosed and controlled shopping environment offered by free standing centers. The latter also offer an entertainment value inherent in its sheer scale of shoppers and stores against which an older suburb pedestrian mall simply cannot compete.

A less expensive CBD refurbishing strategy deserves consideration. Relatively low cost amenities should be provided by Englewood retailers and/or the city. Examples include vandal-proof benches, planters, information booths, waste receptacles and bicycle racks. These items provide needed creature comforts. In addition, creatively placed and designed, they can enliven the main shopping street and provide focal points to visually segment the 2,400 foot Palisade Avenue main street into more appealing, smaller sections.

Further visual improvement would be provided by a more uniform store facade-sign treatment replacing the current discord of Palisade Avenue. Common themes, materials, etc., for signs and facades offer a sense of symmetry and continuity. Thoughtfully done, common signs and facades can also play an important marketing role, wooing and informing customers.

Englewood currently has a sign review committee and related ordinances designed to achieve some of the advantages cited above. These efforts do not go far enough because they are not mandatory; they merely regulate changes contemplated by retailers rather than forcing all merchants to provide a united visual front. Consideration should therefore be given to adopting mandatory facade and sign standards. Such an approach has worked well in other older retail areas such as Baltimore's Old Town:[45]

> The merchants agreed, and the ordinance to approve the Old Town plan provided for mandatory standards....
>
> Surprisingly, the mandatory standards were attractive to many merchants who were willing to rehabilitate their stores, but who doubted that their neighbors would do so without mandatory controls. In many cases, merchants were disturbed less by the cost of rehabilitation than by the thought that their neighbors might do nothing and benefit from rehabilitation by others. The thought of a "free ride" for some merchants was almost unbearable.

To lessen the financial demands and sometimes hardship of the mandatory standards, Englewood should allow a reasonable period, say two to three years, for their satisfaction. Financial assistance is also in order. Englewood's Downtown Facade Improvement Loan Program (DFILP) provides an in-place vehicle for such financial aid. DFILP draws on public funds as well as low cost private monies made available by local financial institutions concerned about downtown revitalization. It makes available reduced interest rate loans, small grants, as well as facade design and construction specification-inspection services. CUPR's survey revealed that most Englewood merchants were favorably disposed towards DFILP, albeit many knew little about the program. (It had been in existence only a short period of time when the survey was conducted.) This favorable attitude, coupled with the fact that DFILP does not demand deep public subsidies, makes this in-place program an ideal base for financing mandatory facade and sign improvements.

As a further financial prop, Englewood should not penalize merchants making improvements by automatically increasing their property assessment and thus taxation. A more constructive approach should be adhered to. The city should consider property tax abatement-reduction whereby assessments would not be increased or would be adjusted only marginally in cases of facade or sign improvements. (Possible state statutory restrictions/encouragement for such a policy should be checked.) At minimum, Englewood should not immediately nor automatically increase assessments in instances of commercial improvements. Such sensitive taxation treatment has worked effectively in other jurisdictions:[46]

> Store owners also were concerned about the impact of expenditures for rehabilitation on property tax assessment. With the assessor's assistance, however, the planners were able to convince the merchants that assessment would not be increased merely because improvements were made. Only when actual sales and rents indicated a rise in property values would assessments be raised. (An eager assessor increased the assessment of the first merchant to get a permit by the cost of rehabilitation, but he was successfully overruled when planners and merchants protested.)

A further older suburb retail problem -- apprehension concerning
security -- demands a significant response. Would-be shoppers will
tolerate parking, shabby appearance, and other annoyances, but will go
elsewhere if they fear that the downtown is unsafe. Such concern requires treatment at its source. Pedestrian-auto conflicts can be reduced by signaling changes at busy interchanges so as to give shoppers
protected passage, free from turning cars. This change was recommended
by many Englewood retailers and shoppers for the busy Palisade-Dean
and Palisade-Engle crossings. As commented on by retailers:[47]

> Need red signal in all directions for 30 seconds at intersections
> to allow pedestrians to cross safely. We had it in the past, but
> was discontinued.

> Palisade Avenue and Grand and Engle Street corner is the most
> hazardous pedestrian crossing in the U. S. of A. Let us deal with
> this with better signaling.

Crime in the older suburb CBD is far less tractable. Improved lighting is one deterrent. Expanded, visible police patrol is another important step, one recommended by numerous Englewood retailers and
shoppers:[48]

> Police need to walk the beat or use motorized bikes.

> Visibility of police should be more prominent in CBD. Many shop-
> pers comment on their concern for safety on W. Palisade Avenue.
> Loitering by groups of youths should be discouraged by police.

> We must have visible protection during shopping hours and during
> night hours to entice people to shop. This worked during Christ-
> mas. Why can't the city provide patrols year round?

In addition, the public's image of crime as a problem in older suburbs could, in part, be neutralized by pointing to growing crime problems at shopping centers. The "universalization" of crime theme would
stress that:[49]

> Safety is not a major differentiating factor between
> malls and older suburbs -- it has deteriorated every-
> where. Malls have loiterers and roving youths. Malls have
> purse snatchings, auto thefts, car break-ins, and so on.

We thus far have been concentrating on addressing the negative aspects of the mature suburb retail environment. Equally as important is
accentuating and publicizing positive characteristics. Shoppers come
to an older suburb in part because of convenience. This benefit should
be stressed via a marketing campaign. Possible marketing efforts,
using Englewood as an example, include: "Time is money -- shop Englewood," "Englewood -- 300 stores five minutes from home," or "Englewood

-- a $200 million retail giant at your doorstep." A loyalty theme can also be emphasized such as "shop local, shop Englewood," "Englewood -- local merchants serving you," or "Englewood -- your downtown."

The special retail characteristics of the mature suburb -- personal service and superior quality merchandising -- deserve special emphasis to differentiate these older downtowns from shopping centers. Englewood is again illustrative. A marketing campaign for this community should emphasize such features as: "Englewood -- knowledgeable merchants who know you," "Englewood -- quality individual stores instead of malls," or "Englewood -- for the smart shopper." Such image promotion should be coupled with informational advertising to dispel possible negative shopper perceptions of the Englewood CBD relative to shopping centers such as higher prices, limited selection, and/or reluctant return policies. As discussed in a prior Englewood retail study:[50]

> Image advertising can also help overcome certain consumer feelings, e.g., embarrassment about returning something to a small local store. It is often helpful to just acknowledge consumer feelings, with a question headline that is answered in the copy, with individual store examples where relevant. For example, a headline might be: "Do you feel embarrassed to return something in a small local store?" Copy would then reassure, with reason-why....

> Bold question headlines can work very well. For example, DO YOU THINK THE PRICES AT ENGLEWOOD STORES ARE HIGHER THAN AT MALLS? NOW LEARN THE TRUTH! Followed by illustrations of actual price comparisons for specific items at specific stores....

> Also, merchants should clarify what they carry, since many customers are unaware of their variety of merchandise. Some might consider running a left-hand panel in all their full-page advertising, with a heading: DID YOU KNOW THAT WE STOCK ALL THE FOLLOWING? Followed by a complete list of types of merchandise.

Accentuating the retail attributes of the older suburb must go beyond mere advertising. Superior service, products, and merchandising must be reinforced constantly. Englewood is again illustrative. Its CBD could be bolstered by:

1. Expanding Englewood's retail line to include more boutique-specialty stores such as a "French bakery," "Zabars food emporium," better quality junior size women's clothing, etc.[51]

2. Merchandising with a theme, e.g., numerous retailers could display, advertise, and in other ways, promote goods with a unified theme such as imported cameras, clothes, rugs, paintings, and accessories.

3. Providing quality, convenience and amenities ranging from better
   eating facilities to special events such as lunch-hour concerts.
   Numerous Englewood retailers and shoppers pointed approvingly to
   the Railroad Cafe (a first-class restaurant converted from an
   older railroad station) and the John Harms Englewood Plaza (a
   cultural complex converted from an old movie house; see chapter
   five) as two downtown resources reinforcing Englewood's quality
   image.

The point of these activities is not to have the older suburbs directly compete with shopping centers but rather to differentiate the
former from the latter so as to secure a special, enduring retail
niche. Concede most general shopping goods to shopping centers. Admit
that older downtowns simply do not have the scale, controlled physical
environment, and entertainment value of freestanding malls. Fight,
however, for the local, convenient, quality goods-merchandising, retail role of the older suburb.

Who should be responsible for the mature suburb retail revitalization? Cooperative public and private action is necesary.[52] City government must do its part. In Englewood's case, the municipal government should:

1. provide the police manpower to actively and visibly patrol the
   CBD;

2. address the anti-pedestrian conflict at hazardous intersections
   such as Palisade and Grand;

3. examine ways to encourage off-Palisade parking and in general
   should reconsider its CBD parking enforcement via ticketing; provide assistance for small-scale downtown -- streetscape improvements such as adding signs, trash receptacles, etc.;

4. provide assistance for small-scale downtown streetscape improvements such as adding signs, trash receptacles, etc.;

5. adopt a mandatory sign-facade ordinance as discussed in this
   chapter;

6. continue/expand the facade improvement loan program and seek continued private-public financing (e.g., combine local bank participation and CBDG funds);

7. adopt a sensitive property tax assessment policy to encourage
   rather than discourage sign-facade improvements;

8. support/expand current revitalization efforts by the Englewood
   Economic Development Corporation (EDC). (The EDC has assisted the
   adaptive reuse of the Railroad Cafe and is considering other en-
   deavors such as purchasing/renovating properties near the John
   Harms Theatre); and

9. be receptive to supporting organizational/taxation mechanisms to foster coordinated retail marketing and improvements such as a special assessment district (see discussion later in this chapter).

Vocalized city recognition of the importance of and support for the downtown is also recommended. Numerous retailers surveyed by CUPR felt that city officials were not always sensitive to their needs and did not push hard enough to further their, and ultimately Englewood's, interests. While such griping is common, express actions demonstrating the city's concern and commitment to the downtown would be constructive. Possible examples include city council resolutions citing the importance of the CBD and pledging long-term support and/or appointing a city official to act as an ombudsman for retailers.

Merchants must also do their part. A retailers organization should be formed. The Englewood Chamber of Commerce already serves such a function. Its effectiveness would be enhanced if more local merchants could be encouraged to join and more importantly they played an active role. To this end, the Chamber must promote itself as an effective, self-interest organization which has the ears of city officials and represents all merchants -- small and large, west and east Palisade Avenue, etc.

Whatever its guise, the Englewood retailers entity should press for collective merchant support for downtown improvements. Example activities include: educating its members to curb Palisade Avenue parking abuses, supporting current Englewood revitalization initiatives such as those effected by EDC and DFILP, and lobbying for the public intervention discussed previously (e.g., streetscape and security improvements). It is especially important for the retailers group to develop merchant consensus for and support of changes entailing expenditure on their part such as mandatory sign and facade standards.

Consideration should also be given to expanding the retail association's role from just education and lobbying efforts to selected, centralized management and marketing as well. Older retail areas are characterized by disparate ownership and operation; many stores go their own way to attract customers. Such individuality, in part, is a virtue for it gives each merchant a stamp of uniqueness. The absence of a united advertising and marketing front, however, also puts mature retail areas at a disadvantage vis à vis the centralized arrangement of the freestanding mall:[53]

> The biggest difference between suburban shopping centers and older business districts is in the area of management....Shopping centers promote very actively, with coordinated advertising programs....Many shopping centers have regular special events such as style shows, sidewalk sales, and exhibits....Most...centers have professional administrators with the full-time responsibility to maintain records, coordinate maintenance, provide for security systems...do market research to identify types of busi-

nesses that could be located to meet identified demand for goods
and services...and have people call on businesses that might expand into or relocate in the center.

Older downtowns do not have coordinated management nor marketing
because they grew and developed piecemeal. This historical fact does
not mean that these locations cannot introduce after the fact at least
certain aspects of a centralized retail strategy. The Englewood retailers association discussed earlier might assume such a role. Other
organizational approaches are possible including: 1) creating a new
management organization to work under contract with the merchants'
group; or 2) contracting with existing real estate management-devel-
opment and/or advertising-public relations firms.

Whatever its specific guise, the centralized entity could perform
such tasks as: promoting the retail attractions of the older suburbs
(e.g., loyalty, convenience, quality); coordinating downtown special
events, thematic marketing, etc.; conducting retailer-shopper surveys
to ascertain gripes and perceptions concerning the downtown; effecting
other market-related studies as needed; acting in a liaison role with
city government agencies to ensure that retail interests are heard;
searching for public and private financial sources to continue-expand
programs such as the DFILP; working to reduce misunderstanding between
retailers and to catalyze merchant support for revitalization activities necessitating their investment; and promoting ancillary efforts
to bolster the downtown such as assisting the John Harms Englewood
Plaza (see chapter five).

The above activities necessitate expenditures for staff and other
resources. Centralized management and marketing costs in a shopping
mall are paid for directly by mandatory fees and the imposition of
percentage leases. A similarly secure financing source is needed for
older retail areas. One possibility is to form a special assessment
district (SAD).[54] A special assessment is defined as "a compulsory
charge on selected property for a particular improvement or service
which presumably benefits the owners of the selected property and is
also undertaken in the interests of the public."[55] Imposing a special assessment in a prescribed area constitutes a SAD. It is a vehicle increasingly turned to as a means to revitalize older retail
areas:[56]

> As downtown retailers exit to suburban shopping centers and fed-
> eral purse strings tighten, local officials and business owners
> are relying more and more on their own powers and finances to
> revitalize their CBDs. One of the most popular ideas being tested
> across the country is the downtown benefit or improvement dis-
> trict. This district, known by various names, is actually a mod-
> ern version of the 500-year-old concept of special assessments
> ....It enables communities to plan, finance, implement, and man-
> age improvements.

Numerous states including New Jersey have enacted comprehensive legislation enabling municipalities to create assessment districts. Englewood could thus authorize a SAD for its CBD. (A model ordinance was specified in the Stadtmauer Associates Englewood study.[57]) With the SAD in place, an extra property assessment would be imposed on CBD property owners on the basis of their front footage, property area, or other equitable, agreed upon allocation criteria. The income generated by the special assessment would be used to finance centralized marketing and management activities, streetscape improvements, and whatever other revitalization activities are agreed upon by the CBD business community.[58]

In short, mature suburb retail areas must walk the tightrope of adopting those shopping center features which will improve their competitiveness while at the same time working to improve and promote their unique retail features.

NOTES

1. See Raymond Vernon, The Changing Economic Function of the Central City (New York: Committee for Economic Development, 1959); George Sternlieb, The Future of the Downtown Department Store (Cambridge: The Joint Center for Urban Studies of MIT and Harvard University, 1962); George Sternlieb, "The Future of Retailing in the Downtown Core," Journal of the American Institute of Planners (May 1963), Vol. 29, No. 2, p. 102; Spindletop Research, Inc., The Suburbanization of Retail Trade -- A Study of Retail Trade Dispersion in Major U.S. Markets, 1958-1967 (New York: Spindletop Research, 1970); Brian J. Berry, "Conceptual Lags in Retail Development Policy," in George Sternlieb and James Hughes (editors), Shopping Centers: U.S.A. (New Brunswick: Rutgers University Center for Urban Policy Research, 1981), p. 29; Thomas Muller, "Regional Malls and Central City Regional Sales: An Overview," in Sternlieb and Hughes, Shopping Centers: U.S.A.; Real Estate Research Corporation, Lessons for States and Cities: Impacts of New Developments in Older Commercial Areas (Washington, D.C.: Government Printing Office, 1982).

2. George Sternlieb, "The Future of Retailing," p. 102.

3. Spindletop Research, The Suburbanization of Retail Trade, p.vii-viii.

4. P. O. Muller, Contemporary Suburban America (Englewood Cliffs: Prentice Hall, 1981); P. O. Muller, "Geographical Consequences of the Urbanization of the Suburbs" (Washington, D.C.: Association of American Geographers, 1976), Research Paper No. 25-2; R. Boyce and D. Fausler, "A Quarter Century of Downtown Decline -- The Case of CBD Retail Sales in American Cities: 1948-1972." Paper presented at Regional Science Association Meeting 1977.

5. Muller, "Regional Malls and Center City Regional Sales," p. 180.

6. See Vernon, The Changing Economic Function of the Central City.

7. D. Bennett Mazur, People, Politics and Planning: The Comparative History of Three Suburban Communities, Ph.D. Dissertation, Rutgers University, May 1981.

8. Ibid., p. 125.

9. Ibid., p. 124.

10. Ibid., p. 126.

11. Ibid., p. 127.

12. Ibid., p. 150.

13. Ibid., p. 572.

14. Ibid.

15. Ibid.

16. Ibid.

17. Urban Land Institute, <u>Englewood, New Jersey Recommendations for a Central Area Revitalization Program</u> (Washington, D.C.: ULI, 1974).

18. Urban Land Institute, <u>Dollars and Cents of Shopping Centers: 1981</u> (Washington, D.C.: ULI, 1981), p. 9.

19. One final methodological note concerns the representativeness of the CUPR surveys -- how closely the sample respondents parallel the composition of the universe of Englewood retailers/shoppers. The retailer questionnaire is strong in this respect; CUPR was able to elicit responses from a cross section of downtown merchants, retailers both on and off Palisade Avenue on both East Palisade (typically selling higher priced goods) and West Palisade (typically selling lower priced merchandise) and so on. The shopper questionnaire is less representative. This bias is a function of: 1) customers agreeing to return the distributed questionnaire are likely a "self-selected group" of more affluent individuals concerned about the future of the Englewood CBD; and 2) the League of Women Voters membership likely shares this affluence-civic interest emphasis. To improve the representativeness of the shopper survey, CUPR conducted a number of on-the-street interviews. It is likely, however, that the shopper survey still reflects some respondent bias.

20. Lawrence A. Alexander and Company, Inc., <u>Englewood Economic and Marketing Factors.</u> Report No. 1, August 1973; Lawrence A. Alexander and Company, <u>Englewood, NJ: Downtown Development Plan and Program</u> (New York: Lawrence Alexander, 1975); Urban Land Institute, <u>Englewood, New Jersey Recommendations for a Central Area Revitalization Program</u> (Washington, D.C.: ULI, 1974); Virginia Miles, "Research Findings and Retail Marketing Plan," prepared for the Retail Division, Englewood Chamber of Commerce, May 1977; Stadtmauer Associates, "Revitalization Program for Palisade Avenue, Englewood, New Jersey," September 1978.

21. Alexander, "Economic and Marketing Factors."

22. Ibid.

23. Ibid., p. 23.

24. Ibid., p. 23.

25. Ibid., p. 23.

26. Ibid., p. 28.

27. See note 20.

28. Center for Urban Policy Research survey of Englewood CBD shoppers, Spring 1982. Hereafter referred to as CUPR shoppers survey.

29. Center for Urban Policy Research survey of Englewood CBD retailers, Spring 1982. Hereafter referred to as CUPR retailer survey.

30. Miles, "Research Findings and Retail Marketing Plan," p. 10-11.

31. CUPR shopper and retailer surveys.

32. Ibid.

33. Miles, "Research Findings and Retail Marketing Plan," p. 8-9.
34. CUPR shopper survey.
35. Ibid.
36. Ibid.
37. Miles, "Research Findings and Retail Marketing Plan."
38. CUPR shopper survey.
39. Ibid.
40. CUPR retailer survey.
41. Barry Berman, <u>An Evaluation of Selected Business Districts in Nassau, Suffolk and Queens Counties</u> (Hempstead, New York: Hofstra University, 1980), Hofstra University Yearbook of Business, Series 15, Vol. 5; See also Rouse Corporation, Paramus Park (1975) and Summary of Findings, Paramus Park Survey (1979).
42. Ibid.
43. See, for example, Iowa Office for Planning and Programming, <u>Downtown Improvement Manual for Iowa Cities</u> (Des Moines: Iowa Division of Municipal Affairs, 1978); National Development Council, <u>Neighborhood Business Revitalization</u> (Washington, D.C.: The Council, 1978); Real Estate Research Corporation, <u>Analysis of Major Commercial Districts</u> (Chicago: RERC, 1978); Marie Nahikian, "Here's One City Where Commercial Rehab Works," <u>Planning</u>, Vol. 43, No. 6; (July 1977), Benjamin Goldstein, "Revitalization of Commercial Areas in Urban Neighborhoods, <u>Practicing Planner</u>, Vol. 6, No. 3 (June 1976); Michael Calvert, "Baltimore's Old Town Mall, a Prototype of Urban Neighborhood Commercial Rehab," <u>Practicing Planner</u>, Vol. 7, No. 1 (March 1977); John Sower, "Revitalizing Older Business Districts," <u>Journal of Housing</u>, Vol. 34, No. 11 (December 1977); Pennsylvania Department of Community Affairs, <u>Reports -- Central Business Districts</u> (August-September 1982); Lawrence A. Alexander, Editor, <u>Financing Downtown Action: A Practical Guide to Private and Public Land Funding Sources</u> (New York: Downtown Research and Development Center, 1975), Emanuel Berk, <u>Downtown Improvement Manual</u> (Chicago, IL: ASPO, 1976); Downtown Research and Development Center, <u>An Inside Look at Current Downtown Action Ideas</u> (New York: Downtown Idea Exchange, DRDC, 1978).
44. See note 20.
45. Calvert, "Baltimore's Old Town," p. 47.
46. Ibid.
47. CUPR retailer survey.
48. Ibid. and CUPR shopper survey.
49. Miles, "Research Findings and Retail Marketing Plan," p. 20.
50. Ibid., p. 29.
51. CUPR shopper and retailer survey.
52. See for example Adrienne Levatino, <u>Neighborhood Commercial Rehabilitation</u> (Washington, D.C.: National Association of Housing and Redevelopment Officials, 1978); National Development Council, <u>Neighborhood Business Revitalization</u> (Washington, D.C.: Council, no date).
53. Sower, "Revitalizing Older Business Districts," p. 571.
54. Ibid.
55. National Municipal League, <u>Special Assessments: A Means of Financing Municipal Improvements</u> (New York: League, 1929). Cited in

Mercurius and Werth, "Downtown Benefit Districts: New Use of an Old Tool," in PAS Memo, July 1980 (Chicago: American Planning Association, 1980). See also Downtown Research and Development Center, The Downtown District Action Guide (New York: Center, 1980).

56. Mercurius and Werth, Downtown Benefit Districts, p. 2.

57. Stadtmauer Associates, Revitalizing Englewood.

58. See Real Estate Research Corporation, Analysis of Major Commercial Districts, p. 75.

Chapter Five
The Arts As a Downtown
Revitalization Mechanism

INTRODUCTION

The previous chapter considered the most important traditional economic activity of the older suburb CBD -- retail sales. Its prognosis was sobering. Mature suburbs have been buffeted by competition from freestanding shopping centers. While the former's retail prospects can be strengthened by emphasizing its special attractions, the mature suburb realistically will never be able to achieve its yesteryear grandeur as a retail hub.

If past economic roles are no longer applicable, new identities must be searched for. A glimpse of one such new persona -- the older suburb acting as an office-hotel center -- was seen in chapter three of this study. Further new economic roles must be explored, especially for the vital downtown.

If people don't come to the mature suburb's CBD to shop as they once did, perhaps they will be attracted by cultural facilities and activities. In the past few years, many older suburbs have blossomed with theatres, often converted movie houses and similar structures, offering dance, shows, symphony, recital, opera, and other cultural events. The Arts, as this ensemble of activities will be referred to by this chapter, not only plays an important cultural role in its own right, it has the added benefit of an economic pump-priming mechanism. Cultural facilities purchase local goods, hire local residents, etc. In addition and perhaps more importantly, the Arts attract audiences who in turn patronize local restaurants, retail establishments, and hotels.

This chapter considers the Arts as a strategy to strengthen the older suburb CBD. It commences with a discussion of the merits of this approach and its application in older downtown areas across the country. The analysis then turns to the case study community, Englewood. It focuses on an existing Englewood cultural center, the John Harms Englewood Plaza (JHEP). JHEP's current economic impact is explored followed by recommendations to strengthen its beneficial effect to the community.

BACKGROUND: THE ARTS -- ECONOMIC PROP FOR OLDER DOWNTOWNS

In recent years many downtown renewal programs have incorporated a cultural facility/theme as a major constituent component.[1] Examples include:

New York City - Lincoln Center Urban Renewal project; 42nd Street
Development Corporation Arts Complex; and Soho Theatre Area.

Boston - Combat Zone-Theatre District Revitalization.

Philadelphia - Academy of Music - Hotel Complex (Broad and Locust
Street Project).

Chicago - New Central Library Area Redevelopment.

San Francisco - Opera Plaza Redevelopment Zone.

While Arts-related renewal has received the most attention in large
cities, it is not limited to such communities. Many smaller localities
have followed suit. The Reading (Pennsylvania's) "Downtown East" redevelopment effort incorporates the adaptive reuse of the downtown Astor
Movie Theatre as a cultural complex.[2] Springfield, Illinois, has opted for a similar strategy, the renovation of its turn-of-the century
Symphony Hall.[3]

In some instances, the Arts have served as the primary revitalization theme. Winston-Salem (North Carolina) is a leading example. Like
many sister communities, Winston-Salem's downtown declined in the post
World War II era. Nostrums of the day proved ineffectual. Urban renewal in the 1950's-1960's tore down much yet accomplished little. The
1970's prescription, a downtown pedestrian mall to revitalize retail
trade, also fared poorly:[4]

  The city's greatest downtown revitalization debacle has been the
  Trade Street Mall. The downtown pedestrian mall was hailed as the
  savior of the central business district. Like nearly all such
  downtown malls, the one in Winston-Salem proved a dismal failure.
  Trade Street Mall was completed in 1970, but by 1975, it was a
  dying venture; in that year Hanes Mall, a huge two-level shopping
  center four miles from the city center, opened, taking with it
  several major department stores that had been the mainstays of
  the downtown. Security became a problem in the Trade Street Mall
  as derelicts began to congregate there. All the stores closed --
  "even the pawnshop on the corner." In the fall of 1980, the mall
  area was reopened to traffic.

Business-government leaders sought a new rallying theme for the
downtown. They found it in the Arts. Winston-Salem now hosts scores of
cultural facilities including the Southeasten Center for Contemporary
Art, North Carolina School of the Arts, North Carolina Dance Theater,
Piedmont Chamber Orchestra, Symphony Orchestra, and assorted galler-
ies. Two new major redevelopment projects, Winston Square and the
Roger Stevens Center, are also Arts-based:[5]

By bringing to the downtown a performance place for the School of the Arts and relocating the Arts Council, evening activities will be provided to complement the convention center and associated motels. Residents as well as tourists will come downtown at night. Thus a relatively modest public investment should generate several times the amount in private investments while providing other public goods as well.

Are cultural facilities, in reality, potent economic generators? In certain cases there is little doubt they are. Lincoln Center surely acted as a catalyst, albeit one of many, to the physical and economic revitalization of Manhattan's west side. Is the Lincoln Center Arts-based economic prop found elsewhere? Many studies conducted over the past decade answer in the affirmative.[6] To illustrate, an Indianapolis analysis concluded that cultural facilities in this city were responsible for over $30 million in economic activity.[7] A comparable Philadelphia study cited a $160 million benefit and noted that this community's cultural organizations were responsible for more local employment than Philadelphia's advertising or hospitality industries.[8] A regional investigation concluded that New England Arts centers had a $6 billion effect on the economy of the six-state area.[9]

Many of these early studies had questionable methodologies. Often authored by arts councils and similar far-from-disinterested groups, they understandably attempted to show a maximum fiscal benefit ensuing from cultural activities.[10] For instance, all expenditures from all non-local residents attending the Arts were credited to the presence of a local cultural attraction despite the fact many of these individuals (e.g., businessmen) availed themselves of hotels, restaurants, etc. for reasons only incidentally related to community cultural facilities. Undocumented, and therefore questionable multipliers, were also utilized such as stating that every direct Arts-dollar expenditure (e.g., for stage props) resulted in four to six dollars of secondarily induced outlays (e.g., purchases/hiring to produce the stage materials).

Considerably more rigorous economic impact analysis is evident in the studies conducted by David Cwi and others at Johns Hopkins University.[11] While Cwi et al. point to a lesser Arts economic benefit than many prior investigations, for instance a less generous secondary multiplier, their findings still document that the Arts serve as an important economic catalyst. Arts facilities incur staff, equipment, and other purchases on their own behalf. They attract audiences who typically spend half again as much as their ticket and other admission costs for incidentals -- parking, eating out, etc. Moreover, a sizeable share of Arts audiences are typically not local residents. While surely only a fraction of these non-locals have come specifically because of a community's cultural resources, those that do constitute a significant "import" spending group.

Multiple chains of economic activity are illustrated in Cwi's survey
of 50 Arts institutions in six cities. This probe revealed that the
facilities cumulatively attracted an audience of over seven million.
In addition to ticket purchases, audience members spend anywhere from
$2 to $3 per capita for local residents to $60 to $100 per person for
non-local visitors. Cultural facilities themselves incurred operating
budgets ranging from $2 to $22 million. In the aggregate, the Arts
activities in the six cities were responsible for $70 million in di-
rect expenditures and about $130 million in secondary business volume.

When matched against other economic sectors, the Arts industry is
small. The findings of the Cwi six-city study are illustrative. Arts
spendings in these urban centers, while amounting to millions of dollars, still represent only one to two percent of total retail sales,
manufacturing activity, etc., prevailing in each locality. It is thus
important not to overrepresent the financial significance of cultural
activities. At the same time, we should not overwork its benefits.
While the Arts may not be a prime economic function for the city as a
whole, it does play an important economic role in the specific neighborhoods where cultural facilities are located, e.g., west side, mid-
town and SoHo neighborhoods in Manhattan. The Arts also bestow an
important positive community image to present as well as would-be
residents and businesses. As summarized by Cwi:[12]

1. Expansion of the local Arts sector can change the negative images
   held of many cities as boring or otherwise not livable.

2. Development of cultural facilities can create an awareness that
   some negative images are not based in fact and that efforts are
   underway to build in more amenities and lessen disamenities.

3. The local Arts sector can be a part of the emerging service-based
   economy and thus generate -- not result from -- economic development. As such, Arts involvement acts as a people magnet.

4. All or any of the above, in tacit and indirect ways, reinforce
   possible locational choices by citizens, businesses, and institutions....

THE ARTS AND OLDER SUBURBS

Much of the research concerning the financial importance and downtown revitalization role of the Arts has focused on central city locations. Such an urban emphasis is not surprising for unlike retail and
other economic sectors, the Arts are still concentrated in central
cities. In recent years, however, the incidence of suburban cultural
activities-facilities has grown. These do not replace urban Arts for
the latter have continued to flourish. Instead, suburban Arts functions are likely responding to an enhanced public appetite for culture, especially when conveniently located and moderately priced.
More and more suburban communities are thus becoming the home for
local and/or regional theatre, dance, music and other companies.

Suburban Arts activities are often found in the mature as opposed to growing suburbs. New Jersey is illustrative. Many of the older suburbs referred to in this study house cultural functions or centers. Examples include Millburn's Papermill Playhouse, Red Bank's Monmouth Culture Center, Montclair's Center for Mime, New Brunswick's George Street Playhouse, Plainfield's Tweed Art Gallery, Morristown's Performing Art Center, and Ridgewood's Playhouse.

Arts activities cluster in older rather than newer suburbs for numerous reasons. The former offer a variety of physical facilities which can readily be used or adaptively reused for cultural events. Examples include large vaudeville-era movie houses which were designed for live performances; auditoriums of church, service (e.g. Elks, Rotary Club), school, and other private-public organizations; and department store and other retail establishments which have closed or are marginally used. To illustrate, cultural events and instruction are housed in New Brunswick's State Theatre, a 1920's movie house. The Mason Gross School of the Arts is housed in the former P.J. Young Department Store which closed due to competition from nearby shopping centers. Similarly, New Brunswick's Crossroads Theatre stages productions in an abandoned industrial loft. Older suburbs offer other Arts attractions besides suitable physical locations. These communities, typically spending more for culture and recreation than newer suburbs, often are more willing to lend municipal financial and other support for local Arts facilities. There is also a sense of function. Cultural activities have traditionally been inspired by and have flourished in places where there is diversity and density of people, activities, etc. Such a critical mass is personified by a city environment. It is most closely duplicated outside urban areas in older suburbs and thus these locations, rather than their newer sister communities, are inculcating the Arts.

The Arts are viewed as an important strategy to revitalize mature suburbs. Hempstead Long Island, for example, has turned to it as a major revitalization theme:[13]

> The cultural component of the plan is far more ambitious: it aims to transform Hempstead into the "arts capital" of Nassau County. Hopes ride on the creation of a multi-block cultural district comprising a performance arts complex, museums, "SoHo-type" galleries, restaurants, and shops. Already in place are the Nassau County Fine Arts Museum and the Nassau County Black History Museum. The 2,435 seat Calderone theater has been taken over by Adelphi University for use as a concert and dance facility, with joint cultural offerings being planned by Adelphi, Hofstra, and C.W. Post College. The New York State Urban Development Corporation is expected to recommend Hempstead as the site of a multi-million dollar Long Island Cultural Center for the Performing Arts soon.

We can obtain a better sense of the nature and impact of cultural facilities in older suburbs by describing and analyzing the John Harms Englewood Plaza (JHEP).

JOHN HARMS ENGLEWOOD PLAZA: BACKGROUND

"Meet me at the Plaza" evokes the image of a New York City hotel for
most people in the metropolitan area, but in late 1920's advertise-
ments, these words referred to another meeting place: the Englewood
Plaza movie-vaudeville house.[14] Completed at the end of 1926 in the
heart of Englewood's downtown, the theater offered superb acoustics,
2,000 seats, a $50,000 Welte-Mignon organ, and a symphonic orchestral
ensemble to accompany motion picture programs and shows. The design of
the theater combined elements of late-Victorian luxury with the more
austere art deco style it presaged.

By the 1930's, a popular innovation, "talking movies," had arrived,
but attendance at the Englewood Plaza slumped during the Depression.
To lure customers, movie theaters of the day gave away free prizes.
The Plaza offered ten tons of coal along with the more usual household
items.

In the 1940's and 1950's, the Plaza flourished as did other movie
houses of the day. Patriotic films were shown during the war and popular flicks afterwards. Television's growing strength as an entertainment medium soon took its toll, however. Starting in the late 1950's,
patronage of the Plaza and sister theatres fell dramatically. Physical
alterations were made to the Plaza in a desperate move to maintain its
lure. In the early 1960's, these included installation of a new wide
screen, plush upholstery, and carpeting. Management changes were also
tried such as a takeover of the Plaza by a succession of movie chains
(Skouras and then United Artists). These physical and management improvements proved ineffectual against the challenge of increased television viewing and competition from newer theaters, typically located
in free-standing malls. Like many downtown movie houses, the Englewood
Plaza ceased operations in the early 1970's.

Unlike many sister movie theaters, the Englewood Plaza did not remain permanently closed. Under the leadership of impresario John
Harms, the theater reopened in October, 1976 with the performance of
Russian pianist, Lazar Berman. This launched the theater in its new
role as the John Harms Englewood Plaza (JHEP), a regional performing
arts center bringing live music, dance, and theater to northern New
Jersey. The Great Artists Series, sponsored by John Harms Concerts,
has attracted such outstanding performers as Isaac Stern, the Boston
Symphony Orchestra, Richard Tucker, and the Beaux Arts Trio. Many
regional groups have used JHEP for performances, including the Pro
Arte Chorale, the Arts Musica, the New Jersey Symphony, the Classic
Ballet of New Jersey, and the Garden State Ballet. In addition, the
Creative Theatre for Children, a non-profit group which produces two
children's plays a year, is housed at JHEP.

JHEP is maintained and operated by John Harms Concerts, a nonprofit
corporation. A board of directors, selected from the community and
serving without compensation, establishes policies and guidelines for
the professional staff in charge of day-to-day operations.

As is the case with other Arts facilities, JHEP is financed by a combination of private and public monies. Ticket sales account for approximately 40 percent of its roughly $400,000 annual operating budget. Contributions from individuals, foundations, and corporations are responsible for a similar 40 percent share. Theatre and store rentals, government grants, and miscellaneous sources pay for the remaining 20 percent of operating expenditures.[15] Capital improvements to the theatre, averaging approximately $150,000 to $200,000 yearly, have been made with some private but largely government funds, primarily from the Community Development Block Grant program.

JHEP is an attractive cultural addition to the greater Bergen County area. Its management also emphasizes the theatre's economic revitalization role, claiming that JHEP brings audiences downtown, makes the city safer through "round the clock" activities, and contributes to attracting industry to the area. Economic development strategies prepared for Englewood by numerous consultants have all recommended support and expansion of the Plaza theater and related cultural facilities.[16] Similar suggestions have been made in other older suburbs.

What is the reality of Arts-based downtown revitalization in mature suburbs? Some answers are provided in the following analysis.

IMPACT OF THE JOHN HARMS ENGLEWOOD PLAZA

JHEP has a combined operating plus capital budget of about $600,000 annually. This sum, even if increased by two or three times to take into account secondary effects, is still quite small when matched against the current level of Englewood's economic activity. For instance, the community's 1982 retail sales most probably amount to at least $200 million.

JHEP's greatest significance lies not in its outlays but rather in the audience it attracts. The theatre's records indicate that about 60,000 individuals attend performances every year. About 10 percent of this group are children, leaving an annual adult audience of about 50,000. Who are these people? Why do they attend? To what extent do they patronize local restaurants or retail establishments? What changes would induce more frequent theatre or local facility usage?

To answer these questions, the Center for Urban Policy Research conducted a survey of JHEP audiences at two separate performances in March 1982. The two events were selected as being representative of JHEP's cultural offerings. On both occasions, attendees were handed a survey form containing questions on audience demographic profile, cultural interests, and so on. Approximately 600 questionnaires were distributed and 160 were returned. Ten forms were largely blank and/or illegible, leaving a remainder of 150. Analysis of these surveys reveals that the JHEP audience (see Exhibit 5-1):

- is middle-aged or older;

- is very affluent;

EXHIBIT 5-1

Older Suburb Audience Profile: John Harms Englewood Plaza (JHEP)

AUDIENCE PROFILE	JHEP AUDIENCE SURVEY RESPONSES (n=150)[a]
Age	
Below 20	0.7%
20-29	7.5
30-39	18.7
40-49	29.9
50-59	25.4
60 and over	17.9
Total	100.0
Annual Household Income	
Under $15,000	9.0%
$15,000-29,999	21.3
$30,000-44,999	21.3
$45,000-59,999	21.3
$60,000-74,999	4.1
$75,000 and over	23.0
Total	100.0
Residence	
Englewood	17.4%
Nearby communities	39.4
Remainder Bergen Co.	22.7
Remainder New Jersey	9.8
Outside New Jersey	10.6
Total	100.0
How Often Attend John Harms Theatre Performances	
1-2 times annually	52.7%
3-4 times annually	16.3
5-6 times annually	10.9
7-8 times annually	6.2
9-10 times annually	3.9
More than 10 times annually	10.1
Total	100.0

AUDIENCE PROFILE	JHEP AUDIENCE SURVEY RESPONSES (n=150)[a]
Why Attend JHT	
Quality	39.2%
Convenience	20.7
Loyalty	7.7
Personal reasons[b]	8.5
Other[c]	24.9
Total	100.0
Attend Other Arts Centers	
Yes	91.9%
No	6.0
Other	2.0
Total	100.0
Where	
New York City	64.0%
New Jersey	10.8
New York City and New Jersey	20.9
Other	4.3
Total	100.0
Regularly Shop in Englewood	
Yes	30.3%
No	65.2
Other	4.5
Total	100.0

AUDIENCE PROFILE	JHEP AUDIENCE SURVEY RESPONSES (n=150)[a]
Patronize Englewood Restaurants When Attend JHEP	
Frequently	12.4%
Sometimes	30.3
Never	49.7
Other	7.6
Total	100.0
Patronize Englewood Retailers When Attend JHEP	
Frequently	6.3%
Sometimes	13.2
Never	75.0
Other	5.6
Total	100.0

Notes:

[a] Number of actual respondents to each question may be less than 150.

[b] Specified in survey.

[c] Includes "nostalgia," "good value for money," etc.

Source: Rutgers University Center for Urban Policy Research survey of JHEP audience, Spring, 1982.

- attends JHEP for various reasons ranging from performance quality to convenience;

- attends other Arts facilities, primarily in New York City;

- for the most part does not live in Englewood nor does the audience regularly shop the Englewood CBD; and

- while attending JHEP performances, rarely patronize Englewood restaurants or retail establishments.

Most Arts audiences are middle-age or older. The landmark American Arts Audience: Its Study and Its Character[17] indicated that the median age of Arts attendees was 35. The median age of performing Arts audiences in New York City was an identical 35.[18] JHEP patrons are relatively older. According to the CUPR audience survey, only 10 percent were under 30 years, while 60 percent were 40 to 60 (see Exhibit 5-1). Their median age roughly was 45 -- a third again the age profile indicated by the national and New York City studies.

Leisure time, admission costs, and other prerequisites to Arts attendance limits most such patronage to middle-income or more affluent households. The American Arts Audience study indicated a median 1976 attendee income of about $19,000.[19] Adjusting this figure for inflation implies a 1982 income of roughly $30,000 -- a sum well above the national average. The New York City Performing Arts survey reveals similar audience affluence. Fifty percent of Broadway attendees, 60 percent of the symphony orchestra audience, and almost 70 percent of opera patrons earned $30,000 or more.[20]

JHEP's audience is even more affluent: only one-tenth had an annual 1982 household income of $15,000 or less; one-quarter earned $75,000 or more. Their median household income was about $45,000. This affluence characteristic reflects the fact that JHEP draws from the wealthiest suburbs of the New York metropolitan area, a feature we shall shortly discuss.

What is the attraction of JHEP? Patrons of older suburb Art centers such as John Harms typically have access and surely have the means to attend urban Arts. CUPR's survey reveals they take advantage of city cultural resources. Ninety percent of the JHEP's audience frequented other cultural facilities, for the most part (two-thirds of the time) located in New York City.

Given New York's cultural abundance and the proximity of these resources to the JHEP audience (most live 20 to 40 minutes from midtown Manhattan) why do these individuals come to Englewood? This question is roughly analogous to the one posed as to why shop Englewood in the face of the nearby multitude of suburban shopping centers and Manhattan's retail clustering? Interestingly, the factors motivating cultural patronage of the older suburb are roughly similar to the retail attractions of such communities -- quality, loyalty, convenience, and "personalized service." When asked "Why do you attend the John Harms theatre?" 40 percent of respondents cited the quality of the offerings. As elaborated on by one individual, "first-class, world-quality entertainment from Isaac Stern to the Vienna Boys Choir." While equivalent, if not superior, Arts quality is surely available in next door Manhattan, there are numerous special Englewood-JHEP attractions. Twenty percent of the respondents to the CUPR survey cited a convenience advantage, namely that JHEP was near their residence; 10 percent cited loyalty to a local institution; and 15 percent were attracted for personal reasons such as "Performances are on a human scale, not like (Lincoln Center's) Philharmonic Hall," "It's nice to know the people in charge," and "We are friends ("or relatives") of the performers, organizers, ushers, and others assisting the production." Additional attractions of JHEP included "good value for the money," and "nostalgia -- I remember going to the Plaza as a teenager."

These features have attracted a loyal cadre of attendees. JHEP has about 1,000 subscribers per year, individuals who commit themselves to pay for, if not always attend, a season's worth of events as opposed to purchasing tickets for individual performances. The CUPR survey reveals another facet of JHEP audience loyalty -- the repeat nature of their patronage. When asked "How often do you attend performances at the John Harms theatre?" about half of the respondents indicated a one-to-two event annual frequency, a quarter replied they came four times a year, while the remaining quarter patronized six events annually.

These figures permit the calculation of how many different individuals attend JHEP as opposed to its total audience size. Theatre records indicate a total adult attendance of about 50,000 per year. At the patronage ratios cited in the previous paragraph (e.g. 50 percent of the audience attend 1.5 times annually; 25 percent, 4 times; and 25 percent, 6 times), the 50,000 total audience would translate into about 22,000 different persons frequenting JHEP. If we assume that most JHEP attendees come as two-member "couples" (this overstates the case), then the 22,000 figure cited above translates into about 10,000 households.

Where do these people come from? Most are not Englewood residents but instead live in the greater Bergen County area. This non-local characteristic is revealed in different ways. Of the approximately 1,000 seasonal subscribers to JHEP, only 300 live in Englewood. An additional 200 are residents in neighboring Teaneck and Tenafly. The remaining 500 come from throughout Bergen County: 50 from Fort Lee, 25 from Leonia, 25 from Franklin Lakes, 20 from Ridgewood, 20 from Demarest, 15 from Hackensack, 10 from Paramus, and so on. CUPR's audience survey confirms the wide geographical draw of JHEP. When asked "Where do you live?" only one-sixth of the respondents said Englewood. Forty percent were residents in an arc of communities close to Englewood, such as Englewood Cliffs, Tenafly, Teaneck, Dumont, Cresskill, Alpine, and Hackensack (see Exhibit I-1). An additional 20 percent lived in the remainder of Bergen County, and a roughly similar share were residents outside of this county, coming from Manhattan, Rockland County, etc.

The extralocal nature of the JHEP audience is evident in another way. When asked "Do you regularly shop in Englewood?" only about one-third of the respondents to the CUPR survey replied in the affirmative. In short, the overwhelming majority of the JHEP audience do not live in Englewood nor patronize its CBD.

If they don't regularly draw upon Englewood retailers and restaurants, do JHEP attendees at least frequent these establishments when they attend the theater? The answer is unfortunately very little, especially with respect to retail stores. When asked "Do you patronize Englewood restaurants either before or after coming to John Harms?" only 12 percent of the respondents replied they did so frequently, only 30 percent did so at all. When queried "Do you patronize Englewood retailers when attending John Harms?" only 6 percent did so frequently, only 13 percent did so at all. The significance of this as well as other JHEP audience characteristics is discussed below.

JHEP AUDIENCE: COMPARATIVE ANALYSIS

It is instructive to compare the profile of those who attend Englewood's John Harms Plaza to shoppers in this community's CBD. Both groups are predominantly middle-aged or older. The median age is about 40-45 in both instances. Both groups are for the most part affluent; however, the JHEP audience is considerably wealthier than the CBD shopper. Median household income is $45,000 in the former case and $25-$30,000 in the latter. The biggest difference concerns the geographical pull of the two functions -- older suburb Arts attendance versus retail patronage: John Harms patrons are predominantly non-local residents; roughly 60 to 80 percent live outside of Englewood, for the most part scattered throughout the surrounding county and beyond. Retail shoppers, in contrast, are overwhelmingly local; about 60 percent live in Englewood and even non-residents typically dwell in immediately adjacent communities.

The fact that the JHEP audience is predominantly non-local and as indicated not regular shoppers of the Englewood CBD, makes them a most attractive group for Englewood retailers/restaurants to attract. The audience's affluence further enhances their desirability. It was previously estimated that about 10,000 separate households attend JHEP yearly. At a median household income of roughly $45,000, the John Harms audience, in aggregate, has a $450,000,000 annual income -- a most tempting target for local businesses.

Unfortunately for downtown Englewood, JHEP attendees rarely frequent local establishments. The retail promise of the Arts' draw is thus not realized. Why the absence of retail throughput? Part of the answer lies in the nature of the older suburb audience. These individuals live relatively close by and can conveniently eat at home or can patronize restaurants/stores in their own communities rather than having to draw on the retail resources of the older suburb hosting the Arts facility. The mature suburb Arts audience is roughly analogous to the local patrons of urban Arts centers which Cwi documented spend very lit'le for hotels, meals, etc. Englewood's case is illustrative. JHEP attendees, while predominantly non-locals, draw very little on Engle-

wood retailers. They do not need lodging, can eat at home, or can
conveniently draw upon their hometown downtowns of Teaneck, Bergenfield, Tenafly, Fort Lee, and so.

The inconsistency of the timing of cultural versus retail activities
is another impediment to the former fueling the latter. Very simply,
older suburb Arts functions are frequently scheduled when local retailers are closed for business. Englewood is again illustrative.
Most of its retailers are not open nights or on Sunday -- the very
periods when most JHEP performances are held. We are thus not seeing a
concatenation of Arts and retail because the two are not scheduled simultaneously.

Specific features of the older suburbs may further deter Arts audiences from shopping local stores or eating at local restaurants. Englewood serves as an example. Respondents to the CUPR John Harms survey explained their minimal or non-patronage of local merchants to
such factors as "security apprehensions after dark," "a confusion of
stores, especially to one unfamiliar with the area," and "the absence
of good restaurants, with the exception of the Railroad Cafe."

USING THE ARTS TO STRENGTHEN THE OLDER
SUBURBS' DOWNTOWN: RECOMMENDATIONS

Before proceeding to specific suggestions, it is important to set
the tone for the discussion. As with the case of older suburb retail,
one must be realistic in assessing the revitalization potential of
mature suburb' Arts activity. Even under optimal conditions, cultural
facilities in these communities could not replace once-vital economic
functions such as serving as a regional retail hub. Furthermore, it is
most difficult to initiate or expand suburban cultural facilities at
the current time because of recent cutbacks in federal and state Arts
funding.

What then can be expected of an Arts strategy to revitalize older
suburban CBDs? Cultural facilities are potent vehicles to lure relatively large numbers of people to the downtown. The fact that the Arts
audience is relatively quite affluent, and for the most part would not
otherwise be coming to the host older suburb, makes it particularly
welcome to local businesses. Unfortunately, the retail patronage promise of the older suburb Arts audience has not always translated into
reality. This lack of throughput can be addressed by numerous recommendations which shall be illustrated by reference to Englewood and
the John Harms Theatre.

The timing of Arts-retail functions must be synchronized so that
they can be mutually supportive. One possibility is for the Arts
facility such as JHEP to offer weekday matinees -- a period when CBD
stores are open. Such a strategy has certain drawbacks, however. For
one, there may not be much audience interest in this time slot. CUPR
asked John Harms patrons if they "would attend weekday matinees," and
only one-quarter responded in the affirmative. Another problem is that
a weekday matinee audience may compound some of the traffic and parking problems already bedeviling the older suburb CBD.

Another suggestion is for downtown merchants to modify their hours of operation so that they are open when JHEP performances are held. One possibility is for them to extend their evening hours to capitalize on JHEP events conducted say Wednesday or Thursday nights. A more radical proposal is for the CBD merchants to stay open on Sundays to take advantage of John Harms matinees scheduled on that day. In effect, this latter change attempts to mimic the historical clustering of Sunday afternoon activities characteristic of, and once constituting an important financial prop for, many older downtowns, e.g., going to the movies, restaurants, etc. The combination of evening/Sunday Arts and retail activity offers other advantages. Traffic-parking would not be as problematical during these periods. In addition, Sunday matinees are a very popular time slot. In a survey conducted by JHEP management, Sunday afternoon was deemed the most desirable period for scheduling events by a two-to-one margin over other possibilities.

The evening/Sunday Arts-retail relationship will have to be encouraged. Wherever possible, JHEP management should attempt to schedule events when downtown merchants are open. Retailers should consider offering special discounts to holders of John Harms tickets or stubs. The opening of stores in evenings and on Sundays and possible special promotions or sales during these periods will have to be publicized. In this regard, competing Sunday amusement and shopping activities at freestanding malls should be dealt with head-on with such advertising themes as "Why go to a movie in a mall? See a show and shop in Englewood."

Bringing together a clustering of cultural institutions (e.g., theatre, ballet, and opera) in the older suburb as opposed to one isolated facility would increase the audience-drawing power of an Arts-based revitalization strategy. This, in turn, would enhance the Arts' economic pump-priming. Keeping stores open on evenings or Sunday, for instance, would be more feasible if numerous cultural facilities conducted events during these time periods. Combining Arts-instruction with performances would serve a similar critical mass role. Possibilities include a ballet school and company, cinematography training and art-film moviehouse, and so on. New Brunswick is following such an Arts aggregation approach by bringing to its downtown the George Street Playhouse, Crossroads Company, State theatre, Mason Gross School of the Arts, Princeton Ballet Company, etc. A similar regional Arts role has been envisoned for Englewood in the guise of locating a Bergen County Cultural Arts Center in this community and developing a town center with a strong cultural motif. High interest rates and cutbacks in federal-state support for the Arts, however, make it quite difficult to bring such ambitious Arts strategies to fruition.

A further important consideration is making the older suburb retail environment more appealing to Arts audiences. Recommendations detailed in the previous chapter, ranging from providing more parking to emphasizing quality merchandise and service, would help realize this objective. The mature suburb Arts facility itself could also be made more attractive. JHEP attendees, for example, made the following recommendations:

1. provide better lighting and security especially for evening performances;

2. distribute a map showing available parking in the immediate area;

3. rehabilitate adjacent buildings (The Englewood Economic Development Corporation is considering this action); and

4. continue refurbishing of the John Harms Englewood Plaza. (This is
   being done as funding permits.)

NOTES

1. See David Cwi et al., The Role of the Arts in Urban Economic
Development (Washington, D.C.: Government Printing Office, no date);
Edward Duensing, The Arts and Urban Economic Development (Monticello:
Ill: Vance Bibliographies, November 1980, p. 844); Advisory Council on
Historic Preservation, The Contribution of Historic Preservation to
Urban Revitalization (Washington, D.C.: Government Printing Office,
1979); Jerry Hagstrom, "Bringing People Back Downtown with a Little
Help From the Arts," National Journal, December 15, 1979; "Art Grants
Help Revitalize Downtown Areas," Uptown, December 1978, pp. 2-3;
(Boston) Mayor's Task Force on Urban Theaters, Report to Kevin H.
White, Mayor (Draft Recommendations for Action) (Boston, MA: The Task
Force, 1975); Boston Redevelopment Authority, Boston's Theater Dis-
trict: A Program for Revitalization (Boston, MA: The Authority, 1979);
Boston Redevelopment Authority, Return of the Boston Opera House: A
Proposal for Converting Music Hall Theater and Performing Arts Complex
(Boston, MA: The Authority, 1974); Ralph Burgard, "Arts Draws Urban
America into its Public Places," Planning (October 1977), pp. 10-13;
Andrea Dean, "Linking a Civic Symbol to its City," AIA Journal, August
1978, pp. 40-45; Peter Green, "Arts Contribute to Commercial Renais-
sance in Galveston," Urban Land (November 1977), pp. 13-15; Donald A.
Wilcox, "Attractions Management is Key to a Revitalized Downtown's
Success," Journal of Housing (July 1980), pp. 377-382; American Prac-
tice Management Inc., Assessing Market Feasibility of Ten Theaters on
42nd Street (N.Y.C. Public Development Corp. and UDC, January 1981);
The City at 42nd Street. A Proposal for the Restoration and Redevelopment of 42nd Street (January 1980); University of California -- Los
Angeles. School of Architecture and Urban Planning. Urban Innovations
Group, The Arts in the Economic Life of the City (New York: American
Council for the Arts, 1979); Business/Labor Working Group, Culture &
the Arts: Major Contributors to the Economy of New York City (November, 1976); American Council for the Arts, The Arts and City Planning
(1980).
2. Cwi, The Role of the Arts, p. 23.
3. Ibid.
4. Susan Hollis, "The Arts and Center-City Revitalization" in Caroline Violette and Rachelle Taqqu (editors), Issues in Supporting the
Arts (Ithaca, N.Y.: Cornell University, 1982), p. 39.

5. Ibid., p. 43.

6. Arkansas Arts Council. The Arts are Big Business (Department of Natural and Cultural Heritage, Little Rock: 1979); Murray Frost and Garneth O. Peterson. The Economic Impact of Non-Profit Arts Organizations in Nebraska, 1976-77 (Nebraska Arts Council, August 1978); Hammer, Siler, George Associates, Economic Impact of Selected Arts Organizations on the Dallas Economy (City of Dallas, November 1977); John J. Sullivan and Gregory H. Wassall, The Impact of the Arts on Connecticut's Economy (Connecticut Commission on the Arts, March 1977); Ibid.

7. Metropolitan Arts Council, The Economic Impact of the Arts on Indianapolis.

8. Greater Philadelphia Cultural Alliance, An Introduction to the Economics of Philadelphia's Cultural Organizations (February 1975).

9. New England Foundation for the Arts, The Arts and the New England Economy, 2nd Edition (1981).

10. David Cwi, "The Focus and Impact of Arts Impact Studies," in Violette and Taqqu, Issues in Supporting the Arts, p. 23.

11. Cwi, The Role of the Arts; David Cwi and Associates, The Economic Impact of the Arts: A Study of 49 Cultural Institutions in 6 U.S. SMSA's (New York: Publication Center for Cultural Resources, n.d.); David Cwi and Associates, "Models of the Role of the Arts on Urban Economic Development" in William S. Hendon, et al., eds., Economic Policy for the Arts (Cambridge, Massachusetts: Abt Associates, 1980); David Cwi and Albert Diehl, In Search of a Regional Policy for the Arts (Baltimore, Maryland: Regional Planning Council, 1975); David Cwi and Katherine Lyall, Economic Impacts of Arts and Cultural Institutions: A Model for Assessment and a Case Study of Baltimore (National Endowment for the Arts Research Division Report No. 6), Baltimore, Maryland: Johns Hopkins University Center for Metropolitan Planning and Research, 1977.

12. David Cwi, The Role of the Arts in Urban Development. Cited in James L. Shanahn, "Cultural and Economic Development: How They Come Together" in Violette and Taqqu, Issues in Supporting the Arts, p. 27.

13. Susan Tenenbaum, "Hempstead: Can the 'Hub' be Recapped?" New York Affairs, Vol. 7, No. 2, 1982, p. 85.

14. John Harms Englewood Plaza, "1981-82 Great Artist Series" (no date). John Harms Englewood Plaza. "Brochure" (no date).

15. John Harms Englewood Plaza "Brochure."

16. See for example, Howard-Settro, "Englewood, A Town Center for Tomorrow."

17. Paul Dimaggio et al., American Arts Audience: A Study of Its Character. (Cambridge, Mass.: Center for Study of Public Policy, 1977).

18. Consumer Behavior Incorporated, A Study of the Performing Arts in the New York Metropolitan Area (February 1980).

19. See note 17.

20. See note 18.

Chapter Six
Rethinking Municipal Expenditures
and Service Strategies

INTRODUCTION

Chapter one of this study documented the fiscal stress of older suburbs in general and Englewood in particular. Chapter two focused on a
major factor causing distress -- high municipal spending -- and concluded that growth, whether in residential or nonresidential guise,
would improve the mature suburb's financial condition. This recommendation prompted the detailed probes of the fiscal implications of selected development and redevelopment options open to the case study
community, Englewood. Chapter three evaluated the fiscal impact of
constructing single-family dwellings, townhouses, and office-hotel
complexes; chapter four examined the financial health and future of
downtown retail functions; chapter five considered how the Arts could
give new life and health to Englewood's CBD.
All of these development and redevelopment approaches are important.
The fiscal health of older suburbs demands more, however, namely, to
severely temper municipal expenditures. This goal, as indicated in
chapter two, can be achieved most vigorously by reducing "factor
costs" such as the number of public employees and their compensation
and by reconsidering "qualitative service factors" including the span,
type, and means of service delivery. This chapter considers how these
actions may be taken in older suburbs in general and Englewood in particular. It examines strategies to: 1) lower service provision costs;
2) reduce service commitments and standards; and 3) modify service
delivery strategies.

HISTORICAL PERSPECTIVE

Before delving into the specifics of these different financial belt-
tightening measures, it is important to realize that such changes are
not new. Municipalities have encountered fiscal hard times before and
have risen to the challenge. Our discussion, thus, suggests how they
once again must respond.
Englewood is illustrative. During the 1930's it was forced, as were
sister communities, to react to strained economic conditions.[1] In
1931:

Englewood cut down on the scale of the new High School by eliminating the proposed auditorium. Plans for construction of a
municipal incinerator to replace the odorous garbage dumps in the
Fourth Ward were abandoned. Municipal salaries were cut 10 percent -- although Englewood continued throughout the Depression to
pay in cash when many other municipalities resorted to payments
in scrip. The Board of Education reduced its teaching staff and
also cut salaries. Economy became the byword....

In 1933 a local committee was appointed to study Englewood's financial situation.[2] Its report, released in 1936, concluded:[3]

that taxes were too high and that municipal expenditures should
be reduced drastically....It was also of the opinion that both
long and short term capital debt of $4.5 million was excessive
...[further] that the high level of expenditures and the cost of
the debt service made it difficult for taxpayers to meet their
obligations and were directly responsible for the difficulties in
collecting taxes....The report urged that Englewood drastically
reduce expenditures and forego any capital improvements until all
outstanding obligations were retired....

These belt-tightening recommendations were heeded. Public operating
expenditures were cut, so much so that welfare and other social services previously provided by tax dollars were now made available by
eleemosynary organizations such as the Social Service Federation
(operating Memorial House) and Mount Carmel Guild. Capital plans were
shelved or scaled down. For instance, bids for a "grand" post office
building were abandoned in favor of a much more modest structure.
These cutbacks paved the way to fiscal recovery. By 1936, Englewood
had to borrow only $20,000[4] to cover expenditures. A year later, the
city restored the 10 percent salary reduction imposed on its employees. The improving economy of the war years and early post-World War
II era was the final push to fiscal recovery. By 1947, Englewood's
budget returned to a cash basis -- it no longer had to borrow to meet
its expenditures.
During the 1950's and 1960's Englewood expanded its public sector
profile. A luxurious slate of services was provided, new public
buildings, especially schools were added, public employees were paid
on time and often quite handsomely, and so on. These expenditures demanded relatively high taxes which were approved although not always
without public complaint. For instance, a 10 percent property tax increase in the 1960's:[5]

caused protests from the Englewood Taxpayers' Association which
had argued that a tax peak had been reached beyond which Englewood should not go. Pointing out that the cost of government had
been increasing steadily due to wage increases, undertaking of
long-deferred maintenance work, and the high cost of labor and
materials, the association contended that Englewood had reached
the point where salaries were adequate and where it could not un-
dertake any further services.

During the early 1970's Englewood continued to spend and tax at very
high rates, a spiral documented in chapter one of this study. In the
latter part of the decade, however, the community began to restrain
its outlays (see chapter one). Spending constraint continued into the
1980's, with the recently adopted 1982 budget exhibiting rather severe
cuts. In real (inflation-adjusted) dollars, Englewood's 1982 municipal
operating expenditures are about 10 percent lower than in the late
1970's. Thus Englewood has recently turned once again to fiscal belt-
tightening, albeit not on the scale of its Depression-era retrenchment. Our discussion below points to both cost-cutting actions which
the community has taken already as well as additional strategies de-
serving consideration.

RETRENCHING THE PUBLIC SERVICE SECTOR:
THE RESPONSE STRATEGIES OUTLINED

This chapter considers the following four approaches to moderate
municipal spending:

1. Reduce service provision costs by cutting non-personnel outlays,
   and public employee staff size and their remuneration;

2. Reduce service expenditure commitments and standards by scaling
   back the range, quantity and quality of public services, equipment, and capital plant;

3. Modify service delivery strategies by altering public service
   provision borders (e.g., a municipality pay other units of government to deliver services if such an arrangement is more efficient); and

4. Modify service delivery strategies by shedding a public sector
   approach in favor of: a) turning to private firms (e.g. private
   scavengers); or b) relying on citizen volunteers (e.g., volunteer
   fire department).

These approaches differ to the extent to which they alter the status
quo. The first retains current arrangements concerning which services
are provided and by whom, and merely attempts to reduce out-of-pocket
expenditures. The second goes further and reduces service standards;
effectuation by the local unit of government is retained, however. The
third and fourth strategies alter the parties providing services: the
former retains public sector involvement but modifies service delivery
boundaries; the latter goes further and sheds public sector implementation in favor of the private sector and/or local citizens.
    A more detailed specification and evaluation of these four changes
follows.

REDUCE SERVICE PROVISION COSTS

Mature suburbs can provide public services at a lower cost. Frills such as non-critical travel and photocopying can be cut. Improved inventory controls can reduce warehouse and interest costs while improving product availability. Inexpensive energy conservation measures such as adjusting thermostats and caulking windows can lower heating and air conditioning bills. Self insurance may offer relief to spiralling insurance premiums. Purchasing telephones, as opposed to renting them, can often provide both cost and operating benefits. Rental of city offices from private owners should also be scrutinized: are the rents fair; is free space available in underutilized or surplus city-owned properties?

Englewood has implemented or has at least considered most of these approaches. In 1980, for instance, it opted for self insurance. In 1981, spending for "conventions and conferences" was slashed by one-half in many municipal departments. The 1981-82 budgets have also cut outlays for such "frill" items as photocopying, telephone, office supplies, etc.

The above shopping list offers some financial relief of non-personnel costs. For true service delivery savings, however, attention must be focused on employee expenses. These latter outlays dominate total service expenditures. In Englewood's case, salaries and wages alone amount to about 50 to 60 percent of total budgeted municipal operating expenditures. Reductions in payroll costs can be accomplished either by decreasing the total number of municipal employees or by scaling down in real dollars the compensation package offered each worker.

Work force cuts have become commonplace in financially hard-pressed cities and suburbs. Detroit and New York both experienced large-scale layoffs in their uniformed forces, albeit the latter city has recently been able to augment its police and fire department staffing as its fiscal posture has improved. In the wake of Proposition 13, many California cities reduced their public staffing, especially in service areas considered "non-essential."[6] For instance, in response to reduced library funding, California's largest libraries effected a painful one-fifth staff cut.

How can the municipal work force be pruned? A common and relatively painless approach is to let attrition take its toll -- freeze or severely restrict new hiring and do not replace those who leave, retire, etc. A more painful way to trimming staff size is to terminate a portion of the public payroll. Non-civil service workers (e.g., CETA employees) are often let go first. Next are civil service staff affected by reductions in force -- layoffs following the elimination or consolidation of whole departments or service areas. One example is sanitation and fire department workers terminated when a locality drops municipal refuse collection and fire protection in favor of having homeowners contract with a private scavenger and them serving on a volunteer fire force. Another illustration is surplus staff let go when individual departments are consolidated or are in other ways reorganized -- a common action as shown in Exhibit 6-1. Police and fire departments, for example, are increasingly being joined into singular

EXHIBIT 6-1
Local Government Productivity Improvements: ICMA National Municipal Survey, 1981

Community Classification	PRODUCTIVITY STRATEGIES						
	New Technology (b)	Internal Reorganization/ Consolidation (c)	Staff Motivation (d)	Work Measures/ Standards (e)	Interjurisdictional Service Cooperation/ Consolidation (f)	Contracting Out (g)	Volunteers (h)
	Percentage of Municipalities With Indicated Strategy (a)						
TOTAL, ALL CITIES	57.2%	39.9%	32.4%	30.5%	56.5%	55.3%	56.5%
POPULATION GROUP							
100,000-249,999	81.0 (i)	60.8	34.8	43.1	67.1	57.7	56.9
50,000- 99,999	70.1	50.7	38.6	31.0	60.1	63.0	59.5
25,000- 49,999	57.1	38.3	33.9	29.7	54.1	53.6	55.9
10,000- 24,999	41.0	28.2	25.7	27.6	54.4	52.1	55.4
5,000- 9,999							
GEOGRAPHIC REGION							
Northeast	50.7	34.7	27.3	31.3	48.3	59.6	60.6
North Central	58.3	36.3	29.9	29.8	58.0	56.2	54.4
South	53.2	37.4	35.9	30.2	52.9	41.1	53.1
West	67.8	54.6	38.5	31.1	68.0	65.2	58.8
FORM OF GOVERNMENT							
Mayor-council	46.7	30.0	28.8	21.8	51.6	53.7	53.8
Council-manager	63.4	45.9	35.2	35.9	60.9	56.7	57.8
Commission	58.3	20.0	10.0	0.0	41.7	41.7	41.7
Town meeting	50.0	39.3	25.0	30.4	26.9	53.6	69.2
Rep. town meeting	60.0	40.0	40.0	40.0	75.0	50.0	50.2

Notes:

(a) The share of respondents in each community category (e.g., 5,000-9,999 population versus 10,000-24,999 population, or Northeast versus Southern localities) adopting indicated strategy. Sample sizes of respondents are indicated in the notes below.

(b) Acquiring or adopting new technology such as purchasing new equipment. A total of 851 communities responded to the ICMA questionnaire concerning new technology, of which 487 indicated they adopted this strategy.

(c) Modification of a local government's organizational structure via reorganizing internal departments or program area. A total of 795 communities responded to the ICMA questionnaire concerning reorganization, of which 317 indicated they adopted this strategy.

(d) Strategies to improve employee performance via such motivational approaches as merit pay systems, quality circles, and employee suggestion programs. A total of 780 communities responded to the ICMA questionnaire concerning motivational approaches, of which 253 indicated they adopted this strategy.

(e) Adopting work measurements and standards. A total of 793 communities responded to the ICMA questionnaire concerning work measures and standards, of which 242 indicated they adopted this strategy.

(f) Modification of the local government's organizational structure via consolidation or cooperation with other local governments to provide particular services. A total of 820 communities responded to the ICMA questionnaire concerning consolidation/cooperation of which 463 indicated they had adopted this strategy.

(g) Using nongovernmental personnel to deliver services. A total of 810 communities responded to the ICMA questionnaire concerning contracting out, of which 448 indicated they had adopted this strategy.

(h) Using citizen volunteers to provide services. A total of 807 communities responded to the ICMA questionnaire concerning volunteers, of which 456 indicated they had adopted this strategy.

(i) Insignificant response.

Source: International City Management Association, "Productivity Improvements in Small Governments," *Urban Data Service Report*, Vol. 14, No. 7 (July 1982).

public safety divisions.[7] The final staff cut typically entails civil service employees terminated from ongoing departments such as trimming personnel from an administrator's or assessor's office.

Englewood has effected all of these personnel strategies. It has incorporated hiring freezes whereby new positions requested by department heads have not been granted. Staff lines left vacant from attrition have not been filled. Entire departments have been eliminated such as community development. Organizational changes have been made or at least considered to reduce the need for administrative staff, e.g., the recreation department would become a division under a newly created department of health and recreation, and the fire department would similarly be consolidated with police to form a department of public safety. Englewood has also made the hard decision to terminate some currently funded and/or occupied staff lines. The 1981 budget, for example, eliminated 34 formerly budgeted positions for a net reduction of over $400,000, roughly 3 percent of that year's municipal operating budget.

In addition to reducing the size of the public payroll, mature suburbs must scrutinize the remuneration offered to their workers, both direct salaries and fringe benefits. Compensation package review is most meaningful if conducted on a comparative basis -- what do city workers receive versus the salary/fringes accorded to employees in sister jurisdictions or the private sector?

An example of a comparative compensation analysis is shown in Exhibits 6-2 through 6-4 which list the cost of sanitation workers, policemen, and firemen respectively in Englewood and other New Jersey mature suburbs. Englewood's sanitation workers are relatively well paid with annual salaries for workers reaching almost $17,000 compared to about $14,000 in Millburn, Montclair, and Ridgewood (see Exhibit 6-2). Such a salary differential is not evident in Englewood's police (Exhibit 6-3) and fire (Exhibit 6-4) services, however. The community's public employee salary scales are thus average to slightly above average relative to those offered in comparable New Jersey suburbs.

In contrast, Englewood's public employee fringe benefits are appreciably more generous, especially for its uniformed services. Sanitation workers, for example, are allowed 20 to 25 vacation days after 10-15 years of service compared to 10 to 20 days in other communities (see Exhibit 6-2). Englewood patrolmen and firemen receive 24 vacation days in their first to fifteenth years of employment (see Exhibits 6-3 and 6-4). Police-fire service vacation allotments in most of the other older suburbs are far shorter. Morristown, for example, allows only 15 days after 11-15 years of service. Furthermore, Englewood offers its uniformed fire and police services a handsome bonus of 1.5 percent of base salary for every four years of employment. Sister mature suburbs typically provide lesser bonuses (e.g., Morristown grants a $200 to $750 stipend; see Exhibits 6-3 and 6-4). There are further examples of generous fringe benefits granted to Englewood public employees. Englewood historically credited to its terminated or retiring workers all of their unused sick pay (see Exhibit 6-5). An employee with many years service leaving active duty would thus often be compensated for many months of accumulated sick leave.

EXHIBIT 6-2

Contract Terms for New Jersey Mature Suburbs
Municipal Sanitation Departments

MUNICIPALITY	UNION	CONTRACT TERM	HIGHEST WORKER'S SALARY	WORK HOURS PER WEEK	LONGEVITY BONUS	VACATION DAYS[a]	PERSONAL LEAVE DAYS[1]
ENGLEWOOD	Local 29 R.W.D.S.U.[1] Dept. of Public Works	1980	$16,654	40	--	10-15 yr.=20 DPY 15+ yr. =25 DPY	1 DPY 3 or more; then charged to sick leave
HACKENSACK	N.J. Civil Service Bergen Council #3	1980	$14,900	40	11-15 yr.=5% base pay 16-25 yr.=7% base pay	10-15 yr.=15 DPY + 1 DPY for each additional year	2 DPY
LONG BRANCH	N.J. Civil Service Assn. Monmouth Council #4	1980	$15,230	40	11-15 yr.=3% base pay 16-25 yr.=6% base pay	11-15 yr.=10 DPY 1 DPY for each additional year	3 DPY
MILLBURN	N.J. Civil Service Assn. Essex Council #1	1978	$13,520	40	11-15 yr.=4% base pay 25 yr.+=10% base pay	5-16 yr.=18 DPY 1 additional DPY with 22-day maximum	3 DPY
MONTCLAIR	N.J. Civil Service Assn. Essex Council #5	1980	$13,530	40	11-15 yr.=4% base pay 25 yr.+=10% base pay	10-15 yr.=12 DPY 16-25 yr.=15 DPY	3 DPY
MORRISTOWN	Municipal Employees Assn. of Morristown	1980-82	$17,600	40	11-15 yr.=$200. 16-20 yr.=$300. 21-25 yr.=$450. 26-30 yr.=$600. 31+ yr. =$750.	11-15 yr.=15 DPY 16-30 yr.=20 DPY	2 DPY
RIDGEWOOD	Service Emp. Int. Union #550	1978	$13,422	40	12-16 yr.=6% base pay 20 yr.+=10% base pay	10-15 yr.=16 DPY 1 additional DPY for each year	1 DPY

Notes:

[a] DPY = Days Per Year

+ = or more years

Source: Rutgers University Center for Urban Policy Research telephone survey, 1982.

EXHIBIT 6-3

Contract Terms for New Jersey Mature Suburbs
Municipal Police Departments

MUNICIPALITY	UNION	CONTRACT TERM	HIGHEST PATROLMAN SALARY	WORK HOURS PER WEEK	LONGEVITY BONUS	VACATION DAYS	PERSONAL LEAVE DAYS
ENGLEWOOD	N.J. State P.B.A. Assn. Local #216	1980	$19,000.00	40	every 4 yrs., 1½% base pay	1-15 years, 24 days; 15 years +, 28 days (maximum)	1 day (annually)
BERGENFIELD	Policeman Assn. P.B.A. Local #83	1978- 1980	$19,476.00	40	9-11 years, 2% base pay; 27 years +, 8% base pay	11-15 years, 18 days; 20 years +, 25 days (maximum)	1 day (annually)
HILLSIDE	P.B.A. Assn. Local #70	1978	$16,020.00	37½	10th anniver- sary, 40% base pay; 25th anniver- sary, 10% base pay	10-15 years, 18 days; 15 years+, 21 days	3 days (annually)
LYNDHURST	P.B.A. Assn. Local #202	1981- 1982	(1981) $21,000.00 (1982) $23,000.00	40	4 years, 1% base pay; 20 years, 5% base pay	1 year, 5 working days; 25 years, 30 working days (maximum)	--
MAPLEWOOD	P.B.A. Assn. Local #44	1981- 1982	$20,810.08	40	10-15 years, 4% base pay; 25 years +, 10% base pay	10-20 years, 25 days; 20 years +, 30 days	3 days (annually)
MILLBURN	P.B.A. Assn. Local #34	1981- 1982	$20,017.00	40	5-10 years, 2% base pay; 25 years +, 10% base pay	1-5 years, 12 days; 30 years + 27 days	2 days (annually)
MORRISTOWN	P.B.A. Assn. Local #43	1980- 1982	$21,851.00	40	11th year, $200.00 ↓ 31st year, $750.00	11-15 years, 15 days; 16-30 years, 20 days	2 days (annually)

EXHIBIT 6-3 (continued)

MUNICIPALITY	UNION	CONTRACT TERM	HIGHEST PATROLMAN SALARY	WORK HOURS PER WEEK	LONGEVITY BONUS	VACATION DAYS	PERSONAL LEAVE DAYS
RIDGEWOOD	P.B.A. Assn. Local #20	1980-1981	$20,300.00	40	10% base pay after 10 years (maximum)	9-15 years, 14 days + 1 day for every additional year worked	1 day (annually)
ROSELLE	P.B.A. Assn. Local #99	1980-1981	$19,512.00	40	10-15 years, 4% base pay; 25 years +, 10% base pay (maximum)	10-14 years, 25 days; 20 years +, 30 days	2 days (annually)
SUMMIT	P.B.A. Assn. Local #55	1982-1984	(1982) $21,367.00 (1983) $23,076.00	40	5-10 years, 2% base pay; 25 years +, 10% base pay (maximum)	1-10 years, 12 days; 25 years +, 25 days	2 days (annually)

Source: Rutgers University Center for Urban Policy Research telephone survey, 1982.

EXHIBIT 6-4

**Contract Terms for New Jersey Mature Suburbs
Municipal Fire Departments**

MUNICIPALITY	UNION	CONTRACT TERM	HIGHEST FIREMAN SALARY	WORK HOURS PER WEEK	LONGEVITY BONUS	VACATION DAYS	PERSONAL LEAVE DAYS
ENGLEWOOD	F.M.B.A. Assn. Branch #24	1980	$18,750.00	42	every 4 years, 1½% base pay	1-15 years, 24 days; 15 years +, 29 days	1 day (annually)
BERGENFIELD	Bergenfield Paid Fire Dept.	1978-1980	$20,995.00	40	9-11 years, 2% base pay; 27 years +, 8% base pay	6-10 years, 13 days; 21 years +, 25 days	1 day (annually)
CRANFORD	F.M.B.A. Assn. Local #37	1979-1980	$18,096.00	42	merit rating	11-20 years, 12 days; 21-40 years, 24 days	1 day (annually)
HILLSIDE	F.M.B.A. Local #35	1978	$16,020.00	42	10th anniversary, 4% base pay; 25th anniversary, 10% base pay	10-15 years, 18 days; 15 years +, 22 days	3 days (annually)
MORRISTOWN	F.M.B.A. Local #43	1980-1982	$21,851.00	42	11th anniversary, $250.00; 26th anniversary, $750.00 (maximum)	11-15 years, 15 days; 16 years +, 20 days	2 days (annually)
RIDGEWOOD	F.M.B.A. Assn. Local #47	1980	$19,980.00	56	10th anniversary, 10% base pay (maximum)	10-20 years, 24 days (maximum)	3 days (annually)
ROSELLE	F.M.B.A. Assn. Local #55	1980-1981	$19,269.00	42	10-15 years, 4% base pay; 25 years + 10% base pay (maximum)	10-14 years, 25 days; 20 years +, 30 days	1 day (annually)
SUMMIT	F.M.B.A. Local #54	1981-1982	$19,784.00 (1981) $21,367.00 (1982)		5 years, 2% base pay; 25 years +, 10% base pay (maximum)	1-10 years, 10 days; 24 years, 25 days (maximum)	2 days (annually)
CLIFTON	F.M.B.A. Local #27	1981	$21,000	42	11-20 years, 4% base pay; 25+ years, 10% base pay	11-20 years, 16 days; 20-25 years, 20 days	1 day (annually)
DOVER	F.M.B.A. Local #47	1980-1982	$20,180	42	11-15 years=$250. 16-20 years=$400. 21-25 years=$600. 26+ years =$700.	11-15 years, 15 days; 16+ years, 20 days	2 days (annually)

EXHIBIT 6-4 (continued)

MUNICIPALITY	UNION	CONTRACT TERM	HIGHEST FIREMAN SALARY	WORK HOURS PER WEEK	LONGEVITY BONUS	VACATION DAYS[1]	PERSONAL LEAVE DAYS[1]
LONG BRANCH	F.M.B.A. Local #17	1981	$20,170	40	11-15 years, 4% base pay;	11-15 years, 15 days;	1 day (annually)
					15-25 years, 7% base pay	16-25 years, 20 days	
MAPLEWOOD	F.M.B.A. Local #37	1980-1982	$18,130	42	15-20 years=$200. 20+ years =$325.	11-15 years, 15 days;	2 days (annually)
						16-25 years, 20 days	
MILLBURN	F.M.B.A. Local #39	1980-1982	$18,534	40	16th year=$220. 21st year=$350.	11-15 years, 15 days;	2 days (annually)
						16-25 years, 20 days	
MONTCLAIR	F.M.B.A. Local #41	1980-1982	$20,150	40	15-20 years=$250. 21-25 years=$350. 26+ years =$400.	11-15 years, 15 days;	2 days (annually)
						16-25 years, 20 days	
PLAINFIELD	F.M.B.A. Local #28		$16,766	42	16th year=$220. 21st year=$350. 25th year=$400.	15-20 years, 10 days;	2 days (annually)
						20+ years, 15 days	
TEANECK	F.M.B.A. Local #57	1979-1981	$16,920	42	18th year=$420. 26th year=$525.	15-18 years, 12 days;	2 days (annually)
						19-24 years, 15 days;	
						25+ years, 20 days	

Source: Rutgers University Center for Urban Policy Research telephone survey, 1982.

EXHIBIT 6-5

A Comparison of Fringe Benefits for New Jersey Mature Suburbs Municipal Police, Fire, and Sanitation Departments

MUNICIPALITY	SICK LEAVE			TERMINATION PAY			OTHER
	POLICE	FIRE[5]	REFUSE	POLICE	FIRE[5]	REFUSE	
Englewood	15 DPY	15 DPY	15 DPY	50-100% Unused Sick Pay	50-100% Unused Sick Pay	50-100% Unused Sick Pay	For Police, Fire and Public Works: 100% of Unused Days Prior to August, 1981. 50% Thereafter. Some Contracts Have a Maximum Limit of $12,000.
Bergenfield	Up to 1 yr. Not Cum.	Up to 1 yr. Not Cum.	12-15 DPY[6] Cum.	3 Mo. After 15 Yrs. + 1 mo. for each add. 4 yrs. up to a total of 8 mos.	3 Mo. After 15 Yrs. + 1 mo. each add. year up to a total of 8 mos.	25 yrs. = 5 mos. 30 yrs. = 6 mos.	Termination Leave Does Not Include Sick Leave or Vacation Days - Refuse Collection Dept.; No Termination Pay for Less Than 24 Years of Service.
Cranford	15 DPY Dum.	15 DPY Cum.	15 DPY Cum.	2 Days for Each Year of Service	2 Days for Each Year of Service	2 Days for Each Year of Service	Sick Days Can Accumulate for a Maximum of 90 Days. 2 Days Term Pay for Every 5 Unused Sick Days.
Hillside	Up to 1 Yr. Not Cum.	Up to 1 Yr. Not Cum.	12-17 DPY[6]	1-17 yr. = 1 DPY >17=1½ DPY	1-17 yr. = 1 DPY >17=1½ DPY	1 DPY After 3 Yrs.	Under 17 Years of Service, 1 DPY; Over 17 Years of Service, 1½ DPY. For Police and Fire Termination, Pay Calculation.
Lodi	15-30 DPY[6] Cum.	Vol.[2]	15-30 DPY[6] Cum.	3 Months	Vol.[2]	3 Months	Police and Refuse Sick Leave Accumulate to a Maximum of 1 Year.
Lyndhurst	Up to 300 DPY Not Cum.	Vol.[2]	12 DPY Cum.	Unused Sick Pay	Vol.[2]	50% of Sick Leave Up to 120 Days	Police Termination is Calculated by Subtracting Paid Days in Past Year from $300. Paid for Remaining Days.
Ridgewood	15 DPY Cum.	15 DPY Cum.	15 DPY Cum.	50% Unused Sick Pay	50% Unused Sick Pay	50% Unused Sick Pay	Unused Sick Pay Accumulates to a Maximum of 6 Months for Termination Pay.
Roselle	Up to 1 Yr. Not Cum.	15 DPY Cum.	15 DPY Cum.	None	50% Unused Sick Pay	50% Unused Sick Pay	
Scotch Plains	15 DPY[1] Cum.	15 DPY[1] Cum.	Contract Out[3]	30 + 50%[4] Unused Sick Pay	30 + 50%[4] Unused Sick Pay	Contract Out[3]	
Summit	12-15 DPY[6] Cum.	12-15 DPY[6] Cum.	12-15 DPY[6] Cum.	30 + Unused Sick, Vacation Days[4]	30 + Unused Sick, Vacation Days[4]	2 Weeks + Unused Sick Pay[4]	

EXHIBIT 6-5 (continued)

MUNICIPALITY	SICK LEAVE			TERMINATION PAY			OTHER
	POLICE	FIRE[5]	REFUSE	POLICE	FIRE[5]	REFUSE	
Fort Lee	12-15 DPY[6] Cum.	Vol.[2]	Contract Out	1/3 Sick Pay + 30 Days[4]	Vol.[2]	Contract Out	Sick Days Paid Lump Sum, then 2 Reg. Pay Periods.
Hackensack	12-15 DPY Cum.[6]	12-15 DPY Cum.[6]	12-15 DPY Cum.[6]	30 + 50% Sick Pay[4]	30 + 50% Sick Leave[4]	30 + 50% Sick Leave[4]	14 + 1/3 Sick Pay.[4]
Montclair	15 DPY Cum.	15 DPY Cum.	15 DPY Cum.	Unused Sick Pay Up to 130 Days	Unused Sick Pay Up to 130 Days	After 15 Yrs. Service, 50% Unused Sick Pay	P., F.: Paid in Lump Sum.
Teaneck	12-15 DPY[6] Cum.	12-15 DPY[6] Cum.	12-15 DPY[6] Cum.	Years x 50%/25 of Unused Sick Days	Years x 50%/25 of Unused Sick Days	Years x 50%/25 of Unused Sick Days	Calculation of Termination Pay: (Number of Years Employed ÷ 25) x 1/2 the number of accumulated unused sick days.
Flemington	10 DPY	Vol.[2]	Contract Out[3]	30 + Unused Sick Pay[4]	Vol.[2]	Contract Out[3]	Police: Sick Days Accumulate to Maximum of 30.
New Brunswick	15 DPY[1] Cum.	15 DPY[1] Cum.	15 DPY Cum.	60 + Unused Sick Pay[4]	60 + Unused Sick Pay[4]	30 + 50% of Unused Sick Pay[4]	
Long Branch	15 DPY	15 DPY	15 DPY	30 + Unused Sick Pay[4]	30 + Unused Sick Pay[4]	30 + 50% Unused Sick Pay[4]	
Red Bank	15 DPY Cum.	Vol.[2]	12-15 DPY[6] Cum.	30 + Unused Sick Pay[4]	Vol.[2]	All Unused Sick Pay	
Dover	12-15 DPY[6] Cum.	12-15 DPY[6] Cum.	12-15 DPY[6] Cum.	30% Unused Sick Pay	30% Unused Sick Pay	25% Unused Sick Pay	
Clifton	30 DPY Cum.	30 DPY Cum.	12-15 DPY[6] Cum.	50% of Unused Sick Leave	50% of Unused Sick Leave	50% of Unused Sick Leave	Paid in Lump Sum.
Wayne	12-15 DPY[6]	Vol.[2]	12-15 DPY[6] Cum.	30 + Unused Sick Pay	Vol.[2]	30 + Unused Sick Pay	Maximum Unused Sick Days for Termination Pay Calculation is 90 Days for Police and 60 Days for Public Works.
Plainfield	15 DPY	15 DPY Cum.	Contract Out[3]	1 DPY + Unused Sick Pay	1 DPY + Unused Sick Days	Contract Out[3]	
Maplewood	90 DPY Cum.	90 DPY Cum.	15 DPY Cum.	50% Unused Sick Days	50% Unused Sick Days	50% Unused Sick Days	
Millburn	12-15 DPY[6] Cum.	12-15 DPY[6] Cum.	12-15 DPY[6] Cum.	50% Unused Sick Days	50% Unused Sick Days	50% Unused Sick Days	Termination Pay Paid in Lump Sum.

Notes: Cum. = Cumulative
Not cum. = Must be used within a 1-year period or forfeited.
DPY = Days per year
Source: Rutgers University, Center for Urban Policy Research telephone survey, 1982.

[1] Up to 1 year if job-related illness or injury
[2] Volunteer department
[3] Contract out refuse collection to private firms
[4] Number of days of regular pay and any extra pay
[5] Only fully-paid personnel; not volunteers
[6] Number of days for 1st year/2 or more years

In summary, as indicated in chapter two, Englewood's public staff "factor costs" are above average. It is important to note, however, that these costs are being trimmed. To illustrate, as of August 1981, only 50 rather than 100 percent of unused sick leave is credited, a provision closer to that offered by comparable communities (see Exhibit 6-5).

Improving Productivity Given Reduced Resources

Following the service cost reduction steps outlined above -- eliminating unnecessary nonpersonnel outlays, reducing the city's work force, and bringing staff compensation costs in line with new fiscal realities -- the municipality will be left with fewer people and support resources with which to service its population. Given this contraction, it behooves mature suburbs to explore how they can increase their service delivery efficiency -- "getting more bang from each buck being spent." The detailed means for achieving this goal could be the subject of an entirely separate monograph; some critical steps are outlined below, however.

As a first action toward achieving heightened productivity, communities must establish a management data base. Few localities measure the output of their services -- what activities/assistance is being made available or goods produced -- as opposed to simply accounting for what is being spent.[8] This is not a new problem. In 1938, a landmark work, Measuring Municipal Activities, bemoaned the fact that municipal administrators did not "think...in terms of (service) accomplishments."[9] Coterminous with this study was Herbert Simon's pre-World War II work on quantifying service outputs as well as costs in the San Francisco Bay area (see discussion in chapter two). Such research sparked efforts to develop municipal service measures. A National Committee on Municipal Standards was established to develop means to measure the performance and impact of local services.[10] The International City Management Association (ICMA) has actively participated in this endeavor. Its 1958 "Checklist on How to Improve Municipal Services" spoke to the issue.[11] More detailed measurement standards were promulgated by the ICMA in a 1970 Management Information Service Report, "Measuring Effectiveness of Municipal Services,"[12] and in subsequent monographs authored jointly by ICMA and the Urban Institute.[13] An outpouring of work in this area has followed.[14]

This research has affected field practice. A 1976 national survey of municipalities revealed widespread adoption of performance measures.[15] Four categories of indices were identified: (1) "work load" -- activities performed and/or level of services provided (e.g., tons of garbage collected or miles of streets paved); (2) "unit cost" -- level of resources (dollars or worker hours) expended to produce a service (e.g., 2.5 violations abated per inspection hour); (3) "effectiveness" -- extent to which the general goals of local government services are satisfied (e.g., service responsiveness, accessibility, reliability, citizen satisfaction, etc.); and (4) "goals and objectives" -- description of the overall mission and long-range intent of

specific programs (e.g. provide diversified recreational opportunities) and realization of these targets.[16] Perhaps because of its
simplicity relative to the other indices, the "work load" measure was
most commonly used by municipalities. More recent surveys reaffirm
that output measures have become a widespread municipal management
tool (see Exhibit 6-1), albeit simple first generation indices are the
norm as opposed to more encompassing scales.

Developing municipal service output can be a demanding task especially to pinpoint and monitor "effectiveness" and "goals and objectives"-type standards. In many cases, however, workable measures of
the "work load" and "unit cost" variety can be devised without much
strain to municipal administrators. Exhibit 6-6 gives examples of such
simple output indices for a municipal public works department including "road miles sealed" for the pavement repairing division and "cubic
yards snow removed" for the highway division. With output scales in
place, it is then possible to create productivity or "unit cost" indices (e.g., "direct labor hours or cost per road mile sealed or cubic
yard of snow removed" -- see Exhibit 6-6). Such measures, in turn,
allow municipal administrators to chart the progress with which services are delivered and efficiency is being improved. Interestingly,
the gathering of such management information was one of the first
responses undertaken by New York City in the height of its fiscal
crunch. City officials benefitted immensely by translating the line
item dollar budget into an aggregation of service output and efficiency measures. It is not meant to resurrect PPBS here; a mere listing of services by function, and a provision of first generation out-
put/outlay measures will suffice. All that is needed is a vehicle to
show what is provided at roughly what cost.

Such data management will hopefully spur municipal officials to seek
and implement more productive means of providing services. Productivity gains can be realized from a spectrum of strategies (see Exhibit
6-1).[17] Departmental consolidation and/or reorganization can prune
excess managerial staff so as to improve the output of remaining employees. This was the goal of Englewood's departmental shifts described earlier. Employer performance can also be enhanced by motivational approaches such as merit pay systems, job enrichment, quality
circles, staff suggestion programs, and the like. Englewood attempted
to improve the efficiency of its perennially rather unproductive public works department (chapter two indicated its relative overstaffing
and high costs) by changing work assignments from a "time basis"
(e.g., a sanitation crew worked an eight hour shift plus overtime if
necessary) to an "achievement basis" (e.g., a sanitation crew was assigned a pick-up route: finishing it early would give the crew free
time; no overtime, however, would be paid in the case of tardiness).

"Hardware" additions in the form of new equipment and/or better
technology can also enhance employee output. Examples range from
larger, side-loading garbage trucks to word processing equipment.
Ironically, one of the first responses to municipal fiscal austerity
is to delay or forego such hardware and technology improvements. Police cars are kept past their replacement cycle, small rear-loading

EXHIBIT 6-6

Work Output/Productivity Measures:
A Public Works Department Example

Program	Cost Center	Work Load Measures	Productivity Measures
Pavement Repairing	Pothole Filling Crack Sealing	Tons Asphalt Applied Lane Miles Sealed	Cost/Ton Applied Cost/Lane Mile Sealed
Street Resurfacing	Asphalt Overlay Chip Seal Coating	Lane Miles Overlayed Lane Miles Coated	Cost/Lane Mile Overlayed Cost/Lane Mile Coated
Concrete Repair	Sidewalk Repair Curb/Gutter Repair Crosspan Repair Radii Repair	Lineal Ft. Repaired Lineal Ft. Repaired Crosspans Repaired Radii Repaired	Cost/Lineal Foot Repaired Cost/Lineal Feet Repaired Cost/Crosspan Repaired Cost/Radii Repaired
Snow Removal	Snow Plowing Snow Removal	Lane Miles Plowed Cu. Yds. Snow Removed	Cost/Lane Mile Plowed Cost/Cu. Yd. Snow Removed
Street Cleaning	Street Sweeping	Lane Miles Swept	Cost /Lane Mile Swept
Street Grading	Gravel Streets Shoulders	Lane Miles Graded Miles of Shoulders Graded	Cost/Lane Mile Graded Cost/Mile Shoulder Graded
Vegetation Control	Right-of-Way Mowed Mowing City Lots Weed Control	Miles Mowed Acres Mowed Acres Mowed	Cost/Mile Mowed Cost/Acre Mowed Cost/Acre Mowed
Drainage Maint.	Ditch Mowing Debris Clearanc	Miles of Ditch Mowed Miles of Ditch Cleared	Cost/Mile Ditch Mowed Cost/Mile Ditch Cleared

Source: Donald Oatman, "It's Time for Productivity Accounting in Government," <u>Governmental Finance</u>, Vol. 8, November 1979, p. 11.

refuse vehicles are retained, manual typewriters are kept, etc. These
and kindred actions are short-term responses which will reap long-term
problems in employee efficiency if not morale.

Clearly many strategies can enhance productivity. An extensive literature has developed on this subject.[18] Robert Poole, author of
<u>Cutting Back City Hall</u>,[19] terms such productivity measures "thinking
smarter" and cites numerous examples of their application. A selected
group of approaches, organized by service function, is shown below.

Garbage/Solid Waste/Public Works

- Replace old rear-loading garbage trucks with side-loading
  vehicles. The latter can be operated with a smaller crew.

- Provide garbage transfer stations so as to reduce lengthy trips
  to incinerator or landfill sites.

- Assign more efficient garbage pickup routes.

- Modify work crew scheduling so as to better correspond to need;
  decentralize the city yard to reduce time spent traveling to work
  sites; limit overtime expenses (night or weekend work) to emergencies only.

Fire Protection

- Unless otherwise indicated, respond with a mini-pumper as opposed
  to a full-size fire truck. The mini-pumper is less costly to purchase and requires fewer firemen to operate.

- Since most fires are reported by telephone, eliminate all but
  essential fire boxes. This change will allow significant capital
  and routine maintenance savings.

Police/Criminal Justice/Other Public Safety

- In areas which permit, assign one as opposed to two officers per
  patrol vehicle; replace full-size sedans with compacts.

- Wherever possible, allow lower cost civilians to perform tasks
  which do not require a uniformed officer (e.g., dispatching,
  record keeping).

- Hire professional court administrators.

- Improve scheduling of police officer courtroom appearances so as
  to reduce wasted time.

In some cases, scheduling and other changes along the lines cited above can reap significant benefit. Sensitive allocation of police manpower as per need is illustrative. As expressed by Poole:[20]

> Your city's police force can nearly double its strength during high-crime hours without increasing the police budget. A few police departments are doing just that, because they've thought up a smarter way to schedule their patrol officers. Analyzing the records of calls for service by hour of the day, they saw that in most cases demand for police response was three or four times higher in the evening hours than in the early hours of the morning and twice as high as in the morning and afternoon hours. In cooperation with their officers, they devised a new shift schedule based on a ten-hour day, four days a week. Using ten-hour shifts, they could arrange things so that 6 of the 24 hours in a day were covered by overlapping shifts -- putting twice as many officers on duty during the overlap. This overlap, of course, was programmed to occur during the high-crime peak hours.

While work measurement, and management-productivity changes are welcome, they are an inadequate response by themselves to municipal fiscal austerity. Current services simply cannot be provided given constrained public sector resources, no matter how efficiently these resources are applied. Older suburbs therefore face the added task of retrenching their municipal service offerings.

REDUCE SERVICE EXPENDITURE COMMITMENTS AND STANDARDS

Fiscal austerity has forced many localities to scale back the range and quantity of the services, equipment, and capital plant they provide their citizens. One of the first items to go are new capital facilities. Financially hard-pressed communities have had to replace the dream of the new and gleaming infrastructure with the reality of making do with older highways, bridges, police-fire stations, libraries, schools, and so on. Even maintenance of the existing capital plant has been severely curtailed.

There are myriad such examples. Following Proposition 13, California's library system almost eliminated capital spending; this expense item fell from about 15 percent of total library outlays in 1975-76 to 2 percent just two years later.[21] A survey by the United States Conference of Mayors of local responses to recent federal aid cutbacks revealed:[22]

> Sixty-three percent of the cities have deferred capital spending as a result of federal budget cuts or plan to do so....Denver stated that it had "almost totally" deferred capital spending, particularly affecting expansion of libraries, bridges, and wastewater drainage....Allentown...has deferred a sewer run-off system; Buffalo, street resurfacing, street lighting, and an updating of city water lines; Des Moines halted a major sewer project, which had been in planning for several years; in Omaha,

two fire stations, three senior citizen centers, and water and sewer projects have been deferred...and Youngstown has noted that bridges and streets that need repair are not being repaired.

Englewood has trimmed its capital spending activity for both small and big items. Its police department is keeping patrol cars far longer than in the past and has delayed purchase of a backup communication system.[23] Plans for a new town hall, considered for many years, have been shelved. Proposals for a new town center complex, parking garage, pedestrian mall and so on are no longer being given serious thought in a period of spending cutback. Maintenance of the existing physical infrastructure has also been reduced. The Englewood public works department, for instance, reports that "emergencies are responded to as usual but maintenance and preventive services are severely curtailed, especially with reference to the drainage department and the shade tree commission."[24] Further maintenance cutbacks loom in the future. Englewood is considering whether it should continue to maintain curbs, sidewalks, and the like at public expense as opposed to having private property owners assume responsibility.[25]

Fiscal austerity has also forced many municipalities to cut operating services. In the aftermath of Proposition 13, California libraries reduced non-book lending (records, films, art) and interlibrary loan transactions -- two "luxury" activities requiring relatively more staff time.[26] Library hours were also curtailed. Englewood has also trimmed its service offerings. Weekend library hours have been shortened.[27] Police escort services have been curtailed. The recreation department has cut back sports instruction. Certain housing inspections have been discontinued or else are done on a nonroutine basis by the fire department.

Additional Englewood service retrenchments should be considered. Chapter two indicated that Englewood offers thrice weekly pick-up of residential refuse, two times of which are rear yard collection. This cycle is a luxurious one. Nationally, about half of the municipalities in the United States have once-a-week refuse collection and 40 percent, twice weekly.[28] Over two-thirds have curbside as opposed to rear yard pickup.[29] Englewood's sanitation services are thus far in excess of the national "norm" and even exceed the rather comprehensive coverage of its sister, mature New Jersey suburbs (see discussion in chapter two). Sanitation service cutbacks should thus be considered, a suggestion already under review. Englewood's 1982 budget report for example, recommended: [30]

> Twice a week curb-side service for all residential and business properties in the City. Anyone requiring service beyond that, for rear yard purposes, etc., would have to pay extra. This would take the costs out of our tax rate, which is distorted in comparison to other communities because of it and would allow us to restore a more reasonable service level, except where people wanted to pay for it separately.

Reducing the scope of Englewood's sanitation service would reduce municipal spending. E.S. Savas has found that twice-a-week curbside refuse pick-up is about 10 percent more expensive than a once-a-week curbside cycle, and backyard pick-up is roughly 25 percent more costly than curbside (see Exhibit 6-7).[31] Given these ratios, it is possible to project the cost-savings potential of changing Englewood's refuse collection standards. In 1978, Englewood spent about $600,000 for garbage removal (1978 is chosen for illustration purposes because it was the year referred to in chapters two and three). If the community would turn from frequent backyard pick-up to less frequent curbside service it could shave approximately 10 to 25 percent of 1978 sanitation outlays -- a savings of roughly $50,000 to $150,000 or approximately one percent of that year's total municipal operating budget.

The strategies considered thus far maintain traditional service arrangements, albeit these are of a diminished range and quality and are provided by a smaller, less well-paid, and hopefully more efficient public staff. The fiscal crunch of the older suburb demands more: a fundamental rethinking of municipal service approaches. Such changes are explored in the following sections.

MODIFY SERVICE DELIVERY STRATEGIES:
INTERGOVERNMENTAL AGREEMENTS

The suburban landscape typically consists of a cluster of small to mid-size communities each offering separate police, fire, recreation, and other public activities. Such an approach clearly does not allow for economies of scale. Expensive capital equipment is not amortized over an optimally large population base; prices of the multitude of goods needed for the operation of a municipal government are higher than they would be than if bought in greater bulk; and operating services such as police-fire patrols are not as efficient nor as effective as possible for they stop at "artificial" municipal boundaries.

One solution to this service delivery disaggregation is governmental consolidation, whereby individual local units of government merge into a single encompassing governing entity. With the exception of Nashville-Davidson Tennessee, Lexington-Fayette County Kentucky, and a few other cases, political consolidation has met with little success, however.[32] It is not even seriously considered in a strong home rule state such as New Jersey.

Municipal transfer of functional responsibilities (e.g., welfare, health inspection, etc.) to higher levels of government (such as the county, regional district, or the state) is a much more common activity. A study by the International City Management Association concluded:[33]

> Nearly one-third of the 3,319 municipalities responding to the survey have transferred responsibility, voluntarily or involuntarily, for a function or a component of a function to another governmental unit during the past ten years. The most commonly

EXHIBIT 6-7

**Annual Cost of Refuse Collection Per Household
By Service Arrangement and Service Level:
National Municipal Survey**

Service Arrangement	Once-a-week Curbside			Twice-a-week Curbside			Once-a-week Backyard			Weighted Mean Cost ⑥	Total Number of Cities
	Mean	Std. Dev. ⑤	No. of Cities	Mean	Std. Dev. ⑤	No. of Cities	Mean	Std. Dev. ⑤	No. of Cities		
Municipal ⓐ	$24.41	$8.86	26	$28.83	$ 8.22	31	$38.71	$11.42	8	$28.28	65
Contract ⓑ	22.42	8.98	30	29.14	10.79	23	31.63	20.39	4	25.78	57
Franchise ⓒ	27.94	10.23	22	29.85	8.57	8	27.48	10.50	9	28.23	39
Private ⓓ	35.91	7.96	27	38.71	12.32	9	46.24	10.87	9	38.54	45
TOTAL ⓔ	$27.54	$9.95	105	$30.30	$10.04	71	$36.66	$14.03	30	$29.82	206

SERVICE LEVEL

Notes: ⓐ Local government agency provides service.
ⓑ Private firm operates under contract with the municipality.
ⓒ Private firm with territorially-exclusive rights provides service.
ⓓ Private firm without franchise provides service.
ⓔ Average for all service arrangements.
⑤ Standard deviation.
⑥ Weighted by number of cities.

Source: E.S. Savas, "Policy Analysis for Local Government: Public Versus Private Refuse Collection," *Policy Analysis* Vol. 3, No. 1, Winter 1977, p.66.

transferred functions, in order of frequency of transfer, were
solid waste collection and disposal, law enforcement, public
health, sewage collection and treatment, taxation and assessment,
social services, building and safety inspections, and planning.
As was anticipated, the greatest number of municipalities that
transferred functions shifted responsibility for only one function, and the favorite recipients were the county and the special
district. Social services, however, were most often shifted to
the state.

Municipalities transferring functions often welcome such a move as a
means to shed both a service and expenditure responsibility. Conversely, jurisdictions to whom the service load is shifted are often
understandably hesitant and acquiesce to such change only if compelled
to do so by law and/or in the case of extreme local fiscal stress. To
illustrate, in response to New York City's fiscal crunch in the late
1970's, New York state began to pay for the city's college system
(CUNY). Similar considerations led the state and county levels of government to assume the major financial responsibility of Newark's
largest municipal health facility, Martland Hospital. Such statutory
and/or fiscal preconditions are typically not present in the case of
older suburbs (e.g. they are not so financially hard-pressed as to
compel service takeover by another unit of government). It is therefore unlikely that mature suburbs will be able to shed service obligations and cost via a transfer mechanism.

A much more realistic consideration for older suburbs is an Intergovernmental Service Agreement (ISA) whereby one governmental body
(contractor) provides a public service for another (contractee),
typically for a fee or other compensation. An ISA may also entail
joint provision of services with a joint sharing of costs, e.g., a
combined police department for two municipalities. An ISA differs from
a municipal transfer of responsibility in numerous ways.[34] With an
ISA, local service decision making and the ultimate service cost
responsibility do not change while it does shift in a transfer situation. In addition, the ISA remains in effect only for the time period
specified in the contract agreed upon, in contrast to the usual perma-
nent arrangement of a municipal transfer of responsibility.

The ISA's features make it attractive to local governments, especially relative to other service shift alternatives.[35] Unlike with
consolidation, an ISA does not entail the radical step of dissolving
political boundaries. Instead, the ISA merely alters traditional service delivery borders and in so doing hopefully achieves economies of
scale and other efficiencies. Another consideration is the recompense
for the governmental body assuming the service responsibility. Since
compensation is provided with an ISA but not a municipal transfer of
responsibility, the latter is often effected under duress. Furthermore, an ISA can be tested, implemented on a trial basis, and if found
wanting, discontinued. Such flexibility is absent with both consolidation and transfer strategies. Finally, an ISA is a flexible instru-
ment for it can be put in place for only those services for which

sharing is deemed practical or desirable (e.g., public works or
library) while traditional arrangements can be left intact for local-
ly-sensitive areas (e.g., general governments or police functions).
Such selectivity is absent with consolidation and is often not a
voluntary choice in a transfer situation where the pressing immedi-
acies of a fiscal crisis may dictate which service obligations are
shifted.

These ISA advantages make it an attractive mechanism to improve the
efficiency and hence lower the cost of public services. In recent
years increasing attention has been paid to remove the statutory, administrative, and other hurdles to ISA implementation. In 1957, the
Council of State Governments drafted a model interlocal contracting
act.[36] Over forty states have adopted a close variant permitting
intergovernmental cooperation in providing services.

New Jersey's legislative efforts in this regard are illustrative.
For many years, individual New Jersey communities effected cooperative
service arrangements on an ad hoc basis. To further encourage such
efforts, the state enacted relevant enabling legislation.[37] In 1966,
cooperative purchasing was permitted,[38] in 1967, joint tax assessment.[39] This legislation opened the way to such efforts as joint
purchasing by numerous Sussex County municipalities, joint property
assessment by the boroughs of Caldwell and Essex Fells, joint revalua-
tion by numerous Warren County communities, and the county-wide Bergen
Cooperative Purchasing Program. To induce further municipal cooperation, the state enacted sweeping legislation[40] in 1974:[41]

> The Interlocal Services Act provides authority for local govern-
> ments to get together and work out contractual arrangements for
> the joint provision of services. Municipalities, counties, school
> districts, regional authorities and even intramunicipal authori-
> ties (with municipal approval) can now get together to provide
> common services. Local units getting together may agree to pro-
> vide jointly, or through the agency of one or more of them, any
> service which any of the parties may legally perform for itself.
>
> The means of entering into such agreements is by a contract...
> containing a description of the services to be performed, some
> statement of standards and allocation of responsibility, esti-
> mated cost and allocation of cost by fixed amounts or by formula,
> the length of the contract and the payment procedures....The
> party who performs the service becomes the general agent of all
> the other parties with respect to that function, and assumes
> commensurate authority and responsibility....

Many other states have adopted ISA statutes similar to New Jersey's.
Such legislation has encouraged cooperative service arrangements
throughout the nation. A national study of almost 6,000 incorporated
municipalities of over 2,500 population revealed the following (see
Exhibit 6-8)[42]:

EXHIBIT 6-8
Municipalities With Interlocal Service Agreements: National Survey, 1972

City Type	Number of Reporting Cities	Having Agreement for Services		NUMBER OF CONTRACTING MUNICIPALITIES CONTRACTING WITH:													
				Municipality		County		School District		Other Special Districts		Public Authority		State		Other	
		n	%	n	%	n	%	n	%	n	%	n	%	n	%	n	%
TOTAL, ALL CITIES	2,375	1,491	63	600	40	919	62	380	25	412	28	249	17	429	29	217	15
Population Group																	
50,000 or more	180	141	78	64	46	104	74	58	41	62	44	50	35	69	49	42	30
25,000-50,000	236	180	76	81	45	118	66	60	33	60	33	46	46	64	36	31	17
10,000-25,000	532	357	67	156	44	225	63	114	32	106	30	51	14	93	26	41	11
5,000-10,000	618	360	58	141	39	217	60	77	21	86	24	52	14	98	27	41	11
5,000 or less	829	453	55	155	34	255	56	71	16	98	22	50	11	106	23	62	14
Geographic Region																	
Northeast	502	275	55	149	54	83	30	72	26	55	20	67	24	79	29	37	13
North Central	791	513	65	224	44	317	62	126	25	142	28	58	11	122	24	73	14
South	706	380	54	118	31	253	67	66	17	81	21	81	21	123	32	66	17
West	398	313	79	109	35	266	86	116	37	134	43	43	14	105	34	41	13
Form of Government																	
Mayor-council	1,148	645	56	257	40	357	55	136	21	152	24	91	14	167	26	88	14
Council-manager	1,098	762	69	315	41	519	68	249	33	235	31	157	21	233	31	118	15
Commission	78	46	59	11	24	34	74	8	17	9	20	5	11	16	35	4	9
Town meeting	57	30	53	12	40	6	20	15	50	9	30	6	20	11	37	4	13
Representative town meeting	14	8	59	5	63	3	38	2	25	2	25	1	13	2	25	2	25
Metro City Type																	
Central	155	117	75	43	37	81	69	41	35	46	39	37	32	53	45	39	33
Suburban	1,076	762	71	426	56	458	60	201	26	241	29	142	19	201	26	112	13
Non-Metropolitan	1,164	612	53	131	21	380	62	128	21	127	21	70	11	176	29	76	12

Source: Cited in Joseph F. Zimmerman, "Alternative Service Delivery Mechanisms and Areawide Tax Savings." (See reference 36 in footnotes.)

- Over 60 percent of the respondents had entered into formal or informal agreements for the provision of services to their citizens by other governmental units, public authorities, etc.

- Larger units of government (as measured by local population) had a greater propensity to have an ISA (see Exhibit 6-8).

- Service agreements were most common in the west and least popular in the south.

- Urban and suburban communities were more likely to enter into an ISA than non-metropolitan localities.

- An ISA most typically involves an arrangement between individual municipalities or between municipalities and the county. Others also provide services such as the state, school district, special districts, public authorities, etc. (see Exhibit 6-8).

- An ISA typically encompasses one as opposed to many services.

- ISA's are often limited to "noncontroversial functions" such as sewage treatment, civil defense, incarceration facilities, fire protection, emergency medical services, and health/housing inspections as opposed to police or property assessment.

- Existing ISA arrangements are typically viewed with favor by the affected governmental bodies.

Older suburbs should consider an ISA strategy as a means to reduce their municipal expenditures. One possibility is for these communities to cease providing certain services themselves and seek other units of government which can step in and perform the activity more efficiently. Alternatively, the mature suburb can seek others for whom it can provide services so as to reduce per-unit expenses (e.g. costs per mile of road paved, ton of garbage removed, and so on). Older suburbs seeking to act as contractors could point to their experience in delivering a wide range of generally high-quality services. If successful in this campaign to act as a contractor for others, the mature suburb could amortize the cost of its quality services over a population base larger than that contained within its own borders so as to reduce the per capita burden for all involved to a more tolerable level.

Englewood is illustrative. It is one of the most comprehensive purveyors of quality municipal services in northeastern Bergen County. This feature, currently contributing to the community's high local expenditures and tax burden (see chapter two), can be turned to a future asset by possibly attracting other communities to seek Englewood as a service provider under an ISA arrangement. (The latter is permitted by the 1974 Interlocal Services Act discussed previously.) Englewood already acts in such a capacity in a limited fashion. Its fine library is drawn upon by neighboring Englewood Cliffs on a fee basis. The Englewood health department similarly provides some services for nearby localities.

Further cooperative arrangements should be explored. Perhaps neighboring Bergenfield would consider dismantling its own municipal sanitation department in favor of paying Englewood to provide this service. Will Teaneck homeowners, currently contracting with private scavengers, entertain sanitation provision by Englewood's public works department? These arrangements, by amortizing service costs over a more efficient population base, would reduce some of the fiscal pressures confronting Englewood.

Englewood should also consider shedding certain in-house municipal activities in favor of having other, perhaps more efficient, units of government assume responsibility. It already does this in a limited way. For instance, Englewood takes advantage of a purchasing service offered by Bergen County. This "Cooperative Purchasing Service Program" orders stationery, gasoline, and other common supplies in bulk and thus is able to pass along savings to Englewood and sister participating localities. Bolder actions along these lines should be considered. Perhaps Englewood should disband its own fire department if Teaneck's municipal fire force could provide adequate fire protection for an attractive fee.

Detailing specific ISA service transfers available to older suburbs goes beyond the scope of this chapter. The important point is that these communities seriously evaluate service provision by other units of government. Municipal financial stress is already prodding such consideration; even steadfast home-rule local governments are examining cooperative service arrangements. In Bergen County, for example:[43]

> Faced with a trinity of budgetary restrictions, inflation, and taxpayer demands for municipal services, representatives of more than a dozen northern Bergen County communities are planning to meet...to discuss the possibility of regionalizing services and sharing resources.
>
> Mayors and administrators of the towns will explore what areas of local government lend themselves to regionalization and lay the groundwork for future meetings...[as discussed by one mayor] "We've worked together on mutual problems that affect the region, community development block grants, sewerage, and transportation, and now we're going to explore areas where joint action might be taken to solve problems or provide services more cheaply."

MODIFY SERVICE DELIVERY STRATEGIES:
THE PRIVATE SECTOR

The approaches considered thus far, while entailing some tinkering with municipal cost influences, still retain the traditional public gestalt of local service provision -- delivery by public agencies and

financing by public tax dollars. More radical change may be necessary.
One such shift is to inject private market discipline into, if not
private sector implementation of, service provision.[44] A range of
such options, listed in Exhibit 6-9, deserve scrutiny.

EXHIBIT 6-9

Alternative Service Delivery Approaches

STRATEGY	SERVICE IMPLEMENTATION	FINANCING
Traditional	Public (municipal agency)	Public (tax dollars)
User Fee or Public Utility	Public (acting as private sector entity)	Public (paid by service beneficiary)
Contract	Private	Public (tax dollars)
Privatization	Private	Private (paid by service beneficiary)
Voluntarism	Private	Private (paid by donor)

Source: See text.

Expanding the imposition of user charges is one possibility. User
charges are defined as "amounts received from the public for performance of specific services benefiting the person charged."[45] A
charging approach offers not only a new revenue flow but also an advantage as far as service delivery and consumption are concerned. Under a user charge system, there is a direct and strong incentive to
provide market-demanded services at a fair price since doing otherwise
may be met by consumer resistance. In short, a workplace mechanism has
been interjected to guide municipal agencies; no such feedback/re-
straints exist under the current taxation method of financing municipal activities. As summarized by Selma Mushkin of the Urban Institute:[46]

> Under present resource allocation practices within the public
> sector itself, the wrong product is sometimes produced, in the
> wrong quantity, and with no (or inappropriate) quality differ-
> entiation. If it is feasible to determine benefit values and to
> identify the beneficiaries of a public program, pricing (i.e.,
> user charges) becomes a viable means of ensuring that the alloca-
> tion of public resources becomes more efficient.

The advantages of user fees -- added revenues and a "rational" service allocation mechanism -- have led many localities to turn to this mechanism. In fiscal year 1970-71, user charges amounted to about one-fifth of municipal tax revenue in the United States; a decade later about one-third. The impost of such fees by specific service category has been documented in a recent national survey conducted by the International City Management Association.[47] Utility and construction-related charges such as sewerage treatment and plumbing inspection fees were the most common, followed by levies for various recreational-cultural facilities (e.g., swimming pools or golf courses), and then charges for a potpourri of activities going beyond "basic" public services such as non-emergency ambulance pick-up. An interesting finding of the ICMA survey was the recent (post-1978) imposition of charges for activities previously provided gratis. For example, after 1978 between one-quarter to one-third of the surveyed communities began to charge for such "frills" as special police patrols, tennis courts, and local concerts. In short, communities are beginning to disaggregate their service activity into essential or basic areas still to be supported by the public fisc and a less protected group where service beneficiaries are charged.

In a sense, user fees retain public implementation employing the strictures of the private sector. The next two approaches presented in Exhibit 6-9 turn to the private sector even more strongly. Contracting refers to the "purchase of certain services by government from private sources...and financed by tax collections."[48] Privatization similarly entails service implementation by a private entity; however, this entity is paid directly by the party receiving the service. Thus, with privatization there is no transfer of public tax dollars; rather, a fee is paid from one private individual to another. To illustrate, if a municipality hires a private scavenger to collect garbage and then pays for such work with public tax revenues, this arrangement is an example of contracting. If the private scavenger picks up a homeowner's garbage and is compensated directly by the homeowner, this approach is termed privatization.

While there is a distinction between contracting and privatization, this difference should not obscure a close conceptual kinship -- service provision has left the public domain and is being satisfied by private entities. Given the similarities of contracting and privatization, we shall discuss the two together.

There are numerous instances of both of these service approaches on the American municipal scene. A 1982 national survey of municipalities revealed that about half of all local governments had some contracting arrangement (see Exhibit 6-1).[49] This service arrangement is most prevalent in technical and public works services (e.g., architecture, engineering, street construction/repair, and solid waste collection) as opposed to activities not demanding specialized expertise nor equipment (e.g., leaf collection, public recreation, etc.; see Exhibit 6-10).[50]

Refuse collection is illustrative of a public works service for which contracting is often turned to. In 1975, E.S. Savas and col-

EXHIBIT 6-10

Type and Frequency of Contracted-Out Services
By Level of Government

	COUNTY (N = 55)		MUNICIPALITY (N = 170)		TOTAL (N = 225)	
	Number	Percent	Number	Percent	Number	Percent
Architectural services	47	85	134	79	181	80
Engineering services	37	67	112	66	151	67
Street construction	31	56	126	74	149	66
Building repair	29	53	85	50	114	51
Solid waste collection	31	56	64	38	95	42
Equipment maintenance	20	36	67	39	87	39
Legal counsel	13	24	64	38	81	36
Building maintenance	21	38	50	29	77	34
Ambulance services	20	36	61	36	71	32
Vehicle maintenance	15	27	55	32	70	31
Administrative support	14	25	49	29	63	28
Children's day care	6	11	52	30	58	26
Food service, employees	20	36	29	17	54	24
Elderly, nursing	13	24	41	24	51	23
Land use/planning	6	11	45	26	49	22
Halfway houses	11	2	30	17	41	18
Street maintenance	12	22	27	16	39	17
Snow removal	12	22	25	15	37	16
Grounds maintenance	13	24	19	11	32	14
First aid employees	4	7	27	16	31	14
Elderly, recreation	4	7	23	14	27	12
Leaf collection	8	14	8	5	16	7
Public recreation	3	5	12	7	15	7
Misc. police services	4	7	5	3	15	7
Police communications	2	3	13	8	10	4
Building inspection	4	7	6	4	9	4
Janitorial services	3	5	4	2	9	4
Transportation related[1]	2	3	5	3	7	3
Park maintenance	2	3	7	4	7	3
Consulting, miscellaneous	0	0	3	2	7	3
Sewer/water/sanitation[2]	6	11	1	5	7	3
Uniforms - laundry/rental	5	9	2	1	3	1
Escalator/elevator repair	0	0	1	5	1	4

[1]Includes towing, hauling, buses, toll bridges, etc.
[2]Includes treatment, testing, recycling, landfills, meters.

Source: Patricia S. Florestano and Stephen B. Gordon, "A Survey of City and County Use of Private Contracting," The Urban Interest (Spring 1981).

leagues at the Columbia University Center for Government Studies conducted a national survey of sanitation strategies.[51] They found a variety of approaches: municipal -- where local governments deliver services themselves; contract -- where local governments hire and pay a private firm (identical to the contracting approach defined in the chapter); franchise -- where a private firm is granted the exclusive right to provide refuse collection in an area and the firm charges the customers it serves; private -- where households/businesses contract with any private scavenger they desire (identical to the privatization approach defined in this chapter); and self service -- where households/business service themselves (e.g., take refuse to the town dump). As indicated in Exhibit 6-11, municipal collection is in the minority; only about one-third of local governments opted for this strategy. This share was higher in: larger cities than small, central as compared to suburban communities, and for localities located in the south as opposed to other regions (see Exhibit 6-11).

There are several reasons why a municipality prefers private companies to provide sanitation or other services. The municipal corporation often lacks specialized skills and equipment and turns to the private sector to fill this gap. It is for this reason that so much contracting is for engineering, planning and related technical services as well as for activities requiring expensive capital equipment such as road paving or sanitation (see Exhibit 6-10). A further motivation for contracting is the search for economy in service costs. Contracting (and privatization) are looked to as efficient service vehicles because they draw on firms competing in the private market. In this arena, price and product win the jobs. This situation is diametrically opposed to the traditional arrangement of public service delivery with no direct competition and therefore minimal direct incentive to economize or deliver a superior product.

Is the anticipated cost advantage of contracting and privatization realized in practice? Many studies answer in the affirmative, albeit there is considerable "noise" in the analysis because of data inadequacies, service quality variations, and so on.[52] Savas's national refuse collection survey cited earlier discovered the following expenditure declinations (see Exhibit 6-7). Refuse costs were highest in instances of "private" (non-territorially exclusive) collection, perhaps reflecting the inefficiencies of many firms serving the same area.[53] Costs were lower in cases of "municipal" and "franchise" (territorially exclusive) strategies (see Exhibit 6-7). The least expensive outlays were found with "contract" (the municipality arranges with one firm to service the entire community) pick-up. Savas's analysis went beyond the numbers and documented specific areas of "municipal" inefficiency relative to "contract" arrangements:[54]

> For cities of all sizes, contractors use significantly smaller crews and significantly larger collection vehicles than do municipal collection agencies. The absentee rate is significantly higher for public refuse collectors than for private firms. [The] private firm under contract with the city is significantly more

EXHIBIT 6-11
Local Sanitation Collection Strategies by Community
Classification: National Municipal Survey, 1975

Community Classification	COLLECTION STRATEGY [@]												Total Respondents All [①]	
	Municipal		Contract		Franchise		Private		Self-service		Other			
	n	%	n	%	n	%	n	%	n	%	n	%	n	%
TOTAL, ALL CITIES	768	30.3%	421	16.6%	165	6.5%	782	30.9%	376	14.9%	19	0.8%	2,531	100.0%
Population Group														
100,000 or more	89	66.9	13	9.8	1	0.1	19	14.3	8	6.0	3	2.3	133	100.0
50,000-99,999	87	50.6	17	9.9	20	11.6	26	15.1	21	12.2	1	0.6	172	100.0
25,000-49,999	63	31.0	35	17.2	25	12.3	53	26.1	27	13.3	0	0.0	203	100.0
10,000-24,999	179	35.6	117	23.3	34	6.8	117	23.3	54	10.7	2	0.4	503	100.0
5,000-9,999	178	27.8	105	16.4	29	4.5	219	34.2	107	16.7	2	0.3	640	100.0
2,500-4,999	172	19.5	134	15.2	56	6.4	348	39.5	159	18.1	11	1.3	880	100.0
Geographic Region														
Northeast	186	19.0	213	21.7	22	2.2	382	38.9	176	17.9	2	0.2	981	100.0
North Central	143	20.0	111	15.5	16	2.2	330	46.2	107	15.0	8	1.1	715	100.0
South	341	72.7	28	6.0	34	7.2	33	7.0	27	5.8	6	1.3	469	100.0
West	98	26.8	69	18.9	93	25.4	37	10.1	66	18.0	3	0.8	366	100.0
Metro/city Type														
Central	192	62.5	30	9.8	14	4.6	43	14.0	23	7.5	5	1.6	307	100.0
Suburban	576	25.9	391	17.6	51	6.8	739	33.2	353	15.9	14	0.6	2,224	100.0

Notes: ① See text for definition.
② n = 2,531.
③ Percentages may not add to 100% due to rounding.

Source: E.S. Savas and Christopher Niemczewski, "Who Collects Solid Waste," in International City Management Association, The Municipal Year Book, 1979 (Washington, D.C.: ICMA, 1976).

likely than the public collection agency to use vehicles which can be loaded conveniently by the driver or the crew, that is front- or side-loading.

More recent studies similarly document service cost savings realized by private sector as opposed to municipal approaches. In 1980, Eileen Berenyi examined sanitation costs in 10 cities which shifted from municipal sanitation provision to a contract arrangement.[55] After controlling for inflation, quality of service, and other variations, Berenyi found that in all cases, service efficiencies were achieved, with the savings ranging from 7 to 30 percent (see Exhibit 6-12). Berenyi, like Savas, discovered that private sanitation companies were able to achieve a cost advantage by being more innovative and efficient through such means as utilizing larger trucks, using fewer men per truck, and following a more efficient pick-up route.

The fact that savings have been achieved by private sector service approaches does not mean that this advantage will always be realized. For instance, in areas where scavengers are controlled by organized crime or other monopolistic forces, such firms are not competitive in the free-market, Adam Smith sense and hence may be far from efficient. The California State Commission on Government Organization and Economy, for example:[56]

> ...while favoring a constitutional amendment to provide for independent contractors, refused to accept the assumptions of efficiency and economy associated with private contracting, stating ....The commission bases this precaution on a study which it undertook in 1965 entitled Engineering Costs in the Division of Highways, which found that in functions performed by the California Department of Transportation (Caltrans) there was very little cost differential between state government operations and those of an outside contractor; in fact, the commission concluded at that time the cost differential was slightly in favor of in-house operations.

A further consideration is that the fiscal pressures of the past few years have prompted municipal departments themselves to adopt many of the time and cost saving approaches which have given private companies their cost edge. New York City's recent shift to technologically advanced garbage trucks, requiring a smaller crew to man, is illustrative. Wage differentials between municipal employees and workers in private firms have similarly been narrowed as the latter, fearful for their jobs, have consented to fringe and other givebacks.

While there are complex forces affecting the comparative costs of traditional public versus more free market service delivery options, the evidence at hand favors the latter. Consequently, fiscally hard-pressed older suburbs should seriously explore the benefits of employing user fees, contracting and/or privatization. In making such an evaluation, city officials should look beyond the singular objective of economy to the many characteristics on which the different strategies vary. These include (see Exhibit 6-13):

EXHIBIT 6-12

**Cost Comparisons of Residential Refuse Collection
Before and After Privatization**

City	Year of Change	Number of Households	Annual Municipal Cost In Year Prior to Change (per HH)	Projected Municipal Cost In Year After Change (per HH)	Annual Contract Cost (per HH)	Net Transition Gain (per HH)	% Change in Cost
Berwyn, Illinois	1976	15,800	$41.67[2]	$43.31	$40.06[2]	NA[3]	- 7.5
Pekin, Illinois	1976	10,334	$76.18	$81.32	$70.21	NA	-13.6
Covington, Kentucky	1975	17,569	$30.28	$30.28	$26.11	$ 7.22	-13.7
Middletown, Ohio	1972	16,200	$27.34	$29.83	$21.00	$ 4.58	-29.6
Gainesville, Fla.	1977	14,921	$59.17	$62.79	$48.12	$18.60	-23.4
Camden, New Jersey	1974	25,000[1]	$62.81[2]	$67.67[2]	$54.01[2]	$ 4.73	-20.2

[1]Camden's 25,000 figure is the total number of refuse collection customers and includes some commercial stops.
[2]Cost includes disposal.
[3]NA = Not Available.

Source: Eileen Brettler Berenyi, "Contracting Out Refuse Collection: The Nature and Impact of Change," The Urban Interest (Spring 1981).

EXHIBIT 6-13

**Performance of Alternative Service Delivery Approaches
On Selected Criteria**

STRATEGY	EVALUATION CRITERIA[1]					
	Competition	Public Control	Consumer Freedom	Service Universalism	Federal Tax Interface	State Expenditure/ Revenue Interface
Traditional	Decreasing	Increasing	Decreasing	Increasing	Increasing	Increasing
Contract	↓	↑	↓	↑	↑	↑
User Fee	↓	↑	↓	↑	↑	↑
Privatization	Increasing	Decreasing	Increasing	Decreasing	Decreasing	Decreasing

[1]See text.

Source: Rutgers University, Center for Urban Policy Research, 1982.

1. Competition - How many purveyors will likely offer the service?

2. Public control - What is the degree of public control over the service?

3. Consumer freedom - To what extent can an individual consumer pick and choose the type and cost of services consumed?

4. Service universalism - to what degree are the services available to everyone, even the poor?

5. Federal-state tax interface - To what extent are the service costs paid by the consumer deductible from federal or state income taxes (in the form of lowering taxable income)?

6. State revenue-expenditure interface - To what extent are service expenditures-revenues affected by applicable state "caps"?

The service delivery options differ on many of the above-mentioned variables (see Exhibit 6-13). The traditional approach is monopolistic -- there is only one service entity, the designated public agency. In contrast, privatization is characterized by a high level of competition as many firms compete for the consumers' choice. The other strategies are somewhat in between. For example, contracting is more "competitive" than the traditional service strategy, yet is less so than privatization because only a few firms may desire such work -- the learning, paper work, and other costs of responding to a municipal request for services is likely to reduce the number of interested entrants.

Other variations are indicated in Exhibit 6-13. For instance, user fees are not deductible for federal and/or state income tax purposes, nor do they usually count in the enumeration for state expenditure-revenue "caps." In contrast, the tax dollars which pay for contracted services usually are deductible for income tax purposes and usually are included in state "cap" computations.

These service strategy rankings can help guide municipal officials in their determination of when and where different service delivery strategies should be opted for. For instance, in instances where consumer freedom seems to be most appropriate, such as recreation, consideration should be given to those service approaches maximizing this flexibility (e.g., user fees or privatization). Other service areas will have different priorities. Basic health protection such as rodent extermination and infant inoculations may require service universalism -- available to everyone including the poor. Full service coverage, in turn, is usually best achieved by traditional and contract strategies as opposed to user fees and privatization, for the latter approaches may preclude the participation of those of modest income. The affordability issue is an important concern in evaluating the effects of turning to nontraditional service strategies.[57]

These equity concerns can be addressed. Privatization and user fees will not penalize the poor if the latter are given vouchers or other financial assistance to satisfy the charges levied by the company providing services. Such support could be keyed to the importance of the service, e.g., support might be forthcoming to pay for police-fire protection and reduced or withheld for certain types of recreation. This modification would provide a safety net for the poor yet would still realize the service cost savings associated with user fees and privatization.

In summary, municipal officials in older suburbs must carefully analyze whether their current means of service provision should be replaced bv alternatives. In conducting this review, they should consider the differing characteristics of the various strategies and also give thought to how the alternative strategies themselves might be adjusted to best satisfy local needs. The mixed voucher-privatization program mentioned above is illustrative of a conceptually blended approach. Other factors must also be scrutinized. There may be possible legal restrictions in state constitutions or local charters to certain means of providing public services. Further, the interest, expertise and capacity of local private firms to perform once-public functions must also be checked.

Our discussion is not meant as an indictment of existing service patterns but rather as a call to reconsider extant arrangements. Englewood is illustrative. This community currently provides all important services via municipal departments funded by tax dollars. Alternative arrangements should be considered. The community has already turned to enhanced user fees, both in the form of existing levies (e.g., in 1981, the annual fee for alcoholic beverages was raised by one-fifth) to imposing charges for activities once provided gratis (e.g., police fingerprint services). Further user fee imposts should be considered as a means to allocate service consumption and not only as a back door revenue-raising mechanism. Englewood should also evaluate the merits of turning to both contracting and privatization. These service delivery approaches are already in place in many sister mature suburbs. Refuse pick up is illustrative. While Englewood has a municipal collection strategy, Dover and Fort Lee rely on contracting, while Cranford, Plainfield, Scotch Plains, and Teaneck have opted for privatization (see Exhibit 2-10). As evident from Exhibit 2-9 these non-municipal service strategies tend to be less expensive than municipal delivery, albeit there is considerable noise because of differences in service quality (see Exhibit 2-10). There is sufficient evidence, however, from both national studies and our New Jersey analysis to prompt Englewood to reconsider the wisdom of its municipal service emphasis as opposed to private sector alternatives.

PUSHING THE CONCEPTUAL BOUNDARIES -- VOLUNTARISM

The fiscal crunch confronting mature suburbs calls for further pushing of the service delivery status quo. Voluntary assistance by business, civic groups, block associations, and so on could provide

limited assistance. Voluntarism represents an even further shift in
the service delivery spectrum. The traditional concept saw services as
a public monopoly. The trio of user fees, contracting, and privatization conceptually took services to the private sector. Voluntarism
takes the privatization concept one step farther. There are no con-
tractual guides -- assistance is delivered by a private donor to a
private recipient.

Voluntarism is not simply a matter of fiscal necessity, born of a
shrunken public purse, but offers numerous advantages to the pro-
viders. Businesses, neighborhood groups and so on all benefit from
improving the appearance, economic vigor, and security of the area
where they live or work. Tax loads are another consideration; it may
be less costly for a citizen or business to provide certain nominally
"public" services out of its own pocket than to have the same made
available by a costly municipal department supported by public tax
dollars. These factors have prompted growing instances of voluntarism
on the American municipal landscape (see Exhibit 6-1).

Voluntarism could take many forms in an older suburb. In Englewood's
case such service provision would represent a turning back of the
historical clock. In its infancy, Englewood's services and capital
improvements were provided by subscription and other voluntary associations:[58]

> A Village Improvement Society was formed in 1868 to provide for
> and to maintain lighting of streets, the planting of trees, and
> the removal of refuse from public places. The society's funds
> were raised by annual subscriptions and private contributions....
>
> In 1869, a Society for Mutual Protection was formed and given
> police power by an act of the legislature....Its membership at
> first was comprised of almost every able-bodied man in the
> community....In 1872, funds were raised for a "lock-up" which
> later became the first Englewood Police Station.
>
> A volunteer hose company (fire force) was organized in 1887 and a
> subscription raised $1,000 for equipment...
>
> Private institutions were also relied on initially for drainage.
> The Citizens' Sewer Company constructed the main sewer under
> Palisade Avenue with 100 subscribers and another company widened
> the Overpeck Creek into a canal to drain the area....

Over the course of time, Englewood turned from voluntarism to a
municipal service structure supported by tax dollars. One push for
this was the loss to fire at the turn of the twentieth century of both
the Athenaeum Building (a combination post office, retail center, and
800 seat theatre) and the Englewood opera house.[59] Shortly thereafter in 1912, a paid fire department replaced volunteers. At about

the same time, a professional police department was established and the Village Protective Society disbanded. Capital improvements were similarly soon undertaken at the public's expense, leaving the Village Improvement Society a vestigal organization. It was ultimately replaced by the Civil Club which set as its goals socially oriented activities as opposed to more mundane infrastructure improvements.

The turn to municipal services did not totally eliminate voluntary provision. In the 1930's, for example, counseling, day care, recreation, and nutrition supplementary programs were offered by private service federations.[60] The Mount Carmel Guild, founded in 1930, also served the needy throughout the depression. Voluntarism continues until today, albeit nowhere on the scale of a century ago. For instance, arts-related services are made available by the John Harms Englewood Plaza. Local lenders support the facade improvement loan program by making monies available at their cost. Low- and moderate-income housing is sponsored by the Mount Carmel Guild and other eleemosynary organizations. The many faceted involvement of the Chamber of Commerce to improve the central business district is another illustration.

Englewood's fiscal stress may serve to prod further voluntarism -- a return to the community's service roots. As discussed in chapter four, Englewood's retailers could provide security, marketing, and other services to bolster the CBD. Citizens could form block associations, crime watch patrols, and similar self-protection strategies. Counseling, tutoring and other assistance could be made available by volunteers, and so on.

These local resident-business activities would help reduce the burden on municipal departments engaged in recreation, economic development, public safety, etc. In some cases, voluntarism could replace the public delivery and cost of services. Fire protection is illustrative. In 1978, Englewood spent $1.3 of its $10.3 million operating budget for its fire department. Perhaps it should make do with a volunteer force. This is the most common fire protection strategy. About half of the municipalities in the United States rely on volunteer departments, a third have a municipally-paid force, while the remainder have other arrangements (e.g., provision by special districts, counties, etc.)[61] Many of Englewood's sister mature suburbs have opted for firefighter volunteers, including Fort Lee, Scotch Plains, and Wayne. If turning completely to volunteers is too radical a step, then Englewood should at least consider a mixed approach combining a small paid core (e.g., dispatchers and inspectors) with volunteers. This combined strategy is found in numerous mature suburbs including Bergenfield, Millburn, Morristown, Ridgewood, and Summit (see Exhibit 2-8).

A voluntary or mixed fire force clearly offers a municipal expenditure saving over a publicly-paid department. In 1978, New Jersey older suburbs with a volunteer or mixed fire department expended $10 and $30 per capita respectively for fire protection compared to $39 for those with a municipal arrangement (see Exhibit 2-10). National studies indicate approximately the same cost relationship. The landmark Research

Triangle investigation[62] of fire protection services in 200 municipalities indicated that a fully paid force cost anywhere from $5 to
$40 per capita on an annual basis; a volunteer strategy ranged from $5
to $20; while a mixed (paid and volunteer) approach cost from $5 to
about $30 per person (see Exhibit 6-14). In short, a volunteer fire
protection is anywhere from one-quarter to three-quarters less expensive than paid or mixed alternatives.

This ratio permits a rough projection of the expenditure savings
potential open to Englewood in converting its paid fire department to
a volunteer arrangement. In 1978, Englewood expended about $1.3 mil-
lion for fire protection. With a volunteer or mixed force, fire service expenditures could be reduced to roughly $1.0 million (25 percent
savings) to $.3 million (75 percent savings). In sum, Englewood could
realize a savings of say $.5 million (average of the 25 and 75 percent
reductions) or about 5 percent of its 1978 municipal operating budget.

Voluntarism's potential must be nurtured. In part, this will require
encouragement by local municipal officials -- they should not view
voluntarism as competition. Espousal of voluntarism should also stress
private sector self-interest -- "We all rise and fall together." Voluntarism could also be abetted by the federal government. Changes in
federal tax treatment, for instance, is one possibility. To illustrate, under current law, residents volunteering their services to
civic, neighborhood, and similar groups are considered to be "non-
working" and hence are not permitted child care deductions; changing
their status would reduce considerably, out-of-pocket costs for volunteer activities. Voluntarism, while by no means an encompassing
answer to financial austerity, is nonetheless a growing approach to at
least selected public service delivery.

THE SERVICE CHANGES IN PERSPECTIVE: CONCLUSION

This chapter has overviewed numerous municipal expenditures and
service alternatives available to older suburbs in general and Englewood in particular. Where possible, it has projected the cost
savings potential of the different belt-tightening approaches, e.g.,
changes in the Englewood refuse collection schedule could save about
one percent of total operating costs; turning to fire fighting volunteers offers a five percent savings, and so on.

These and other economies come at a "price." All the strategies discussed in this chapter involve inevitable "costs" to the municipal
work force and/or the public at large. Trimming public staff means
remaining personnel must work harder. Cutting back service standards
affects the local quality of life. Altering service arrangements,
whether in the form of turning to other units of government or to
private firms, entails adjustment and a not too infrequent rough
transition. Turning to volunteers poses its own set of risks: will
local citizens-businesses come forward; will they have the expertise
and long term interest to serve as adequate replacements for the
public sector? The trade-offs of altering service arrangements are
dramatically illustrated for fire protection in Exhibit 6-14. The

EXHIBIT 6-14

**Comparison of Property Loss and Expenditures
For Different Types of Fire Service Strategies**

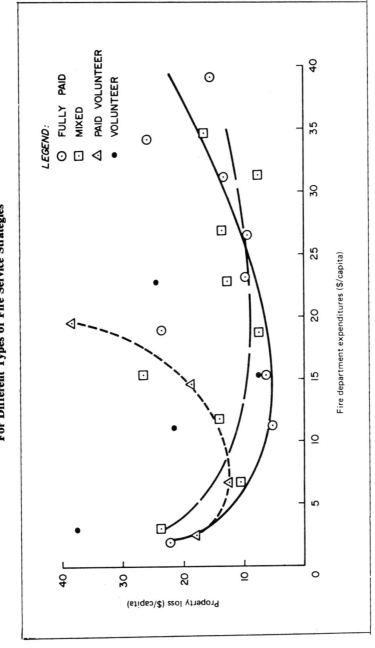

Source: Edward Vickery et al., "Operational Productivity Measures for Fire Service Delivery," The Municipal Year Book, 1976 (Washington, D.C.: International City Management Association, 1976), p. 175.

horizontal axis of this exhibit indicates that fire protection costs
(per capita) are linked to delivery strategy: fully paid fire departments tend to be the most expensive, volunteers the least.[63] The
vertical axis points to the "price" of lesser fire protection outlays -- increasing property losses, albeit there is considerable
"noise" in the relationship and it is not a linear one.[64] Thus,
property losses are highest with low per capita service outlays;
property losses tend to decline at first with increasing service
spending, yet start to rise as service expenditures reach the highest
levels, perhaps reflecting the greater fire hazard inducing the added
spending (e.g. outlays are high in neighborhoods experiencing abandonment). This pattern suggests that a "U" shaped relationship exists
between property loss and service spending.[65]

Our point is not to document the intricacies of fire protection but
rather to point to the inevitable trade-off in altering traditional
service arrangements. Englewood and sister mature suburbs are evaluating these consequences and are making the necessary hard decisions
in an era of fiscal stress. This chapter hopefully will assist their
continued introspection and decision making.

NOTES

1. D. Bennett Mazur, People, Politics, and Planning: The Comparative History of Three Suburban Communities. Ph.D. Dissertation,
Rutgers University, May 1981, p. 490.
2. Ibid., p. 500.
3. Ibid.
4. Ibid., p. 517.
5. Ibid., p. 541.
6. Mark David Menchik, et al., How Fiscal Restraints Affect Spending and Services in Cities (Santa Monica: RAND, 1982).
7. Laurie S. Frankel, "Police/Fire Consolidation in Municipalities
10,000 and Over," The Municipal Year Book, 1978 (Washington, D.C.:
International City Management Association, 1978), p. 137. See also,
Thomas Cowing and A. Holtmann, The Economics of Local Public Service
Consolidation (Lexington, MA: Lexington Books, 1976); James Coke,
Management and Structural Options for City Governments (Columbus, OH:
Academy for Contemporary Problems, 1978); Andrew Glassberg, "Organizational Responses to Municipal Budget Decreases," Public Administration Review, Vol. 38 (1978), p. 325; Charles Levine, "Organizational
Decline and Cutback Management," Public Administration Review, Vol. 38
(1978), p. 316; Carol Lewis and Anthony Logalbo, "Cutback Principles
and Practices: A Checklist for Managers," Public Administration Review, Vol. 40 (1980), p. 184.
8. Donald Oatman, "It's Time for Productivity Accounting in Government," Government Finance, Vol. 8, No. 3, November 1978, p. 9.
9. Clarence Ridley and Herbert Simon, Measuring Municipal Activities: A Survey of Suggested Criteria for Appraising Administrations
(Washington, D.C.: International City Management Association, 1938).
See George Barbour, "Productivity Measurement: The ICMA Viewpoint,"
Governmental Finance (1973).

10. Barbour, "Productivity Measurement."

11. International City Management Association, "Checklist on How to Improve Management Services" (Washington, D.C.: ICMA, 1958).

12. International City Management Association, "Measuring Effectiveness of Municipal Services," Management Information Service (Washington, D.C.: ICMA, 1970).

13. See, for example, ICMA and the Urban Institute, The Challenge of Productivity: Improving Local Government Productivity Measurement and Evaluations (Washington, D.C.: National Commission on Productivity, 1972); Harry Hatry, et al., How Effective Are Your Community Services (Washington, D.C.: Urban Institute and International City Management Association, 1977).

14. See for example, Ernest Enke, "Municipal Accounting," in J. Richard Aronson and Eli Schwartz (editors), Management/Policies in Local Government Finance (Washington, D.C.: International City Management Association, 1975); Allan Drebin, "Criteria for Performance Measurement in State and Local Government," Governmental Finance, Vol. 9 (December 1980), p. 3; Harry Hatry, et al., Efficiency Measurement for Local Government Services -- Some Initial Suggestions (Washington, D.C.: Urban Institute, 1979). See also Walter Balk (ed.), "Productivity in Government: A Symposium," Public Administration Review, Vol. 38 (1978), pp. 1-50; Committee for Economic Development, Improving Productivity in State and Local Government (New York: The Committee, 1976); Elinor Ostrom, "On the Meaning and Measurement of Output and Efficiency in the Provision of Urban Police Services," Journal of Criminal Justice 1 (1973), pp. 93-112; Allan Udler, "Productivity Measurement of Administrative Services," Personnel Journal, Vol. 57 (1978), pp. 672-675; John Ross and Jesse Burkhead, Productivity in the Local Government Sector (Lexington, MA: Heath and Company, 1974); Donald Fisk and Richard Winnie, "Output Measurement in Urban Government: Current Status and Likely Prospects," Social Science Quarterly, Vol. 54 (1974), p. 725.

15. Rackham Fukuhara, "Productivity Improvement in Cities," The Municipal Year Book - 1977 (Washington, D.C.: International City Management Association, 1977), p. 193. See also, Brian Usilaner, "Productivity -- a Management Tool for Controlling Government Spending," Public Productivity Review, Vol. 3 (1978), p. 25; George Washnis, Productivity Improvement Handbook for State and Local Government (New York: Wiley, 1980); David Wilkins, "A Productivity Program for Local Government," Public Productivity Review, Vol. 3 (1979) p. 17.

16. Fukuhara, "Productivity Improvement in Cities," p. 194.

17. International City Management Association, "Productivity Improvements in Small Governments," Urban Data Service Report, Vol. 44, No. 7 (July 1982).

18. James T. Bennett and Manuel Johnson, Better Governance at Half the Price (O'Hara, IL: Caroline Home Builders, 1981); Martha Shulman and W. Maureen Godsey, Local Government Productivity Improvement (Washington, D.C.: International City Management Association, 1982); Robert Poole, Cutting Back City Hall (New York: Universal Press, 1980). See also, Selma Mushkin and Frank Sandifer, Personnel Manage-

ment and Productivity in City Government (Lexington, KY: Lexington Books, 1979); Jeffrey Straussman, "More Bang for Fewer Bucks? Or How Local Government Can Rediscover the Potentials (and Pitfalls) of the Market," Public Administration Review, Vol. 41 (Jan. 1981), p. 150; Daniel Stone, "Productivity and Performance/Providing the Same Services for No Increased Costs," PM Public Management, Vol. 3 (1978), p. 32; John Thomas, "Demand Analysis: a Powerful Productivity Improvement Technique," Public Productivity Review, Vol. 3 (1978) p. 32.
   19. Poole, Cutting Back City Hall.
   20. Ibid., p. 35.
   21. Menchik, How Fiscal Restraints Affect Spending and Services in Cities.
   22. United States Conference of Mayors, The FY 82 Budget and the Cities (Washington, D.C.: Conference of Mayors, 1981).
   23. CUPR telephone interview with Englewood Deputy Police Chief Lucciano, October 1982.
   24. CUPR telephone interview with Ken Albert, Director of the Englewood Public Works Department, October 1982.
   25. Ibid.
   26. Menchik, How Fiscal Restraints Affect Spending and Services in Cities.
   27. CUPR telephone interview with the Englewood library, October 1982.
   28. Robert Bartolatta, "Local Government Solid Waste Programs," The Municipal Year Book 1975 (Washington, D.C.: International City Management Association, 1975), p. 232.
   29. Ibid.
   30. 1982 Budget Recommendations prepared by Kennedy Shaw, City Manager, January 18, 1982.
   31. E. S. Savas, "Policy Analysis for Local Government: Public Versus Private Refuse Collection," Policy Analysis, Vol. 3, No. 1, (Winter 1977), p. 66.
   32. James Mercer, et al., Managing Urban Government Services (New York: American Management Association, 1981).
   33. Joseph Zimmerman, "Municipal Transfers of Functional Responsibilities," Urban Data Service Report, Vol. 7, No. 9 (September 1975), p. 16.
   34. Ibid., p. 13.
   35. Joseph Zimmerman, "Alternative Service Delivery Mechanisms and Areawide Tax Savings." Paper presented at a meeting of "Industries for Amsterdam," New York, November 10, 1981.
   36. Ibid.
   37. J. Peter Braun, "Wherefore Art Thou Joint Services," in Julius Mastro and J. Albert Mastro (editors), Governing New Jersey Municipalities (New Brunswick: Rutgers University, Bureau of Government Research, 1979), p. 439.
   38. N.J.S.A. 40:50-7.1-7.3
   39. Chapter 180 of the Public Laws of 1967.

40. N.J.S.A. 40:8A-1 et seq.

41. James Alexander, Jr., "Interlocal Services: New Tools for Local Cooperation," New Jersey Municipalities (February 1980).

42. Zimmerman, "Alternative Service Delivery Mechanisms."

43. Bergen Record, February 13, 1982, p. C-1.

44. Poole, Cutting Back City Hall; Jeffrey D. Straussman, "Quasi-Market Alternatives to Local Government Service Provision," The Urban Interest (Spring 1981), p. 3; R. S. Ahlbrandt, "Implications of Contracting for a Public Service," Urban Affairs Quarterly (March 1974), pp. 337-359; "When the Government Lets Somebody Else Do Its Job," National Journal (October 1977), pp. 1410-1414; D. D. Fisk, et al., Private Provision of Public Services: An Overview (Washington, D.C.: Urban Interest, 1978); P. S. Florestano, "The Municipal Connection: Contracting for Public Services with the Private Sector," Municipal Management, Vol. 1 (Fall 1978), p. 61; Florestano and S.B. Gordon, "Public Versus Private: Small Government Contracting with the Private Sector," Public Administration Review, Vol. 40 (January-February 1980), p. 29. See also, Sidney Sonenblum, et al., How Cities Provide Services: An Evaluation of Alternative Delivery Structures (Cambridge, MA: Ballinger, 1977); Stephen Mehay, "Inter-Governmental Contracting for Municipal Police Services -- An Empirical Analysis," Land Economics, Vol. 55 (1979), p. 59; Gary Miller, Cities by Contract: The Politics of Municipal Incorporation (Cambridge, MA: The MIT Press, 1981); Daniel Fitzpatrick and Daniel Breuer, "An Experience in Contracting-Out Services," Municipal Management: A Journal, Vol. 3 (1980), p. 171.

45. See Anthony Pascal, "User Charges, Contracting Out, and Privatization in an Era of Fiscal Retrenchment," The Urban Interest (Spring 1981), p. 7.

46. S. J. Mushkin and R. M. Bird, "Public Prices -- An Overview," in S. J. Mushkin, Public Prices for Public Products (Washington, D.C.: Urban Interest, 1972). See also, Patrick Glisson, "Developing Local Government User Charges: Technical and Policy Considerations," Governmental Finance, Vol. 4, No. 1 (March 1982), p. 3; Ross Kory, "Costing Municipal Services," Governmental Finance, Vol. 4, No. 1 (March 1982), p. 21.

47. Maurice Criz, "The Role of User Charges and Fees in City Finance," Urban Data Service Reports, Vol. 14, No. 6 (Washington, D.C.: International City Management Association, 1982).

48. James Alexander, "Contracting Out and the Municipal Budget," New Jersey Municipalities (March 1981), p. 6.

49. ICMA, "Productivity Improvements in Small Local Governments."

50. Patricia S. Florestano and Stephen B. Gordon, "A Survey of City and County Use of Private Contracting," The Urban Interest (Spring 1981). See also, Franklin Edwards and Barbara Stevens, "The Provision of Municipal Sanitation Services by Private Firms: Empirical Analysis of the Efficiency of Alternative Market Structures and Regulatory Arrangements," Journal of Industrial Economics, Vol. 27 (1978), p. 133.

51. E. S. Savas and Christopher Niemczewski, "Who Collects Solid Waste?" The Municipal Year Book, 1976 (Washington, D.C.: International City Management Association, 1976).

52. See for example, Donald Fisk, et al., _Private Provision of Public Services: An Overview_ (Washington, D.C.: Urban Institute, 1978); "Ways Private Firms Can Save Money for Burdened Cities," _U. S. News & World Report_, November 17, 1975, pp. 79-82.

53. Barbara Stevens and E. S. Savas, "The Cost of Residential Refuse Collection and the Effect of Service Arrangement," _The Municipal Year Book, 1977_ (Washington, D.C.: International City Management Association, 1977), p. 200. See also, E.S. Savas, "Municipal Monopolies vs. Competition in Delivering Urban Services," _Urban Analysis_, Vol. 2 (1974), pp. 93-160; E. S. Savas, "Policy Analysis for Local Government: Public versus Private Refuse Collection," _Policy Analysis_, Vol. 3, No. 1, (Winter 1977), p. 49; E. S. Savas, "Intracity Competition Between Public and Private Service Delivery," _Public Administration Review_, Vol. 41 (1981), p. 6; E. S. Savas, "Public vs. Private Refuse Collection: Critical Review of the Literature," _Journal of Urban Analysis_, Vol. 6 (1979), p. 1.

54. Stevens and Savas, "The Cost of Residential Refuse Collection," p. 204.

55. Eileen Berenyi, "Contracting Out Refuse Collection: The Nature and Impact of Change," _The Urban Interest_ (Spring 1981), p. 30.

56. Ibid.

57. Pascal, "User Charges, Contracting Out, and Privatization in an Era of Fiscal Retrenchment," p. 10.

58. Mazur, _People, Politics and Planning_, pp. 118-119.

59. Ibid., p. 133.

60. Ibid., p. 505.

61. Gerard Hoetmer and Amy Cohen Paul, "Municipalities and the Volunteer Fire Service," _Urban Data Service Reports_, Vol. 12, No. 9 (Washington, D.C.: International City Management Association, 1980). See also, Samuel Seward, et al., "Municipal Resource Allocation: Minimizing the Cost of Fire Protection," _Management Science_, Vol. 24 (1978), p. 1740; Robert Dworak, "Maintaining Service Delivery With Reduced Property Taxes," _National Civic Review_, Vol. 68 (1979), p. 299; Gilbert Siegel, "Local Government Cost Reduction and Effectiveness: Radical Manpower Proposals," _Public Personnel Management_, Vol. 7 (1978), p. 49.

62. Edward Vickery, et al., "Operational Productivity Measures for Fire Service Delivery," _The Municipal Year Book, 1976_ (Washington, D.C.: International City Management Association, 1976), p. 167. See also, F. Hitzhusen, _Some Policy Implications for Improved Measurement of Local Government Service Output and Costs: The Case of Fire Protection_, Ph.D. dissertation, Cornell University, 1972.

63. Vickery, et al., "Operational Productivity Measures," p. 167.

64. Ibid.

BIBLIOGRAPHY

Edward E. Duensing and Dorothy Burstyn

I. SUBURBS: GENERAL

Ashton, Patrick J. "The Political Economy of Suburban Development." In William Tabb and Larry Sawers (editors), Marxism and the Metropolis: New Perspectives in Urban Political Economy. New York: Oxford University Press, 1978), pp. 64-89.

Berger, B. "The Myth of Suburbia." Journal of Social Issues, Vol. 17, November 1961, pp. 38-49.

Birch, David L. The Economic Future of City and Suburb. New York: Committee for Economic Development, 1970.

Birmingham, Stephen. The Golden Dream: Suburbia in the Seventies. New York: Harper and Row, 1978.

Bradford, David F. and Harry H. Kelijian. "An Econometric Model of the Flight to the Suburbs." Journal of Political Economy, May/June 1973, pp. 566-589.

Browne, Lynn E. and Richard F. Syron. "Cities, Suburbs and Regions." New England Economic Review, January-February 1979, pp. 41-61.

Chinitz, Benjamin (editor). City and Suburb: The Economics of Metropolitan Growth. Englewood Cliffs, NJ: Prentice-Hall, Inc., 1964.

Devise, Pierre. The Economic Rank of Chicago's Suburban Municipalities in 1970. Chicago, IL: Illinois Regional Medical Program, 1971.

Dolce, Philip C. (editor). Suburbia: The American Dream and Dilemma. Garden City, NY: Anchor Press, 1976.

Donaldson, Scott. The Suburban Myth. New York: Columbia University Press, 1969.

Dornbusch, Sanford M. A Typology of Suburban Communities: Chicago Metropolitan District. Chicago, IL: Chicago Community Inventory, 1952.

Downes, Bryan T. (editor). Cities and Suburbs. Belmont, CA: Wadworth Publishing Co., 1971.

Downes, Bryan T. and John N. Collins. "Community Stabilization in the Inner Suburbs." Urban Analysis, Vol. 4, 1977, pp. 135-159.

Downs, Anthony. Opening Up the Suburbs. New Haven: Yale University Press, 1972.

Farley, Renolds. "Suburban Persistence." American Sociological Review, Vol. 29, February 1964, pp. 38-47.

Gans, Herbert J. "An Anatomy of Suburbia." New Society, Vol. 10, September 28, 1967, pp. 423-431.

Gans, Herbert J. The Levittowners. New York: Panthean Books, 1959.

Goldfield, David R. "The Limits of Suburban Growth: The Washington, D.C., S.M.S.A." Urban Affairs, September 1976, pp. 83-102.

Guest, Avery M. "Nighttime and Daytime Populations of Large American Suburbs." Urban Affairs, September 1976, pp. 57-82.

Guest, Avery M. "Population Suburbanization in American Metropolitan Areas, 1940-1970," Geographical Analysis, Vol. 7 (1975), pp. 267-283.

Guest, Avery M. "Suburban Social Status." American Sociological Review Vol. 43, No. 2, April 1978, pp. 251-263.

Gutowski, Michael and Tracey Field. The Graying of Suburbia. Washington, D.C.: Urban Institute, 1979.

Hawley, Amos H. Urban Society. New York: Ronald Press, 1971.

Hughes, James W. (editor). Suburbanization Dynamics and the Future of the City. New Brunswick, NJ: Center for Urban Policy Research, Rutgers University, 1974.

Kaplan, Samuel. The Dream Deferred: People, Politics, and Planning in Suburbia. New York: Seabury Press, 1976.

Ktsanes, T. and L. Reissman. "Suburbia -- New Homes for Old Values." Social Problems, Vol. 7, Winter 1959-60, pp. 187-195.

Kurtz, Richard A. and Joanne B. Eicher. "Fringe and Suburb: A Confusion of Concepts." Social Forces, Vol. 37, October 1958, pp. 32-37.

Lee, Dorothy. "Suburbia Reconsidered: Diversity and the Creative Life." In Man and the Modern City, Elizabeth Green et al. (editors). Pittsburgh: University of Pittsburgh Press, 1963, pp. 122-134.

Lenk, Richard W., Jr. Hackensack, New Jersey, From Settlement to Suburb 1686-1804. (Unpublished Ph.D. Dissertation) New York University, 1968.

Liebman, Charles. "Functional Differentiation and Political Characteristics of Suburbia." American Journal of Sociology, Vol. 66, March 1961, pp. 485-490.

Linden, Fabian. "Economics of Cities and Suburbs." Conference Board Record, Vol. 13, March 1976, pp. 42-45.

Lineberry, Robert L. "Suburbia and the Metropolitan Turf." Annals of the American Academy of Political and Social Sciences, Vol. 422, 1975, pp. 1-9.

Logan, John R. "Industrialization and the Stratification of Cities in Suburban Regions." American Journal of Sociology, Vol. 84, 1976, pp. 404-416.

Long, John F. Population Deconcentration in the United States. Washington, D.C.: Government Printing Office, 1981.

Masotti, L.H. (editor). "The Suburban Seventies." The Annals of the American Academy of Political and Social Science, 1975, pp. 422.

Merino, James A. A Great City and Its Suburbs: An Attempt to Integrate Metropolitan Boston, 1865-1920. (Unpublished Ph.D. Dissertation) University of Texas, 1968.

Muller, Peter O. Contemporary Suburban America. Englewood Cliffs, NJ: Prentice-Hall, 1981.

Murphy, Thomas P. and John Rehfuss. Urban Politics in the Suburban Era. Homewood, IL: Dorsey Press, 1976.

"The Outer City." New York Times. May 30-June 3, 1971 (5-part series).

Popenoe, David. The Suburban Environment: Sweden and the United States. Chicago, IL: University of Chicago Press, 1976.

Schnore, Leo F. Class and Race in Cities and Suburbs. Chicago: Markham. 1972.

Schnore, Leo F. and Jay K. O. Jones. "The Evolution of City-Suburban Types in the Course of a Decade." Urban Affairs Quarterly, Vol. 4, June 1969, pp. 421-442.

Schnore, Leo F. "The Functions of Metropolitan Suburbs." American Journal of Sociology. Vol. 61, March 1956, pp. 453-458.

Schnore, Leo F. and "The Growth of Metropolitan Suburbs." American Sociological Review, Vol. 22, April 1957, pp. 165-173.

Schnore, Leo F. and V. Z. Klaff. "Suburbanization in the Sixties: A Preliminary Analysis." Land Economics, Vol. 48, February 1972, pp. 23-33.

Sobin, Dennis P. The Future of the American Suburbs: Survival or Extinction? Port Washington, NY: Kennikat Press, 1971.

Solomon, Arthur P. (editor). The Prospective City: Economic, Population, Energy, and Environmental Developments Shaping Our Cities and Suburbs. Cambridge, MA: The MIT Press, 1980.

Stahura, J. M. "The Evolution of Suburban Functional Roles." Pacific Sociological Review, Vol. 21, No. 4, October 1978, pp. 423-440.

Stahura, J. M. "A Factoral Ecology of Suburban America: 1960-1970." Sociological Focus, Vol. 12, 1979, pp. 9-19.

Stahura, J. M. and S. M. Stahl. "Suburban Characteristics and Aged Net Migration." Research on Aging, Vol. 2, No. 1, March 1980, pp. 3-22.

Stanback, Thomas M., Jr. "Suburbanization." In New York is Very Much Alive. Eli Ginzberg (editor). New York: McGraw-Hill, 1973, pp. 42-67.

Stanback, Thomas M. and Richard Knight. Suburbanization and the City. Montclair, NJ: Alanheld, Osmun, 1976.

Sternlieb, George et al. The Affluent Suburb: Princeton. New Brunswick, NJ: Transaction Books, 1971.

Sternlieb, George and W. Patrick Beaton. The Zone of Emergence. New Brunswick, NJ: Transaction Books, 1972.

Teaford, Jon C. City and Suburb: The Political Fragmentation of Metropolitan America, 1850-1970. Baltimore, MD: Johns Hopkins University Press, 1979.

Ward, David. "Comparative Historical Geography of Streetcar Suburbs in Boston, Massachusetts and Leeds, England." Annals of the Association of American Geographers, Vol. 54, December 1964, pp. 477-489.

Warner, Sam. Street Car Suburb: The Process of Growth in Boston, 1870-1900. Cambridge, MA: Harvard University Press, 1962.

Weaver Robert. "The Suburbanization of America." New York Affairs. Vol. 4, No. 3, Summer/Fall 1977, pp. 24-33.

Zikmund, Joseph II and Deborah Ellis Dennis. Suburbia: A Guide to Information Sources. Detroit, MI: Gale Research, 1979.

Zschock, Dieter K. (editor). Economic Aspects of Suburban Growth: Studies of the Nassau-Suffolk Planning Region. Stony Brook, NY: State University of New York at Stony Brook, Economic Research Bureau, 1969.

II. SUBURBS: CHANGES AND PROBLEMS
    (Economic and Social Shifts)

Allman, T. D. "The Urban Crisis Leaves Town and Moves to the Suburbs."
    Harpers, December 1978, pp. 41-46.
"After 160 Billion to Rescue Cities...Experts Wonder Whether Anything
    Can Keep Decay From Invading the Suburbs." U. S. News and World Re-
    port, Vol. 72, April 10, 1972, pp. 42-46.
Benston, G. J. and D. Horsky. "Redlining and the Demand for Mortgages
    in the Central-City and Suburbs." Journal of Bank Research, Vol. 10,
    Summer 1979, pp. 72-87.
Bryce, Herrington J. Small Cities in Transition: The Dynamics of
    Growth and Decline. Cambridge, MA: Ballinger, 1977.
Clay, Phillip L. "The Future of Suburbs and Their Black Populations."
    In Small Cities in Transition: The Dynamics of Growth and Decline.
    Herrington J. Bryce (editor), Cambridge, MA: Ballinger, 1977, pp.
    301-312.
Collver, Andrew and Moshe Semyonov. "Suburban Change and Persis-
    tence." American Sociological Review, June 1979, pp. 480-486.
"Comeback for Cities, Woes for Suburbs." U. S. News and World Report,
    March 24, 1980, pp. 53-54+.
Conklin, John E. and Egon Bittner. "Burglary in a Suburb." Criminol-
    ogy, August 1973, pp. 206-231.
Fernandez, Judith et al. Troubled Suburbs: An Exploratory Study. Santa
    Monica: RAND, 1982.
Grier, George. "Black Suburbanization: Desegregation or Resegrega-
    tion?" Urban Concerns, May/June 1979, pp. 42-44.
Guest, Avery M. "The Changing Racial Composition of Suburbs 1950-
    1970." Urban Affairs Quarterly, Vol. 14, No. 2, December 1978, pp.
    195-206.
Haar, Charles M. The End of Innocence: A Suburban Reader. Chicago, IL:
    Scott-Foresman, 1972.
Haar, Charles M. (editor). United States President's Task Force on
    Suburban Problems. Final Report. Cambridge, MA: Ballinger, 1974.
"Is Flight From the Suburbs Starting?" U. S. News and World Report,
    Vol. 52, June 11, 1962, pp. 86-89.
Isserman, Andrew and Marilyn Brown. Measuring Suburban Need and Dis-
    tress. Washington, D.C.: Government Printing Office, 1981.
Lake, Robert W. Race and Housing in the Suburbs. New Brunswick, NJ:
    Center for Urban Policy Research, Rutgers University, 1980.
Lake, Robert W. "Racial Transition and Black Homeownership in American
    Suburbs." Annals of the American Academy of Political and Social
    Sciences, Vol. 441, January 1979, pp. 423-440.
Linden, F. "Changing Cities and Suburbs." Conference Board Record,
    Vol. 13, February 1976, pp. 14-17.
Loth, David. Crime in the Suburbs. New York: William Morrow and Co.,
    1957.
Loucks, Edward A. "The New Federalism and the Suburbs." Growth and
    Change, Vol. 9, October 1978, pp. 2-7.

Masotti, Louis H. "Urbanization of Suburbia." Real Estate Today, Vol. 5, September 1972, pp. 26-32.

Masotti, Louis H. and Jeffrey K. Hadden (editors). Suburbia in Transition. New York: New Viewpoint Press, 1973.

Masotti, Louis H. and Jeffrey K. Hadden. The Urbanization of the Suburbs. Beverly Hills: Sage Publications, 1973.

Muller, Peter O. Contemporary Suburban America. Englewood Cliffs, NJ: Prentice-Hall, 1981.

Muller, Peter O. The Outer-City: Geographical Consequences of the Suburbs. Washington, D.C.: Association of American Geographers, 1976.

Pratt, Samuel and Lois Pratt. Suburban Downtown in Transition: A Problem in Business Change in Bergen County, New Jersey. Rutherford, NJ: Fairleigh-Dickinson University, Institute of Research, 1958.

Reichlin, Seth. "The Aging of the Suburbs." Fortune, December 15, 1980, pp. 60-67+.

Richards, P., R. A. Berk, and B. Ferster. Crime as Play: Delinquency in a Middle-Class Suburb. Cambridge, MA: Ballinger, 1979.

Schwartz, Barry (editor). The Changing Face of the Suburbs. Chicago, IL: University of Chicago Press, 1976.

Stahura, J. M., C. R. Huff, and B. L. Smith. "Crime in the Suburbs: A Structural Model." Urban Affairs Quarterly. Vol. 15, No. 13, March 1980, pp. 291-316.

Stanfield, Rochelle L. "The Suburban Counties are Flexing Their Muscles: As They Take on More of the Functions of the Cities." National Journal, Vol. 9, May 7, 1977, pp. 704-709.

Sternlieb, George and James W. Hughes (editors). Post-Industrial America: Metropolitan Decline and Inter-Regional Job Shifts. New Brunswick, NJ: Center for Urban Policy Research, Rutgers University, 1975.

"Suburbia: A Not-Always-Green Eden." Sales Management, Vol. 109, October 30, 1972, pp. 86-9.

"Suburbs: A Lucrative (But Not Always Happy) Eden." Sales and Market Management, Vol. 123, October 29, 1979.

Taylor, T. C. "Urbanizing Suburbia." Sales Management, Vol. 102, December 1973, pp. 147+.

Thomas, William V. "America's Changing Suburbs." Editorial Research Reports, August 17, 1979, pp. 583-600.

Weiss, E. B. "Cities, Suburbs Change Character." Advertising Age, Vol. 40, March 3, 1969, p. 52.

William, Roger M. "The Assault on Fortress Suburbia: How Long Can the Poor be Kept Out?" Saturday Review, February 18, 1978, pp. 17-22.

III. MUNICIPAL FISCAL STRESS AND INDICATORS
    (Selected; see also, "Suburbs: Changes and Problems" section)

Aronson, J. R. Municipal Fiscal Indicators. Washington, D.C.: Government Printing Office, 1980.

Brown, M. A. "Do Central Cities and Suburbs Have Similar Dimensions of Need?" The Professional Geographer, Vol. 32, No. 4, 1980, pp. 400-411.

Brown, Marilyn A. "A Typology of Suburbs and Its Public Policy Impli-
    cations." Urban Geography, Vol. 2, No. 4, 1981, pp. 288-310.
Burchell, Robert W. and David Listokin. Cities Under Stress: The Fis-
    cal Crises of Urban America. New Brunswick, NJ: Rutgers University,
    Center for Urban Policy Research, 1981.
Clark, Terry Nichols and Lorna Crowley Fergusen. "Fiscal Strain and
    Private Sector Resources: How Tight Are the Linkages?" In Political
    Processes and Urban Fiscal Strain. (s.l.) (s.n.), (n.d.), pp. 1-32.
"Crowds...Crime...Higher Taxes: City Problems Invade Suburbs." U. S.
    News and World Report, December 10, 1973, pp. 65-68.
Culver, Lowell W. "The Politics of Suburban Distress." Journal of Ur-
    ban Affairs, Vol. 4, No. 1, Winter 1982, pp. 1-19.
Dufault, Roland. "Central City-Suburban Fiscal Disparities in Central
    Massachusetts." New England Journal of Business and Economy. Vol. 3,
    Fall 1976, pp. 1-22.
Fernandez, Judith et al. Troubled Suburbs: An Exploratory Study. Santa
    Monica, CA: RAND, 1982.
"Fiscal Stress in Local Government." Government Finance, Vol. 9, No.
    2, June 1980 (n.p.).
Isserman, Andrew and Marilyn Brown. Measuring Suburban Need and Dis-
    tress. Washington, D.C.: Government Printing Office, 1981.
Levine, Charles H. (editor). Managing Fiscal Stress: The Crises in the
    Public Sector. Chatham, NJ: Chatham House Publishers, 1980.
Livingston, David F. Aggregate Indicators of Suburban Spending Pat-
    terns Among Urbanized Communities in the Philadelphia Area: 1950-
    1960. (Unpublished Ph.D. Dissertation) University of Pennsylvania,
    1970.
Muller, Thomas. Growing and Declining Urban Areas: A Fiscal Compari-
    son. Washington, D.C.: The Urban Institute, 1975.
Municipal Finance Officers Association. "Measuring Governmental Finan-
    cial Condition." In MFOA, Elements of Financial Management, No. 5.
    Washington, D.C.: MFOA, 1980.
Nathan, Richard B. and Charles Adams, Jr. "Understanding Central City
    Hardship." Political Science Quarterly, Vol. 91, No. 1, Spring 1976.
Peterson, George et al. Monitoring Urban Fiscal Conditions. Washing-
    ton, D.C.: Urban Institute, 1981.
U. S. Bureau of the Census. Suburban Classification Project. Washing-
    ton, D.C.: Government Printing Office, 1977.

IV. SUBURBAN NEW DEVELOPMENT
    (Selected, Nonresidential Emphasis)

Armstrong, Regina B. The Office Industry: Patterns of Growth and Loca-
    tion. Cambridge, MA: The MIT Press, 1972.
Berry, Brian J.L. and Yehoshua S. Cohen. "Decentralization of Commerce
    and Industry." In Louis H. Masotti and Jeffrey K. Hadden (editors),
    The Urbanization of the Suburbs. Beverly Hills: Sage Publications,
    Urban Affairs Annual Reviews, Vol. 7, 1973, pp. 431-455.
Breckenfeld, Gurney. "'Downtown' Has Fled to the Suburbs." Fortune,
    October 1972, pp. 80-87+.

Christian, Charles M. and Connie L. Williams. The Suburbanization of
   Industrial Firms and Employment Opportunities: A Bibliography. Mon-
   ticello, IL: Council of Planning Librarians, 1977.
Clark, Frederick P. "Office Buildings in the Suburbs." Urban Land,
   Vol. 13, July-August 1954, p. 7.
Levin, Sharon G. "Suburban-Central City Property Tax Differentials and
   the Location of Industry: Some Evidence." Land Economics, Vol. 50,
   November 1974, pp. 380-86.
Lowenstein, L. K. "Impact of New Industry on the Fiscal Revenues and
   Expenditures of Suburban Communities: Case Study of Three Philadel-
   phia Townships: Lower Merion, Upper Merion, and Radner." National
   Tax Journal.
Mandell, Lewis. "Quality of Life Factors in Business Location Deci-
   sions." Atlanta Economic Review, January-February 1977, pp. 4-7.
Muller, Peter O. "The Suburbanization of Corporate Headquarters." Vi-
   tal Issues, Vol. 27, No. 8, April 1978, pp. 1-4.
The Office Network Inc. National Office Market Report. Houston, TX:
   Office Network, Fall-Winter, 1982, p. 2.
Russell, M.P. "Opportunities in Suburban Office Development." Real Es-
   tate Review, Vol. 9, Fall 1979, pp. 100-102.

V. DOWNTOWN COMMERCIAL REVITALIZATION (URBAN AND SUBURBAN)

Alexander, Lawrence A. (editor). Financing Downtown Action: A Prac-
   tical Guide to Private and Public Land Funding Sources. New York:
   Downtown Research and Development Center, 1975.
Ambrose, David M. "Longitudinal Assessment of Business in a Central
   Business District." Mid-Southern Quarterly Business Review, Vol. 18,
   October 1980, pp. 3-12.
American Public Works Association. Planning and Construction of Munic-
   ipal Malls. Chicago, IL: The Association, 1979.
Balfe, Kevin and Judith Richards. "Neighorhood Commercial Revitaliza-
   tion." Economic Development and Law Center Report, November/Decem-
   ber 1980, pp. 7-17.
Banner, Knox. "Public/Private Partnership in Downtown Revitalization
   Can Be Helped by Downtown Organizations." Journal of Housing, Sep-
   tember 1976, pp. 432-434.
Beardon, W. O. "Determinant Attributes of Store Patronage: Downtown
   Versus Outlying Shopping Centers." Journal of Retailing, Vol. 53,
   Summer 1977, pp. 15-22+.
Bendavid-Val, Avrom. Local Economic Development Planning: From Goals
   to Projects. Chicago, IL: American Planning Association, September
   1980.
Berk, Emanuel. Downtown Improvement Manual. Chicago, IL: ASPO Press,
   1976.
Berman, Barry. An Evaluation of Selected Business Districts in Nassau,
   Suffolk and Queens Counties. Hempstead, NY: Hofstra University,
   1980.
Berry, David et al. "Downtown Redevelopment in Five Cities." Planning
   and Public Policy, Vol. 5, No. 2, May 1979, entire issue.

Bies, Susan Schmidt. "The Future of CBD's as Financial Centers of Metropolitan Areas: A Demand Analysis." _Journal of Regional Science_, December 1977, pp. 431-440.

Boyce, R. R. and D. Fansler. "A Quarter Century of Downtown Decline -- The Case of CBD Retail Sales in American Cities: 1948-1972." Paper presented at the Western Meetings of the Regional Science Association, Tucson (1977).

Breckenfeld, Gurney. "Jim Rouse Shows How to Give Downtown Retailing New Life...." _Fortune_, Vol. 97, No. 71, April 10, 1978, pp. 84-87+.

Calvert, Michael. "Baltimore's Old Town Mall, a Prototype of Urban Neighborhood Commercial Rehab." _Practicing Planner_, Vol. 7, No. 1, March 1977.

Carlson, David and Mary R. S. Carlson. "The Pedestrian Mall: Its Role in Revitalization of Downtown Areas." _Urban Land_, May 1974, pp. 3-9.

Carusone, Peter S. "Decline of the Small-City Central Business District, 1958-1975." _Bulletin of Business Research_ (Ohio State University), Vol. 53, No. 6, June 1978, entire issue.

Cohen, Richard A. "Small Town Revitalization Planning: Case Studies and a Critique." _American Institute of Planners Journal_, January 1977, pp. 3-12.

"Commercial Revitalization." _Challenge!_, February 1979, entire issue.

Cook, Robert S., Jr. _Zoning for Downtown Urban Design: How Cities Control Development_. Lexington, MA: Lexington Books, 1980.

Cunningham, Michael C. "Can Downtown be Reinvented?" _Ekistics_, March 1977, pp. 159-164.

Dalessandro, Mary. _Strategies for Stopping Shopping Centers: A Guidebook on Minimizing Excessive Suburban Shopping Center Growth_. New York: Downtown Research and Development Center, 1980.

Davis, Irwin L. "Seven Requirements Determine the Success of Downtown Revitalization Projects." _Journal of Housing_, Vol. 37, August/September 1980, pp. 448-449+.

Downs, Anthony. "Do Downtowns Really Have a Future?" _Urban Georgia_, June 1979, pp. 41+.

"Downtown Centers: Not Like Suburban Malls." _Chain Store Age Exec_, Vol. 51, January 1975, pp. 25+.

Downtown Research and Development Center. _The Downtown District Action Guide_. New York: Downtown Research and Development Center, 1980.

Downtown Research and Development Center. _Downtown Malls: Feasibility and Development_. New York: Downtown Research and Development Center.

Downtown Research and Development Corporation. _How to Promote to Bring People Downtown: 17 Successful Downtown Promotional Case Studies_. New York: Downtown Research and Development Center, 1980.

Downtown Research and Development Center. _An Inside Look at Current Downtown Action Ideas_. New York: Downtown Research and Development Corporation, 1978.

Duensing, Edward. _Suburban Shopping Center Versus the Central Business Districts: A Bibliography_. Monticello, IL: Vance Bibliographies, February 1980.

Eden Planning Group. _Downtown Revitalization, Surveys and Recommendations: Wake Forest, North Carolina_. Raleigh, NC: N.C. Division of Community Assistance, June 1980.

Engelen, R. E. "What is the Future of Downtown Retailing in Middle
America?" Urban Land, Vol. 38, October 1979, pp. 5-11.

"Faneuil Hall, Harborplace, New Market, and Uncle Sam Atrium." AIA
Journal, June 1981, entire issue.

Gregsen, J. Randolph, II. "New Orleans Creates CBD Tax and Improvement
District." Practicing Planner, December 1976, pp. 43-46.

Grover, Martha. "Trying to Make Main Street All Right Again." Inland
Architect, Vol. 22, No. 5, May 1978, pp. 6-9.

Heard, I., Jr. Neighborhood Commercial Function Revitalization: Factors in Theory and Application. Charlotte, NC: Charlotte-Mecklenburg
Planning Commission, October 1979.

Hill, Richard M. "Is the Central Business District Becoming an Anach-
ronism?" Illinois Business Review, Vol. 34, February 1977, p. 8-
11.

"Inner Suburbs, Cities Get a Closer Look." Chain Store Age Exec, Vol.
51. May 1975, pp. 25-27.

International City Management Association. Bringing Downtown Up: Reju-
venating Commercial Areas in Small and Mid-Sized Cities. Washington,
D.C.: International City Management Association, 1980.

International Downtown Executives Association. Analysis of Major Commercial Districts. Washington, D.C.: IDEA, 1978.

International Downtown Executives Association. Analysis of Major Commercial Districts -- Analysis of National and Regional Trends.
Springfield, VA: NTIS, November 1977.

International Downtown Executives Association. Analysis of Major Commercial Districts. Detailed City Descriptions. Springfield, VA:
NTIS, November 1977.

International Downtown Executives Association. Analysis of Major Commercial Districts. Summary of Finding and Conclusions. Springfield,
VA: NTIS, November 1977.

International Downtown Executives Association. Analysis of Major Commercial Districts. Technical Report, Volume II. Springfield, VA:
NTIS, November 1977.

International Downtown Executives Association. Downtown Revitalization: A Compendium of State Activities. Washington, D.C.: International Downtown Executives Association, 1980.

Iowa Office for Planning and Programming. Downtown Improvement Manual
for Iowa Cities. Des Moines, IO: Division of Municipal Affairs,
1978.

Katon, Phillip B. "Trenton Takes a New Approach to CBD Development."
HUD Challenge, September 1978, pp. 14-15.

Klein, Norman and Walter Arensberg. "Auto-Free Zones: Giving Cities
Back to People." City, Vol. 6, March/April 1972, pp. 45-52.

Kohn, C. F. "Spatial Patterns of Suburban Commercial Retail Services:
The Problem and Present Shopping Habits." Annals of the Association
of American Geographers, Vol. 47, June 1957, pp. 166-167.

Kotler, N. G. and J. Dahms. Neighborhood Economic Enterprises. Dayton,
OH: Charles F. Kettering Foundation, 1978.

Levatino, Andrienne M. Neighborhood Commercial Rehabilitation. Washington, D.C.: National Association of Housing and Redevelopment Officials, January 1978.

Lewis, Stephen E. "Every Downtown is Different." National Real Estate Investor, May 1980, pp. 59-60.

Lewison, Dale M. and Michael J. Showalter. "A Possible Impact of the New Columbia Mall on Columbia's Major Existing Shopping Clusters." Business and Economic Review (University of South Carolina), Vol. 23, May 1977, pp. 2-8.

Lord, J. D. "Intra-metropolitan Area Comparisons in Retailing Productivity: Implications for Central Business District Retail Firms." Annals of Regional Science, Vol. 14, No. 3, November 1980, pp. 95-105.

Madonna, Joseph G. "Public/Private Partnership for Downtown Development." Urban Land, Vol. 39, No. 2, February 1980, pp. 12-19.

McKelvey, Robert A. "Retailing's Future in Downtown: The Marketplace and the Urban Network." Stores, Vol. 55, April 1973, pp. 15-16+.

Melton, R. B. "Can Downtown Live with More Parking and Easy Transportation?" Stores, Vol. 59, March 1977, pp. 14+.

Mercurius, Winston and Joel F. Werth. "Downtown Benefit Districts: New Use of an Old Tool." PAS Memo, July 1980, entire issue.

Mintz, Norman M. "Preservation in Downtown Revitalization." Challenge, July 1979, pp. 2-7.

"Modern Street Lighting Turns CBD Around." Public Works, April 1977, pp. 70-73.

Nakihian, Marie. "Here's One City Where Commercial Rehab Works." Planning, Vol. 43, No. 6, July 1977.

National Development Council. Neighborhood Business Revitalization. Washington, D.C.: The Council.

National Institute for Advanced Studies. Public/Private Strategies for Involving Small Business in Community Economic Revitalization: A Handbook for Local Officials. Springfield, VA: N.T.I.S., 1978.

National Institute for Advanced Studies. Strategies for Revitalizing Neighborhood Commercial Areas: The Role, Application and Impact of Public and Private Resources. Washington, D.C.: National Institute for Advanced Studies, 1977.

Nelson, Carl. "Downtown Shopping Concept Resurrects Central Business District." The American City, November 1973, pp. 86-89.

O'Dell, William F. "A Marketing Strategy for CBDs." Urban Land, June 1972, pp. 14-22.

O'Leary, Rosemary. "The Shopping Center Controversy: A Legal Guide for Municipal Officials." Urban Interest, Vol. 3, No. 2, Fall 1981, pp. 26-36.

Onderdonk, Dudley. "A Commercial Incentive Plan Can Provide Tools for Economic Development." Journal of Housing, Vol. 36, No. 9, October 1979, pp. 465-466.

Onibokun, A. "Comprehensive Evaluation of Pedestrian Malls in the United States." Appraisal Journal, Vol. 43, April 1975, pp. 202-218.

Oyebanji, Joshua O. "Suburban Growth and Regional Shopping Center Development in Northern Virginia." Virginia Social Science Journal, Vol. 12, April 1977, pp. 1-11.

Ramirez, Sylvia. "Wholesale Changes for Downtown Retailers." San Francisco Business, July 1980, pp. 16-20.

Raphel, Murray. "The Gordon's Alley Story; or How to Rebuild a Fading Center City Retail Section Into an...Exciting Place to Shop." <u>Challenge!</u>, April 1979, pp. 22-25.
Real Estate Research Corporation. <u>Lessons for States and Cities: Impacts of New Developments in Older Commercial Areas</u>. Washington, D.C.: Government Printing Office, 1982.
"Rebuilding a Downtrodden Downtown." <u>Builder</u>, January 7, 1980, pp. 144-151.
Redstone, Louis G. <u>The New Downtowns: Rebuilding Business Districts</u>. New York: McGraw-Hill, 1976.
Reece, Beverly. "Shopsteading: Neighborhood Revitalization in Baltimore." <u>Seller/Services</u>, July/August 1980, pp. 12-14.
"Revitalizing Downtown Shopping Requires More Than Cosmetification." <u>Journal of Marketing</u>, Vol. 42, January 1978, p. 13.
Rosenberg, Helen and Dottie Stephenson. <u>Neighborhood Commercial Revitalization</u>. Monticello, IL: Vance Bibliographies, January 1980.
Rosenzweig, P. "Promoting the Central Business District." <u>Buildings</u>, Vol. 71, April 1977, pp. 62-64.
Rubenstein, Harvey M. <u>Central City Malls</u>. New York: Wiley, 1978.
Shah, R. P. and W. L. Trombetta. "Relocating the Black Merchant in Suburbia: A Total Resources Approach." <u>Journal of Small Business Management</u>, Vol. 12, October 1979, pp. 11-17.
Shaw, Steven J. "Some Thoughts on a Main Street Mall in Columbia." <u>Business and Economic Review</u>, Vol. 18, February 1972, pp. 2-6.
Shaw, Whitney R. "Downtown Revitalization: Can it be Done? The Example of One City." <u>Vital Issues</u>, Vol. 30, No. 5, January 1981, entire issue.
<u>Shopping Centers Revisited</u>. New York: Practicing Law Institute, 1979.
"Shopping Malls: Introversion and the Urban Context." <u>Progressive Architecture</u>, December 1978, pp. 49-69.
Simons, Peter L. "The Shape of Suburban Retail Market Areas: Implications From a Literature Review." <u>Journal of Retailing</u>, Vol. 49, Winter 1973/1974, pp. 65-78.
Smith, Al. "The Future of Downtown Retailing." <u>Urban Land</u>, December 1972, pp. 3-10.
Smith, Herbert L., Jr. "Wilkes-Barre Revives its Downtown." <u>Architectural Record</u>, August 1980, pp. 76-79.
Sower, John. "Revitalizing Older Business Districts...." <u>Journal of Housing</u>, Vol. 34, December 1977, pp. 568-572.
Spanbock, Marian H. (editor). <u>Where is Downtown Going? Twelve Expert Opinions</u>. New York: Downtown Research and Development Center, 1979.
Spindletop Research, Inc. <u>The Suburbanization of Retail Trade -- A Study of Retail Trade Dispersion in Major U. S. Markets, 1958-1967</u>. New York: Spindletop Research, 1970.
Stephens, George. "Santa Cruz Cashes in on Downtown Revitalization." <u>Urban Land</u>, October 1979, pp. 12-17.
Sternlieb, George. <u>The Future of the Downtown Department Store</u>. Cambridge, MA: The Joint Center for Urban Studies of MIT and Harvard University, 1962.

Sternlieb, George. "The Future of Retailing in the Downtown Core." Journal of the American Institute of Planners, May 1963, Vol. 29, No. 2, p. 102.

"Suburban Malls Go Downtown." Business Week, November 10, 1973, pp. 90-94.

"Suburbs: Still the Prime Target of Sales Strategies." Sales and Marketing Management, Vol. 121, July 24, 1978 (n.p.).

Tarver, James D. "Suburbanization of Retail Trade in the Standard Metropolitan Areas of the U. S., 1948-54." American Sociological Review, Vol. 22, August 1957, pp. 427-433.

United States. Congress. House. Committee on Small Business. Sub-Committee on General Oversight and Minority Enterprise. Neighborhood Business Revitalization Program: Hearings. Ninety-sixth Congress, First Session, March 7 and 13, 1979. Washington, D.C.: USGPO, 1979.

United States. Department of Housing and Urban Development. Office of Neighborhoods, Voluntary Associations and Consumer Protection. Commercial Revitalization: Neighborhood Focus: A Guide Book. Washington, D.C.: The Office, 1980.

Walters, Jonathan. "Main Street Turns the Corner..." Historic Preservation, Vol. 33, No. 6, November/December 1981, pp. 36-45.

Walzer, Norman and Ralph Stablein. "Small Towns and Regional Centers." Growth and Change, Vol. 12, No. 3, July 1981, pp. 2-8.

Weaver, Clifford L. and Christopher J. Duerkin. "Central Business District Planning and the Control of Outlying Shopping Centers." Urban Law Annual, Vol. 14, 1977, pp. 57-79.

Wilcox, David A. "Attractions Management is Key to a Revitalized Downtown's Success." Journal of Housing, July 1980, pp. 377-382.

Winter, Gary. "The Downtown Revitalization/Redevelopment Dilemma." Current Municipal Problems, Fall 1980, pp. 202-9.

VI. THE ARTS AS A DOWNTOWN REVITALIZATION MECHANISM
     (Selected)

"Arts Grants Help Revitalize Downtown Areas." Uptown, December 1978, pp. 2-3.

Boston Redevelopment Authority. Boston's Theater District: A Program for Revitalization. Boston: The Authority, 1979.

Burgard, Ralph. "Arts Draws Urban America into its Public Places." Planning, October 1977, pp. 10-13.

Cwi, David. The Role of the Arts in Urban Economic Development. Washington, D.C.: U. S. Department of Commerce, Economic Development Administration, September 1980.

Cwi, David and Associates. The Economic Impact of the Arts: A Study of 49 Cultural Institutions in 6 U. S. SMSA's. New York: Publication Center for Cultural Resources, n.d.

Cwi, David and Katherine Lyall. Economic Impacts of Arts and Cultural Institutions: A Model for Assessment and a Case Study of Baltimore. Baltimore, Maryland: Johns Hopkins University Center for Metropolitan Planning and Research, 1977.

Duensing, Edward. The Arts and Urban Economic Development. Monticello,
    IL: Vance Bibliographies, November 1980.
Green, Peter. "Arts Contribute to Commercial Renaissance in Galves-
    ton." Urban Land, November 1977, pp. 13-15.
Hagstrom, Jerry. "Bringing People Back Downtown With a Little Help
    From the Arts." National Journal, December 15, 1979.
Hendon, William S. (editor). Economic Policy for the Arts. Cambridge,
    MA: ABT Associates, 1980.
Logan, Frederick M. "Cultural Patterns and Institutions: Will Suburbs
    Support or Ignore Them?" Arts in Society, Vol. 4, Fall-Winter 1967,
    pp. 451-453.
National Endowment for the Arts. Downtowns -- Reinvestment by Design.
    Selected Grants: Architecture Environmental Arts Program, FY1966-
    1977. Washington, D.C.: National Endowment for the Arts, 1977.
Rockwell, Matthew L. "Cultural Centers in Suburbia." Arts in Society,
    Vol. 4, Fall-Winter 1967, pp. 471-476.
Tenenbaum, Susan. "Hempstead: Can the 'Hub' be Recapped?" New York
    Affairs, Vol. 2, No. 2, 1982, pp. 81-88.
University of California -- Los Angeles. School of Architecture and
    Urban Planning. Urban Innovations Group. The Arts in the Economic
    Life of the City. New York: American Council for the Arts, 1979.
Violette, Caroline and Rachelle Taqqu (editors). Issues in Supporting
    the Arts. Ithaca, NY: Cornell University, 1982.

VII. RETHINKING MUNICIPAL SERVICE STRATEGIES AND STANDARDS

Ahlbrandt, R. S., Jr. "Implications of Contracting for a Public Ser-
    vice." Urban Affairs Quarterly, Vol. 9, March 1974, pp. 337-359.
Alexander, James, Jr. "Biting the Bullet: A Checklist for Budgetary
    Retrenchment." New Jersey Municipalities, Vol. 58, January 1981, pp.
    8-9.
Alexander, James, Jr. "Contracting Out and the Municipal Budget." New
    Jersey Municipalities, Vol. 58, March 1981, pp. 6-7.
Alternatives to Traditional Public Safety Delivery Systems: Civilians
    in Public Safety Services. Berkeley, CA: Institute for Local Self-
    Government, 1977.
Aronson, Richard and Eli Schwartz (editors). Management/Policies in
    Local Government Finance. Washington, D.C.: International City Man-
    agement Association, 1975.
Bahl, Roy W. and Walter Vogt. Fiscal Centralization and Tax Burdens:
    State and Regional Financing of City Services. Cambridge, MA: Ball-
    inger, 1975.
Bennett, James T. and Manuel Johnson. Better Governance at Half the
    Price. O'Hara, IL: Caroline Home Builders, 1981.
Berenyi, Eileen. "Contracting Out Refuse Collection: The Nature and
    Impact of Change." The Urban Interest, Spring 1981, p. 30.
Berenyi, Eileen. "Public and Private Sector Interaction Patterns in
    the Delivery of Local Public Services." Governmental Finance, Vol.
    9, No. 1, March 1980, pp. 3-9.

Bryan, John L. and Raymond C. Picard. Managing Fire Services. Washington, D.C.: International City Management Association, 1971.

Bryce, Herrington J. (editor). Managing Fiscal Retrenchment in Cities. Columbus, OH: Academy for Contemporary Problems, 1980.

California Tax Foundation. Contracting Out Local Government Services in California. Sacramento, CA: California Tax Foundation, 1981.

California University. Institute of Governmental Affairs. Public-Private Collaboration in the Delivery of Local Public Services; Proceedings of a Workshop, April 11, 1980. David, CA: Institute of Governmental Affairs, September, 1980.

Carpenter, P. and G. R. Hall. Case Studies in Educational Performance Contracting: Conclusions and Implications. Washington, D.C.: Department of Health, Education and Welfare, 1971.

"Contracting by Large Local Governments." International Journal of Public Administration. Vol. 1, Summer 1979, pp. 307-327.

Corusy, Paul V. and James F. Gassett. "Assessment Law Notes: Payment in Lieu of Taxes Helps Solve Exemption Problems for Revenue-Starved Communities." Assessors Journal, Vol. 16, No. 2, June 1981, pp. 109-114.

Criz, Maurice. "The Role of User Charges and Fees in City Finance." Urban Data Service Reports, Vol. 14, No. 6., Washington, D.C.: 1982.

Crompton, John L. "Public Services -- to Charge or Not to Charge?" Business, Vol. 30, No. 2, March-April 1980, pp. 31-38.

Drebin, Alan. "Criteria for Performance Measurement in State and Local Government." Government Finance, Vol. 9, December 1980, p. 3.

Edwards, Franklin and Barbara Stevens. "The Provision of Municipal Sanitation Services by Private Firms: Empirical Analysis of the Efficiency of Alternative Market Structures and Regulatory Arrangements." Journal of Industrial Economics, Vol. 27, 1978, p. 133.

Fiscal Containment. Who Gains? Who Loses? Santa Monica, CA: RAND, September 1979.

Fisk, Donald, Herbert Kiesling and Thomas Muller. Private Provision of Public Services: An Overview. Washington, D.C.: The Urban Institute, May 1978.

Fitzpatrick, Daniel and Daniel Breuer. "An Experience in Contracting-Out Services." Municipal Management: A Journal, Vol. 3, 1980, p. 171.

Florestano, P. S. "The Municipal Connection: Contracting for Public Services Within the Private Sector." Municipal Management, Vol. 1, Fall 1978, pp. 61-71.

Florestano, P. S. and S. B. Gordon. "Public Versus Private: Small Government Contracting With the Private Sector." Public Administration Review, Vol. 40, January/February 1980.

Florestano, Patricia S. and B. Gordon. "A Survey of City and County Use of Private Contracting." The Urban Interest, Spring 1981.

Frazier, Mark. "Private Alternatives to Public Services." Transatlantic Perspectives, No. 5, July 1981, pp. 8-13.

Fukuhara, Rackham. "Productivity Improvement in Cities." The Municipal Year Book -- 1977. Washington, D.C.: International City Management Association, 1977, p. 102.

Garson, G. David and D. S. Brenneman. "Resource Rationing for State Agencies: The Management and Political Challenge of Productivity Improvement." Public Productivity Review, September 1980, pp. 231-248.

Glisson, Patrick. "Developing Local Government User Charges: Technical and Policy Considerations." Governmental Finance, Vol. 4, No. 1, March 1982, p. 3.

Gurin, A. and B. Friedman. Contracting for Services as a Mechanism for the Delivery of Human Services: A Study of Contracting Practices in Three Human Service Agencies in Massachusetts. Waltham, MA: Brandeis University, Florence Heller Graduate School for Advanced Studies in Social Welfare, 1980.

Hatry, Harry P. et al. How Effective Are Your Community Services? Procedures for Monitoring the Effectiveness of Municipal Services. Washington, D.C.: Urban Institute, 1977.

Hatry, Harry P. et al. Efficiency Measurement for Local Government Services -- Some Initial Suggestions. Washington, D.C.: Urban Institute, 1979.

Hawley, Willis D., and David Rogers (editors). Improving Urban Management. Beverly Hills, CA: Sage, 1976.

Hayes, Frederick O'R. Productivity in Local Government. Lexington, MA: Lexington Books, 1977.

Hoetmer, Gerard and Amy Cohen Paul. "Municipalities and the Volunteer Fire Service." Urban Data Service Reports, Vol. 12, No. 9. Washington, D.C.: International City Management Association, 1980.

Hyclak, Thomas J., Thomas A. Decorter et al. An Information Base for Fiscal Decision-making. South Bend, IN: South Bend Urban Observatory, 1976.

"Improving Efficiency: Work Planning and Control." Municipal Innovations 12, November 1976, entire issue.

International City Management Association. "Measuring Effectiveness of Municipal Services." Management Information Service, Washington, D.C.: International City Management Association, 1970.

International City Management Association and the Urban Institute. The Challenge of Productivity: Improving Local Government Productivity Measurement and Evaluations. Washington, D.C.: National Commission in Productivity, 1972.

International City Management Association and the Urban Institute. The Challenge of Productivity: Improving Local Government Productivity Measurement and Evaluations. Washington, D.C.: National Commission in Productivity, 1972.

Knight, Fred S. and Michael D. Rancer. Tried and Tested: Case Studies in Municipal Innovation. Washington, D.C.: International City Management Association, 1978.

Levine, Charles. "Organizational Decline and Cutback Management." Public Administration Review, Vol. 38, 1978, p. 316.

Lewis, Carol and Anthony Logalbo. "Cutback Principles and Practices: A Checklist for Managers." Public Administration Review, Vol. 40, 1980, p. 184.

Lodal, Jan M. "Improving Local Government Financial Information Systems." Government Accountants Journal, Fall 1977, pp. 18-29.

Mercer, James et al. Managing Urban Government Services. New York:
American Management Association, 1981.

Miller, Gary. Cities by Contract: The Politics of Municipal Incorporation. Cambridge, MA: The MIT Press, 1981.

Oatman, Donald. "It's Time for Productivity Accounting in Government."
Government Finance, Vol. 8, No. 3, November 1978, p. 9.

Ostrom, Elinor. "On the Meaning and Measurement of Output and Efficiency in the Provision of Urban Services." Journal of Criminal Justice, Vol. 1, 1973, pp. 93-112.

Ostrom, Elinor (editor). The Delivery of Urban Services: Outcomes of
Change. Beverly Hills, CA: Sage, 1976.

Ostrom, Vincent and Frances Pennell Bish (editors). Comparing Urban
Service Delivery Systems: Structure and Performance. Beverly Hills,
CA: Sage, 1977.

Pascal, Anthony. "User Changes, Contracting Out, and Privatization in
an Era of Fiscal Retrenchment." The Urban Interest, Spring 1981, p.
7.

"Police/Fire Consolidation in Municipalities 10,000 and Over." Urban
Data Service Report, September 1977, entire issue.

Poole, Robert W., Jr. Cutting Back City Hall. New York: Universe
Books, 1980.

Ross, John and Jesse Burkhead. Productivity in the Local Government
Sector. Lexington, MA: Heath and Company, 1974.

San Diego, California Organizational Development and Training Team.
Human Factors in Productivity Improvement Project: Team-Building
Workshop Modules. Washington, D.C.: U. S. Department of Housing and
Urban Development, Office of Policy Development and Research, 1979.

Savas, E. S. (editor). Alternatives for Delivering Public Services.
Boulder, CO: Westview Press, 1977.

Savas, E. S. "How Much Do Government Services Really Cost?" Urban Affairs Quarterly, September 1979, pp. 23-42.

Savas, E. S. "Intracity Competition Between Public and Private Service
Delivery." Public Administration Review, Vol. 41 (1981).

Savas, E. S. "Policy Analysis for Local Government: Public Versus Private Refuse Collection." Policy Analysis, Vol. 3, No. 1 (Winter
1977).

Savas, E. S. and Christopher Niemczewski. "Who Collects Solid Waste?"
The Municipal Year Book, 1976. Washington, D.C.: International City
Management Association, 1976.

Sonenblum, Sidney et al. How Cities Provide Services: An Evaluation of
Alternative Delivery Structures. Cambridge, MA: Ballinger, 1977.

SRI International. Human Factors in Productivity Improvement Project:
Assessment Report, San Diego, California. Washington, D.C.: U. S.
Department of Housing and Urban Development, Office of Policy Devel-
opment and Research, 1979.

SRI International. Practical Ideas for Small Governments Facing Big
Problems. Washington, D.C.: U. S. Department of Housing and Urban
Development, Office of Policy Development and Research, 1979.

Stevens, Barbara and E. S. Savas. "The Cost of Residential Refuse Collection and the Effect of Service Arrangement." The Municipal Year
Book 1977. Washington, D.C.: International City Management Association, 1977, p. 200.

Stone, Daniel. "Productivity and Performance: Providing the Same Services for No Increased Costs." PM Public Management, Vol. 3, 1978,
p. 32.

Straussman, Jeffrey D. "Quasi-Market Alternatives to Local Government
Service Provision." The Urban Interest, Spring 1981.

Vickery, Edward et al. "Operational Productivity Measures for Fire
Service Delivery." The Municipal Year Book, 1976. Washington, D.C.:
International City Management Association, 1976.

Washnis, George. Productivity Improvement Handbook for State and Local
Government (New York: Wiley, 1980).

Wilcox, M. C. and S. J. Mushkin. "Public Pricing and Family Income
Problems of Eligibility Standards." In Public Prices for Public
Products, S. J. Mishkin (editor). Washington, D.C.: The Urban Insti-
tute, 1972.

Zimmerman, J. F. "Meeting Service Needs Through Intergovernmental
Agreements." The Municipal Yearbook 1973, Washington, D.C.: International City Management Association, 1973.

Zimmerman, Joseph. "Municipal Transfers of Functional Responsibilities." Urban Data Service Report, Vol. 7, No. 9, p. 16.